£4

geu

17/27.

# SWEET SUMMER

BEBE MOORE CAMPBELL

# SWEET SUMMER

Growing Up With and
Without My Dad

COLLINS
8 Grafton Street, London
1990

William Collins Sons & Co. Ltd
London · Glasgow · Sydney · Auckland
Toronto · Johannesburg

First published in Great Britain by Collins 1990

BRITISH LIBRARY CATALOGUING IN PUBLICATION DATA

Campbell, Bebe Moore *1950-*
Sweet summer: growing up with and without my dad.
1. United States. Biographies
I. Title
973′.0496073024

ISBN 0-00-215626-1

Made and printed in Great Britain by
William Collins Sons & Co. Ltd, Glasgow

# ACKNOWLEDGMENTS

To be raised right is to be given a set of values that see you through the eye of the hurricane and deliver you to the morning calm. Many loving hands shaped the firm foundation on which I stand. I'm thankful for my mother, Doris C. Moore; my father, George L. P. Moore; my grandmothers, Elizabeth Simmons and Mary Moore Griffin; my aunts Ruth, Lela Hawthorne and Edith Seymore; my uncles and their wives, Mr. and Mrs. John Moore, the late Mr. Elijah Moore and Mrs. Moore, Mr. and Mrs. Eddie Moore, Mr. and Mrs. Cleat Moore, Mr. Joseph Moore, Mr. and Mrs. Samuel Moore, Mr. and Mrs. Norman Moore; my godparents, the late Mr. Benjamin Louard and his wife, Mrs. Agnes Louard; and family friends such as the late Mr. Raymond Lee and his wife, Barbara, and my dear departed friend, Pete, and his wife, Anne. Thank you all for your guidance throughout the years, and a special thanks to those of you who helped me put together the pieces of my life and make a book of them. And thank you, Lesley and Michael, for your memories.

I thank God for my husband, Ellis Gordon, Jr., without whose loving support this project would have been impossible to complete. My daughter, Maia, has often been my silent companion in my office as I worked. She is my best cheerleader. My stepson, Ellis III, continues to be a friend and booster.

I am grateful to my agent, Carol Mann, who believed in this project from the beginning and worked hard to bring this work to the public. I'd like to thank my editor, Adrienne Ingrum, whose incisive criticism has helped to shape the book and whose enthusiasm was that of a loving friend.

Finally, I thank God for strong, black men who are good fathers regardless of what else they are not, and whose love for their children is their faith in a brighter tomorrow.

*To my daddy, George Linwood Peter Moore.*
*And to all the fathers who guided me.*

# SWEET SUMMER

# CHAPTER 1

When my father died, old men went out of my life. From the vantage point of my girlhood, he and his peers had always been old to me, even when they were not. In his last years, the reality of his graying head began to hit home. I no longer boogied the weekends away in smoke-clogged rooms that gyrated all night with Motown sounds, where I'd take a breather from the dancing by leaning up against the wall, sipping a sloe gin fizz and spewing out fire-laced rhetoric of "death to the pigs." I was a mature young wife, a mother even, three rungs from thirty, a home owner, a meal planner, who marched for an end to apartheid in front of the South African embassy only often enough to feel guilty. I made vague plans to care for him in his dotage. Care for him on a teacher's salary, in the middle of a marriage that was scratching against the blackboard with its fingernails, in a two-bedroom brick fixer-upper my husband, daughter and I had outgrown the moment we moved in. That was the plan.

When he died in 1977, I suppose, a theoretical weight was lifted, since Daddy was a paraplegic because of a car accident he'd had when I was ten months old. No doubt his senior-citizen years would have been expensive and exhausting for me. And then too,

I had other potential dependents. I mused about the future, fantasized about my role as a nurturer of old people, feeling vaguely smug and settled, maybe a little bourgeois.

The afternoon was muggy as only a D.C. summer afternoon can be. The humidity and my afro were duking it out on the tiny sun porch of our home, the ring being the area immediately above the base of my neck, the hair coffee-colored grandmamas laughingly call the "kitchen." It is the hair I hated most as a child. The rest of my head was covered with a wavy-frizzy mixture that proclaimed my black ancestry had been intruded upon. My "kitchen" has always been hard-core naps, straight from the shores of Dahomey. Benin, they call it now. From time to time I'd tug my fingers haphazardly through the tight web of kinks, trying to make my recalcitrant hair obey me and separate into manageable clumps of curls. The hair was simply too dense back there. I would need my big black comb with the wide-spaced prongs, something heavy like that to pry my rebellious locks apart. All I was doing was hurting my fingers. I raised the window higher for more air. The faint smell of roses wafted in on a thin, damp breeze.

"I am not your responsibility, darling," Mommy had said in a brisk, businesslike tone of voice that still managed to sound loving when, on one of my frequent visits to Philly, I broached the subject of my caring for her when she got old. Each word my mother uttered stood at attention, like a soldier doing battle in the war for improved communication. But what should I have expected from a woman who was absolutely savage about enunciation, pronunciation, speaking co-rrectly, so that *they* would approve. My mother viewed speaking impeccably proper English as a strategy in the overall battle for civil rights. "Bebe, we've got to be prepared," she'd say briskly.

When as a child I said, "He be going," my mother's eyes would widen as big as silver dollars and the corners of her mouth would get dry and chalky-looking. She'd clench her throat with wide, splaying fingers and spring into action, like a fireman sniffing a cigarette in a forest and dousing it before flames erupt. "Don't say that." Her voice would be firm and patiently instructive. "That's a Negro colloquialism. Totally incorrect. They'll think you're dumb if you talk like that." They, always they.

She was sitting at her small mahogany desk in the dining room, her glasses propped on her nose, sorting papers into neat little stacks, bundling them together with rubber bands. Glancing down I saw that the papers were related to her church work, Alpha Kappa Alpha sorority, her volunteer work with a senior citizens' group and her membership on the grievance board of Holmesburg Prison, all overwhelmingly dignified pursuits. Although she was no longer a social worker for the city, my dear mother's retirement consisted of running feverishly from one volunteer gig to the next one, all for the uplifting of the race. My mother has always been and will always be a very lift-every-voice-and-sing type of sister, a woman who takes her Christian duty very seriously. Under the desk she crossed her short, brown legs and tapped her foot a little. "Clara and I will probably take a fabulous apartment together, one of those new complexes with everything inside, a laundry, a grocery store, cleaners, everything. Or by that time, my goodness, the church's senior-citizen complex will be ready and I'll just move in there. Or I'll stay here." She smiled serenely at me for a brief moment, her smooth brown face full of sunshine, then excused herself to continue working on the church bulletins.

"Senior citizens' complex!" I let my words explode in the air. "You *want* to live in an old folks' home? Mommy, that's not our culture." I finished, totally disgusted.

Mommy looked at me, her eyes squinched up in laughter, a grin spreading across her face. She loves for me to mess with her, gets a big kick out of my tongue-in-cheek assaults on her dignity. As if anything could ever put a dent in her dignity.

"Here I am, offering you a secure place in your old age, nutritious hot meals, no abuse, make sure you get your high-blood-pressure medicine. All you have to do is sign over the ole pension, SS check, bonds, CDs, deed to your property, and you get the run of the place. Do whatever you want to do. Want to have the AKAs over? The sorors can come. You get to have a boyfriend. All the sex you want! I'm talking about the best the black extended family has to offer. And you want to go . . ."

"I don't have high blood pressure," my mother said, chuckling and dabbing at her eyes.

"Yet, yet . . ."

My mother whooped.

"What about your arthritis?" I asked in an aha! kind of tone, truly alarmed at the notion of my aged mother hobbling to a dingy basement laundromat, sorting faded bras and well-worn girdles while her ancient sidekick, Clara, threw her yellowed undies into the motley heap.

Doris looked at me as if the word "lunatic" had suddenly become emblazoned on my forehead. Her shoulders and her full upper lip went stiff; the nostrils in her wide nose flared slightly. "What are you talking about, girl? I don't have any arthritis. If you're referring to the occasional stiffness in my knees, I've had that since I was a young girl and it's not going to get any worse. Darling," she said, her tone softening a little, her hands still busily sorting, stacking, writing, "you have your family to look after. A baby. Don't worry about me. I'll go right on, the same as always."

So that was that; my mother was immortal. However, if by some fluke lightning struck or the rapture came and my divine mother was sent soaring away from this earth on diaphanous wings, merrily pumping her way to heaven with stiff knees, then, then I'd be duty-bound to take in Nana.

My feisty grandmother could talk the naps out of any black child's kitchen. Mouth all mighty. Mouth's mammy. I was Nana's sole choice for a caretaker, since her only other children, my Aunt Ruth and my namesake, Aunt Bebe, were dead and her only other grandchild, my cousin Michael, was engaged in a perennial search—finding himself—that made his life-style suspect. Nana wasn't into living with anyone whose phone was on one day and off the next. "Hell, I might as well have stayed in Virginia and picked cotton if I didn't want to do any better," she told me with a snort, referring to her and her parents' migration from the grips of the sharecropping South, aeons ago when she was a baby. For the record, Nana had never picked cotton a day in her life, but all the same, she was fervent about black economic progress and she found Michael's gypsy ways appalling. What was worse, what was intolerable was that her only grandson didn't have a job, at least not a steady one.

"The boy is mad," she said one day as we were snapping string beans in her kitchen. Her large almond-shaped eyes flashed. Nana's eyes were bright, the white part startlingly clear. She was small and plump, the color of a lemon wafer. "Gorgeous in my day, honey," she'd tell you in a minute. "I had all the men frothing at the mouth." Gold hoop earrings dangled at her ears. She gave off subtle whiffs of Estée Lauder, and when she spoke I could smell Doublemint chewing gum. "Smart boy like that. Nice-looking," she said disgustedly. "They need to put him in some government work camp or something." Nana's "they" was different from my mother's. More all-encompassing. Whoever made the rules, set the tone, that was Nana's "they."

"The depression is over, sweetheart. There are no work camps anymore."

"Well, then they should put his ass in the Army!" she snapped.

"Who is 'they'?" I asked, just for fun. Nana laughed. "Anyway, you can't force someone to be in the Army. And besides, he's too old."

Nana put down her beans. Her fingers were motionless in front of her. "You think he's ever gonna get himself together?" Nana's eyes were brimming with concern.

"What do you think?"

Nana sighed and began rubbing at her temples, where her hair was mostly gray, with the base of her thumbs so as to keep her fingers clean. Her eyes stared right into mine as she pulled her hands away from her hair and reached across the table and grabbed my wrist, squeezing it tightly with her thick fingers. "If anything happens to your mother you'll have to take me, Bebe," she whispered.

I simply nodded, too surprised at the sudden serious turn her outburst about Michael had taken. If I had been thinking, I would have said flippantly, "Nuh unh, honey. Sending your butt straight to the old folks' home with your daughter. Come see you every Tuesday." I could have lightened the moment a little, but I chose not to, probably because deep inside I didn't think Nana would outlive Mom. She didn't want to. Nana was seventy-five when we had this little talk and was beginning to show unmistakable signs of a disenchantment with life. Her old folks' blues would become increasingly more sorrowful as she approached her eighties. The older she got, the clearer it was that she was ready to "pass."

At seventy-nine, she called me one late afternoon and wailed into the telephone. "I don't like it anymore. I can't even go out in the winter; I'm so scared I'll fall on the ice and break my ass. And I don't even have a boyfriend," she cried, her voice high and piercing, plaintive. "What kind of life is that?"

A life with no rustling taffeta dresses, no fire-engine-red toes and fingers, no mambo nights, no baritones calling on the phone. For my jazzy grandmother (I still thought of her that way), no life. No life at all.

Whatever frailties owned her, she still possessed the strength to will herself right on out of this world. Seven years after my father's death, I believe she did just that. Only days after her eightieth birthday and a few weeks before the first Philadelphia snowstorm of 1984 could trap her for yet another season, Nana slipped off her red velvet bedroom slippers, lay down on the sofa in the living room of the house I grew up in, and fell into a dreamless, endless sleep.

When I thought about my father I realized that he had a strong will too, and maybe more reasons not to want to live to be older than Nana. You could see that will in the way he jutted out his chin, the quick way he moved and drove. He liked speed because it was powerful, as strong as he always wanted to be. I knew George Moore's mental powers would never be used to precipitate his leaving this earth any sooner than absolutely necessary. Right after the accident the doctors told him he wouldn't live out the year because of the damage that had been done to his kidneys. He made the decision right then. Put away the razor blade he'd been clutching and pressing to his throat when he saw his toes would never move again. Made a decision right then and there. Started drinking gallons of water a day. Doing his exercises. Praying. How he forced the sadness from his eyes I do not know. Only one time did I witness him mourning the life he might have had. It was a terrible moment, but a healing one. That split second taught me that the best part of my father, the jewel stuck deep inside his core, was determination. George Moore was about living life until it was gone, wrested from him, snatched out of his clenched fist. He would play out the hand that had been dealt. My potbellied daddy wouldn't roll off resolutely to some senior citizen's palace to sip tea and play canasta, and he sure as hell didn't know any old guy he'd want for a roommate. Unmarried men living together, unless they were in the Army or Navy or something, seemed weird to him. No, he'd see his old age, his infirmities as something quite naturally to be shared with his only child. He wouldn't want to be a burden; he'd pay his way, share his little Social Security check so he would have a legitimate gripe when there weren't any pork chops in the house. And he'd be very useful; all the Moore men, my father and my seven uncles, have always had a tendency toward workaholism. They get up early and get busy; that's in their blood. Daddy would fix all the broken radios, clocks and televisions in the house. He'd do the plumbing and put in new electrical outlets. And of course, Daddy would tend the garden, since he could make anything grow. And much as he loved children, I'd have had a super built-in baby-sitter. If there was no work, no ball game on television and he couldn't get a decent conversation going, he'd just leave, go for a ride or something. He had a car with hand controls for the accelerator and brakes. Icy streets wouldn't keep Daddy inside a house where there was nothing to do, nobody to chew the fat and trade stories with. And he wouldn't be rushing off to attend some important, purposeful meeting called by the NAACP, the Neighborhood Association, the Coalition of 100 Black Men, or even Omega Psi Phi fraternity, of which he was a very nonactive member. He'd left behind those kinds of gatherings in his other life, the one I knew nothing about, the one he titled "Before I got hurt." No, Daddy would go riding just to hang out. And not alone, either. At least that's what I thought on that day in Washington as the fragrant, moist air mixed in my hair, rendering my kitchen absolutely impassable to my wandering fingers.

I remembered the sweet North Carolina summers of my childhood, my father's snappy "C'mon, kiddo. Let's go for a ride," when life was boring sitting in Grandma Mary's house or the yard. There was a ritual my father had to endure before he and I could zoom away down the one-car-wide dirt lane that led to the larger tar road. He'd roll his wheelchair right up between his open car door and the driver's seat and hoist himself from his chair to the car seat with one powerful thrust of his body. Then he'd clutch his leg, which would invariably start twitching with involuntary muscle spasms. When the shaking stopped, he'd lean out of his car seat, snatch his chair closed, press his body into the steering wheel, pulling the back of his seat up so that he could lift his chair into the backseat of the car. This done, he'd take out a white handkerchief, wipe his drenched forehead and look over at me and grin. Then I'd hop into the seat next to his and we'd take off. In those days I was his partner, his roadie, his little minimama homegirl. In the summer he hardly went anywhere without me. And I believed, as I engaged in my humid, sun-porch reverie, my probing fingers struggling inside the tangle of my kitchen, that I would be all those things again, that when my father got old he would need me.

The thought of our living together for the first time since I was a child delighted me, since it was in such stark contrast to the female-centered home I'd grown up in after my parents separated and my mother and I moved from North Carolina to Nana's house in Philadelphia. Realistically, though, living with my father would present special challenges. There were, of course, the implications of his paralysis, and his lack of mobility was complicated by his size. There were over two hundred pounds of him sitting in that chair. He was the black man's Chief Ironside. Well, maybe Raymond Burr had a couple of pounds on him. He tried to play it off when I teased him about his gut. Daddy would pat his belly, grin and say, "The chippies' playground, baby girl." Still, Daddy would be no fun to heave up and down stairs or in and out of a bathtub, although periodically, when he set his mind on losing weight, my father dieted quite successfully and could knock off thirty or forty pounds. When he was on a diet, I don't care how many pork chops you floated under George Moore's nose, the boy wasn't eating. That kind of doggedness enabled him in his later years finally to cut loose the Winstons he had inhaled with passion when he was younger. When he set his mind on something, that was it. Nobody had more determination than Daddy. So maybe the weight wouldn't have been a problem. What would have irritated me, though, was his innate ability to run the helpless bit into the ground at times, at least with me. Maybe only with me.

The summer before he died I drove from D.C. to the outskirts of Richmond for a visit and stayed with him at the home where he boarded with an elderly widow named Mrs. Murphy. He had only recently begun working for the federal government in personnel. He was, in affirmative-action terms, a twofer: black and disabled. Finally he was beginning to make decent money. He was sick the day I came to see him, something that rarely happened to him. Aside from his useless legs, he was robust. He rarely even got so much as a cold, although, of course, from time to time he had to go into the McGuire VA Hospital for a stay to have his damaged kidneys checked out. The day I went to visit him he had the flu and was coughing like crazy, drinking water like a fiend, snorting, trying to let out his Big Daddy Jumbo Pasquotank County farts on the sly and rattling on and on about the stock market, his latest in a long line of plans to become wealthy. To his dying day he never saw his becoming rich as something out of the realm of ordinary possibilities. His was the American dream: to work hard and have it pay off big. "Yeah, baby. Your ole daddy's gonna make us some money." He tossed off the titles of stocks and prices per share, totally losing me amid the names and numbers. Sensing my disinterest, he said disgustedly, "You ought to listen to this, girl. I'm telling you, we can make us some money." When my only response was to shrug my shoulders, Daddy shook his head. His mood turned bossy. "Bebe, go get Daddy some more cough syrup." "Bebe, go get Daddy a big ole glass of ice water." "Bebe, go empty this urine duct for your ole sick Daddy." Which was pushing it, because I hated rinsing out his urine ducts. And he knew it. But I did it that day, holding way out ahead of me the rubber duct that contained the acrid-smelling waste he could no longer control. I turned my head in the small, cramped bathroom that held his toothbrush at one end of the sink and Mrs. Murphy's teeth in a cup at the other, as I emptied the urine into the toilet, and again as I rinsed the containers out in the special buckets Mrs. Murphy kept right next to the small commode.

When I returned to his bedroom, Daddy was laid up in the bed like some imperial royal highness, flashing me a slightly wan but still very dazzling smile as I handed him his duct; I turned my head as he fiddled under the covers, attaching the thing to himself. The room needed ten shots of Air-Fresh. He cleared his throat when he finished. Then he grinned at me.

My daddy had a killer of a smile and I think he knew it. I know he knew it. His teeth were so white, so perfectly straight they were startling. Big, white, even teeth. Chiclets. And his grin was just a little crooked, and that's what made him such a charming smiler. On that particular day, I wasn't falling for his charm. "Don't ask me to do one more thing, old man," I said, as sourly as I could.

"BebebebebebeMoore," Daddy sang out, throwing his big, heavy arm around my shoulder when I stopped fussing. I was sitting on the side of his bed, one leg under me, the other leg swinging, my big toe just brushing the floor as I looked at a magazine, my hips against his very still legs. The air had returned to normal and I thought to myself, George Linwood Peter Moore, please do not funk up this room with another one of those jumbo farts. I looked up and he was smiling that killer smile. "Don't bother me, old man," I said.

What can I say? Daddy would have run my ass raggedy, but he was so charming I wouldn't have minded. To have my father at the dinner table every night, to watch television with him in the early evening, to discuss books and politics, what Ted Koppel said, to go shopping with him and take rides in his car, I would have emptied his urine ducts to have all that.

But this is what I really wanted to see: Daddy and Maia being crazy about each other. He saw his granddaughter only once before he died. She was an infant at the time and I remember he took her out of my arms because I wasn't burping her right. He showed me how to do it, which didn't surprise me because whenever my father took me to visit people there were usually little kids or babies around. The children would jump up in his lap or climb on the back of his chair. He was used to burping babies. "Where'd you get this little red thing from anyway?" he teased, propping Maia up on his lap and smiling at her, lifting her up and down and shaking her gently. "Hey there, baby girl. Hey, little bit. What her got to say to ole Grandad, huh?"

They would have loved each other. I can see Maia sitting in Granddad's lap for hours, falling asleep in his arms, waking up and giggling as he rolled his wheelchair back and forth to amuse her. I can see her standing on the bracers on the back of his chair, placing her tiny arms around his neck. And when she was older, what a pair they would have made: a little brown-skinned girl and the heavyset man in the chair, she pushing him into the park near the water when they went for rides there. Daddy would go to her school plays and to open house and watch Maia as she pirouetted across the stage or recited a Paul Laurence Dunbar poem in church, his applause the loudest in the audience, his smile the brightest.

And my uncles, my father's seven brothers, would come to visit when Daddy came to live with us. John. Elijah. Eddie. Cleat. Joe. Sammy. Norman. On Sundays my husband and I would have to put the two leaves in the dining room table to accommodate two or three of my uncles and maybe their families. And my father's men friends would visit also. It wasn't such a long ride from North Carolina or Richmond to D.C. I imagine Tank Jackson, who was also paralyzed, but from World War II, driving his block-long Lincoln to our door and the two men rolling their chairs into the backyard to have beer and pretzels and me baking something whenever my uncles or Tank came to visit, a potato pie or a coconut cake, and making lemonade too, even in the winter. It would be easy enough to tear out one of the rose bushes and have a ramp put in that would lead right to the door. When Daddy pulled himself up the ramp, as he got older, I'd stand behind him and say, "Can you make it all right, old man?"

The day before my father died I was a bridesmaid in my best

friend's wedding and was staying with friends in Pittsburgh. My hostess awakened me around three or four o'clock Sunday morning and told me my uncle was on the phone. Uncle Norman's signature has always been brevity, an innate ability to get to the point with a minimum of fanfare or bullshit. When I picked up the phone he said, "Bebe, this is Norman. Your father died in a car accident this morning." Just like that. Then, "Did you hear me? Honey, did you hear Uncle Norman?"

A car accident, I thought, the phone still in my hand, Uncle Norman still talking, another car accident. That wasn't supposed to happen, is what ran through my mind. How did that happen twice in one life? Twice in two lives? Somehow, with the room spinning and my head aching, I listened to the rest of his instructions. I was to return home the next day and Uncle Cleat would take me to Richmond to identify the car and sign papers at the police station. We'd get Daddy's things at Mrs. Murphy's. Uncle Johnny, the eldest of Grandma Mary's eleven children, was having my father's body transported to North Carolina, where he would be buried in the family plot behind Grandma Mary's house. "He was coming to see you, Bebe," Uncle Norman said. "He didn't know you were out of town. You know your daddy, he just hopped in the car and got on the road. He was bringing a camera to take pictures of the baby."

When Uncle Norman said that, I remembered the pictures I'd promised to send Daddy weeks before and felt the first flicker of pain course through my body. Something swept through me, hot as lightning. All at once I was shaking and crying. God. He shouldn't have died like that, all alone out on a highway, slumped over the wheel like some fragile thing who couldn't take a good hard knock. God.

It was cool and dim in the funeral parlor, and filled with a strange odor I'd never smelled before. There were three rooms full of caskets—bronze, dark wood, light wood, pastels. A dizzying array. The funeral director was a friend of the family. Mr. Walson had an uncanny affinity for professional solemnity. He referred to Daddy as "the body." Did I wish to see the body? Was I satisfied with the appearance of the body? Did I care for knotty pine or cherry wood? He said this, his dark face devoid of all emotion, his expansive belly heaving threateningly against the dangerously thin belt around his waist. The same odd smell that filled the room clung to Mr. Walson. What was that smell? I leaned against Uncle Johnny and felt his hand on my shoulder. Upon learning that my grief was buttressed by a healthy insurance policy, Mr. Walson urged me to choose the cherry wood. I looked at Uncle Johnny questioningly; he has always known how to take charge. Maybe it comes from being the oldest. If he tells you to do something, you do it. "We'll take the cherry," he told the funeral director, who assured me he would take care of everything. But he could not, of course, take care of me. My grief was private and not covered.

As we left the funeral parlor, Uncle Johnny took my hand. "Do you know what your big-head daddy wanted to do?"

I shook my head.

"After I retired and moved down here next to Mama, he tried to talk me into doing some hog farming with him. Said we could make a lot of money. I told that joker, 'Man, I came down here to rest.' " Uncle Johnny looked at me. He was smiling. "Your daddy loved making money, didn't he, girl?"

"Loved it."

The cars rolled slowly up the unpaved lane that led to Grandma Mary's house, a fleet of Cadillacs, shiny, long and black, moving quietly, and stirring up dust that flew everywhere, clinging to everyone, coating shoes and suits and dresses, blowing in hair and on faces, where particles finally lodged in eyes that blinked, blinked, blinked then looked away.

It is still cool in North Carolina in April, a perfect time for a family reunion. Crowded in Grandma's yard were all the faces that looked like her face, the resemblance lying somewhere between the chin and the character lines that ran straight across high foreheads. There were others standing next to the ones who looked like her, so many people that their feet would have crushed Grandma's zinnias had they been in bloom.

The people looked up when the Cadillacs drove into the yard. They broke away from the joyous hugs of reunion, of North once again meeting South, put their cameras back into their bags and stood silently, at attention. The gray-haired old ladies fanned themselves with miscellaneous bits of paper, the backs of magazines, newspapers, napkins, even though it wasn't warm. All of a sudden there was a circle, shoulders touching, everyone's breath mingling into a giant sigh. Somebody, my daddy's first cousin, the preacher from New York, was praying, offering to the Lord brief, familiar words that the occasion called for: higher ground, no more suffering, home. The words fell around the crowd like soft pieces of flower petals. An old woman began to sing. The lyrics came back to the people who'd taken that long-ago bus ride from Pasquotank County to Philly, Jersey, New York, in heady rushes. All wiped the dust from their eyes and joined in. The last note had scarcely disappeared before Mr. Walson's assistants began calling the names of immediate family members and leading them to the limousines: ". . . Mr. and Mrs. John Moore, Mr. and Mrs. Elijah Moore." Grandma Mary gripped my fingers as I helped her into the car where my husband and daughter were waiting. I was about to sit down when I felt a hand on my back. I turned around. "How ya making out, kiddo?" It was Sammy, my Marine uncle, the hero of my childhood. Whenever I saw him I thought of starched uniforms, even though he hadn't been in the service for years.

"Okay, so far," I said. I took his hand.

He squeezed my fingers and helped me into the car. "I'm here if you need me," he said.

Later, when I was looking into the layers of expensive satin, blinking frantically as the top of the smooth cherry-wood coffin closed, it occurred to me that more than my father had passed away. Not only had I lost a treasured friend, but gone was the ease with which I could connect to his brothers, his male friends.

After he was buried, Grandma Mary's old friend Miss Lilly or Miss Lizzy, Miss Somebody, whose face had floated in and out of my childhood summers, a wiry woman with lines like railroad tracks on skin the color of a paper bag, put her hand in mine and whispered, "Baby, you sho' put him away nice. Yes you did, chile," then, even more quietly, "God knows best, baby." She gave my arm three hard pats. Be . . . all . . . right. Don't . . . you . . . cry. Hush . . . baby . . . hush. I nodded to her, but later when I was alone I had a singular contemplation: his death wasn't for the best. That clear knowing hit me square upside my head after the last of the heavy North Carolina loam had covered the cherry-wood coffin, after Aunt Edith, my father's youngest sister, had heaved a final mournful wail that pierced through the surrounding fields of soybeans and corn that bordered my grandmother's house, then slowly faded. And what I felt wasn't even pain or grief. Just regret, gripping me like a steel claw.

In a way, it was like the end of an ordinary family reunion. I stood at the edge of the lane with Grandma Mary and watched the last of the out-of-town license plates careen down that narrow dirt road, leaving behind a cloud of dust. Pennsylvania. New Jersey. New York. Tomorrow would be another work day, regular and hard.

In the kitchen my father's mother looked tired, every one of her eighty-six years filling her eyes. She held onto the small table as she walked.

"Grandma, why don't you go to bed," I said.

"I reckon I will," she replied. I kissed her on the cheek. She stumbled and grabbed my shoulder to get her balance. "Is you gone get your daddy's car fixed?"

Her question jolted me. I hadn't given my father's Cadillac any thought since Uncle Cleat and I had left it at the mechanic's in Richmond. Soon I would be whipping around doing a "Detroit lean" out the window of George Moore's hog. Wouldn't he love to see that, I thought. "It's being fixed now, Grandma," I said.

"He sure did like that car," she mused almost to herself. "That boy loved pretty cars." She looked straight at me. "Don't bring it up the lane when you come. Hear?" I had to smile to myself. Grandma was loyal to the end. She stubbornly reasoned it was the machine at fault, and not her beloved son. I understood.

So I cleaned the kitchen, mourning my loss with each sweep of Grandma Mary's broom, each swipe of the battered dish cloth, and thought about this father whose entire possessions had fit neatly into the trunk of his yellow Cadillac, which now was mine.

I took my father's wheelchair back to D.C., even though Aunt Edith asked me if I wanted to give it to one of the old ladies in the neighborhood who was having a hard time getting around. I remember I said, "No, I want it," so fast and maybe so fiercely that Edith blinked and stepped away from me. Though why I wanted it, who knows. I put Daddy's chair in my basement and let it collect dust. Sometimes when I was washing clothes I'd look at it. The most I ever did was touch it occasionally.

In the months that followed, the fat insurance checks my father left me transformed my life-style, but at that moment I could feel his death reshaping my life, or at least the life I thought I was entitled to. There are gifts that only a father can give a daughter: his daily presence, his daily molding, his thick arm across thin girlish shoulder, his solemn declaration that she is beautiful and worthy. That her skin is radiant, the flare of her nostrils pretty. *Yeah, and Daddy's baby sure does have some big, flat feet, but that's all right. That's all right now. Come here, girl, and let Daddy see those tight, pretty curls, them kitchen curls.* I was all prepared to receive a daily ration of such gifts, albeit belatedly, but it was not to be. I would never serve beer and pretzels in the yard to Daddy and Tank. I would never have his company as I cleaned the dishes. He wouldn't see Maia's plays or her recitals. That was the way the cards had been dealt. I would go to my uncles, they wouldn't come to me. And the time for even those visits would later be eroded by obligations and miles. After April 1977 the old men in my life just plain thinned out.

For one thing, I got divorced and later remarried and moved far away to Los Angeles. After Grandma died, Uncle Johnny and Aunt Rena moved to Georgia near Aunt Rena's people. "You come see us," he told me before he left. "Don't forget; I'm your pop now." My Uncle Eddie finally sold his grocery store and moved from Philly to North Carolina, so I couldn't conveniently drop in at his market and chew the fat with him when I came to town to see Mom and Nana. Uncle Elijah died and I couldn't even go to his funeral, because my money was real funny that month. I sent flowers and called his wife, but what could I say? I should have been there.

My Marine uncle became a preacher. Uncle Sammy doesn't whoop and holler; his message is just plain good-sense gospel. He can even get scientific on you. When I hear his message I am thinking the whole time.

Uncle Norman and I still talk, but mostly on the telephone. My youngest uncle would call me up in hell, just to find out how I was getting treated. He is busy with his family and business. We don't see each other often.

The last time I saw Tank was a few weeks after the funeral, when he picked me up at the Greyhound bus station in Richmond and took me to get my father's car. Tank's skin is like a country night—no moon, no stars. You don't know what black is until you look in his face. Daddy always told me he wasn't much of a talker, and he's not, but he was just so nice and polite, sitting up in that big Lincoln, being my chauffeur. "Just tell me where you want to go," he said when I got into the car. We drove all over Richmond. Tank took me to where my father worked, to Mrs. Murphy's, everywhere.

Around two o'clock we pulled into McDonald's and he bought hamburgers, french fries and sodas for our lunch; the car was filled with the aroma of greasy food. We were both famished and we ate without talking at first. All you could hear was our lips smacking against our Big Macs. Al Green was singing, "Love will make a waaay . . ." on the radio. Tank looked at me and said, "Ole Be Be," as though astonished that little girls grow up and become women. He said my name the way older southerners are wont to, two distinct syllables. I love the sound. But it was weird, because as soon as he said my name like that, I caught sight of his wheelchair in the rearview mirror and at the same time thought about Maia, whom I'd left in D.C. with a girlfriend. I was still nursing her and I immediately felt pins and needles in my breasts, and when I looked at my blouse there were two huge wet milk rings. Tank looked, he looked away, then he looked again. Then he said, as if thinking aloud, "That's right. Moore's a grandaddy."

Tank's chair was very shiny in the mirror. His words hung between us real softly for a minute before I started up, which I'd sworn I wasn't going to do. I put my head on his shoulder and I just cried and cried and cried. Tears wouldn't stop. "George was right crazy about you, Be Be. Talked about you all the time. All the time," Tank said shyly. He offered up these words as the gift they were. I just nodded.

There have never been enough idle moments really to straighten out those tight, tight curls at the nape of my neck. Untangling a kitchen calls for a protracted, concentrated effort. You have to be serious. It is not a job for weak fingers on a summer's afternoon. Still, daydreaming fingers, even those caught up in tangles, reveal much.

It has proved to be true, what I felt looking into my father's satin-lined casket: my loss was more than his death, much more. Those men who used to entice me with their storytelling, yank my plaits, throw me quarters and tell me what a pretty girl I was are mostly beyond my reach now. But that's all right. When they were with me they were very much with me. My father took to his grave the short-sleeved, beer-swilling men of summer, big bellies, raucous laughter, pipe smoke and the aroma of cigars. My daddy is really gone and his vacant place is my cold, hard border. As always, my life is framed by his absence.

# CHAPTER 2

I was seven years old, sitting on the front steps waiting for my daddy to come and take me to summer.

I can't remember when this waiting for my father began. Was I four or five or even younger? All I know is, it became an end-of-June ritual, an annual event, something I could set my clock by, set my heart on. I don't know whose big idea it was to divide up my life the way they did. Summer, Daddy. Winter, Mommy. Actually, Mommy had me winter, spring and fall. That was a sensible plan, I suppose, a sensible plan for a little girl, but gradually it began to dawn on me that their division had me lopsided, lopsided and lonely: a girl who sat on the steps in June and waited for her daddy.

It wasn't my ritual alone, of course. I was like a lot of northern black children making the annual trek down south to the Carolinas, to Georgia, Alabama or Mississippi. Across Philly in the summer of 1957, hundreds, maybe thousands of black kids were packed and waiting to be driven to wide open spaces, barefoot living, outhouses, watermelon patches, swimming holes, Grandma. Daddy.

A green Cadillac whizzed by and my heart gave a quick jump inside my chest. Maybe . . . No. Wasn't him. Wasn't he, I thought, correcting myself mentally as my mother's voice invaded my private thoughts. I turned around and took a quick look at the front door. Coast was clear. I stuck my wet thumb back in my mouth and covered it with my other hand, just in case Nana or Mommy came outside. My mother was paying me ten cents a day not to suck my thumb and I'd already collected my dime. The rhythmic sucking flooded my body with tranquility for a minute until the urge for even greater pleasure made me bold and I took away my "cover" hand, reached up and started pulling my ear with it. Ahhhhh. I hadn't been sucking and pulling for a good ten seconds when a green Buick slowed down as it approached my house. I jerked my hands away from my face, wiped my dripping thumb on the inside of my shorts and stood up, craning my neck to see if the person driving the car was my daddy. Daagone. The look-alike vehicle slowly turned the corner. Wasn't he ever gonna get here? I sat down, slipping my thumb back into my mouth. My right fingers rubbed my ear vigorously, so that all I could hear was a thin noise going thickathickathickathicka, as if somebody were playing weird music just for me.

I sucked my thumb, pulled my ear and grabbed one of my plaits. Nana had combed my hair into three fat braids that morning, as she sat on her bed and I sat on the floor, the back of my head between her open thighs. She dipped her fingers into a bright yellow can of Nu Nile hair conditioner. Nu Nile was a gummy grease, a conk in a can. It smelled so good, like peaches cooking. Once when I was little, my cousin Michael told me that it was really candy and I should eat some, and I believed him and swallowed a big glob of it. And he fell on the floor laughing. That sort of turned me against Nu Nile (but not against my beloved Michael). "Nana, please don't put that stuff on me; it's too greasy," I whined, trying to wriggle away, but Nana clamped her thighs shut around my chest and I couldn't move.

"Don't you want your edges and kitchen to look nice?" Nana asked. Nice meant straight and slick. The absence of naps was nice. Nana clipped a white barrette with little combs in it around each plait. I didn't have bangs (I asked Nana to cut me some, but she told me, "Bangs! You want to look like Mamie Eisenhower or something?"), and my high forehead was damp from sweating and a little greasy near my hairline. Nana said Nu Nile made a kitchen behave. Nu Nile mowed down my kitchen.

Bumpety! Bumpety! Bumpety! I bounced my butt from step to step to make the time go faster. When was he coming? When? My heart and all activity stopped at the sight of every dark green car that passed by. I thought about the next day, when I would be in North Carolina, miles and miles away from Mommy. How come, I wondered, sucking and pulling, how come I got to be with my daddy only when school was out? How come, I thought, bouncing from step to step, my thumb in my mouth, my fingers in my ear, Mommy and Daddy and I didn't all live together?

The heat from the brownstone steps warmed my bottom. A trickle of sweat dripped slowly from the top of my neck to the small of my back. I'd been sitting in the sun for two hours, getting browner and sweatier as I waited. Behind me I could hear the ruckus in my house as my mother and Nana prepared for my journey. In the kitchen my grandmother was frying chicken for the long ride south. A cake was baking, and the sweet, doughy odor got tangled with the fragrance of frying chicken and both wafted through the house all the way to the front door. Nana was singing, "Ain't nobody's business if I do-ooooo," while she baked, not fast singing, but a constant, happy tempo that filled her kitchen as much as the smell of food. In the living room Michael was sprawled across the dark green velvet throw pillows that Nana kept on the sofa, pretending he was soooo interested in watching Bugs Bunny running away from some angry cartoon man, but I knew better. Michael's eyes were vacant and he wasn't talking to anybody. He ran his mouth all day long, so I knew something was bothering him. Upstairs my mother was packing. From time to time she would come to the front door to ask me if I wanted to take this doll or that toy or book with me. When I would say yes, she would say, "You do? Really? You think you're going to need this? You don't really need this, do you?"

I held my face in my hands and gulped in the scent of the Jergens lotion I'd soaked myself in earlier that morning. I didn't want to go to North Carolina looking like Queen Ashy Mae. Looking up and down the street, I didn't see a green car in sight.

I went inside and climbed the stairs to my mother's bedroom.

"When is my daddy coming?" I hadn't meant to sound whiny, but that's the way it came out.

My mother looked up from the big tan suitcase on her bed, crammed with my socks and underwear and every piece of summer clothing I possessed, and gazed at me, halfway smiling. "In a little while. Are you in such a hurry to leave your mommy all alone?" She sniffed a little, pretending she was crying.

"Uh huh," I said, laughing. I didn't really want to leave her. Why couldn't she come with me? But I knew better than to ask that question. Mommy would only tell me that she had to go to work, and I knew that already.

I watched cartoons with Michael for a little while, but then my thumb-sucking monkey crawled up on my back and I knew Michael would be only too happy to tell my mother if he saw me. So I eased on out the front door, sat down on the steps and resumed my sucking. I scanned the street. No green cars. Bap! Bap! Bap! I hit the edge of the step with the back of my heel. Where is he! I settled myself on the steps, straightened my bright pink shorts and tucked in my short-sleeved pink and white top. Bending over, I brushed off my new white sneakers. I wanted to look nice for my daddy.

I had sucked all the juice out of my thumb; it was milk-white and wrinkled. I got up, pushed open the front door and yelled inside. "Can I walk to the corner?"

"Do you mean 'may'?" my mother yelled back.

"May I walk to the corner?"

"Yes, but keep an eye out for your father's car."

It was mid-morning on a Saturday and 16th Street was already crowded and noisy. Several people had opened their windows and I could smell eggs and frying bacon as I walked down the street. My new sneakers squeaked as I walked. They made me feel tall and bouncy. Across the street, Mrs. Lewis was coming down the steps, a metal shopping cart clattering behind her. A frail woman, she stopped to catch her breath every time she descended one step. She waved wearily to me as I called out my hello.

Mr. Crawford, who owned the house three doors from ours,

was doing his usual Saturday sweeping. He was the president of the block club, a tall, angular man with crinkly gray hair. This morning his hair was covered with a stocking cap. He was so intent on making his sidewalk spotless that he didn't look up when I passed until I said, "Hello, Mr. Crawford." Then he seemed startled, as though I'd awakened him from a dream.

"Oh, hello there, uh, uh, uh, Sugar. Where you goin'? Grandmama know you out here?"

"Uh huh. I'm waiting for my daddy to come take me to North Carolina."

"Oh, now that's nice," Mr. Crawford said, pausing from his sweeping to lean on the broom. His face brightened and the thin outlines of a smile appeared. "North Carolina is my home too. What part you goin' to?"

"My grandmother lives near Elizabeth City. Do you know where that is?" I asked excitedly. Mr. Crawford's revelation made me feel close to him and much closer to my destination.

"Sure do, baby. That's just down the road from Fayetteville. That's my home." Mr. Crawford was absolutely beaming. "You gone stay a long time?"

I shook my head. "Only till school starts. Then I have to come home."

"Well, that's a long time."

"It's not so long."

"Well, you have a good time. Don't let them mosquitoes eat you up, hear? Mosquitoes is bad down home."

When I got to the corner I turned right around and headed back up the street. Any minute he'd be cruising down 16th Street, looking for me and honking his horn. What if he was outside my house right now, honking away, and I wasn't there and Nana and Mommy didn't hear him? Maybe he would drive away and leave me. A legion of demons suddenly appeared at my back. I ran back to my house as fast as I could, almost bumping into Mr. Crawford, who was bending down over a dustpan. "Have a good time," he called after me. I didn't even turn around, just kept on running.

He wasn't even there. Daagone. I sat down wearily on the top step, panting like a dog, except I kept my tongue inside my mouth. I was just about to suck my thumb when Nana poked her head out of the door and handed me a napkin with a piece of pound cake inside.

"You want soma this?"

"Uh huh."

"What do you say?"

"Thank you, Nana?"

"You're welcome."

I bit into the cake; it was soft and warm. My anxiety dissolved as I concentrated on the sweet lightness in my mouth. The crumbs fell on my blouse and shorts and I stood up to brush them off. I was flicking off the bits of cake with my fingers when I happened to look in the street. Somebody was parking a green Pontiac right in front of our house. Heat pulsed through my body and pulled at my stomach, almost like a cramp, except I didn't feel any pain, just needles and pinpricks, bingbingbingbing, racing from my middle to my feet, my groin, my heart, and when the trail led to my mouth I let out a little scream. "Daddy!"

I rushed down the front steps, flung open his car door and nearly threw myself into my father's chest. I felt his strong arms around me, the stubble of his whiskers grazing my forehead. I looked up and there he was. A big red-brown man in a blue short-sleeved shirt and dark pants. He had on a short-brimmed light-colored hat that sort of angled down over his forehead. "Hey, how's Daddy's little girl?" he whispered.

"Fine," I said. Then everything around me got hazy. Who is this man, I thought, wriggling out of his arms into my seat? His face was out of focus, a mystery. I glanced quickly at my father. He had round, clear eyes. He looked at me, coughed then looked away. "Be . . ." he started, but didn't finish. Who is he? "Da . . ." I started. What should I say? We sat there silently, searching desperately for a road that would lead us back to where we had left off on our last visit.

My father coughed some more, then swallowed. He looked at me carefully, scanning every inch of my body. "Your hair grew," he said finally, holding one of my plaits in his hand. "Lemme see your legs, kiddo."

I knew what he was looking for! I knew! I moved closer to him and held up first the right and then the left leg. I looked at my father's round, smooth face, studied his wide nose (just like mine), his full lips until they became less and less strange to me. Yes. I was used to that face. His hands felt warm and comfortable on my legs. Old friends, those hands. He ran his fingers along my thin calves. "Those sores healed up pretty good, huh?" he said, giving my left leg a little pat. "The mosquitoes are bad this year. Have to get you some repellent."

"Mommy packed some."

"Oh."

"Did Lassie have her puppies yet?" Lassie was my grandmother's dog.

"Yup. She had five or six of 'em. Mama gave 'em all away 'cept for one."

"Ooooh, Daddy, can I play with the puppy?"

"Well, sure you . . ." I looked up at my father. His eyes were blinking quickly. He licked his lips rapidly, then he smiled; it was like a nervous twitch.

"Oh, there you are, Bebe." My mother peered into the car window. She looked pretty even with the stiff little smile on her face. She didn't usually smile that way. My mommy and daddy looked as frozen as the dummies in Wanamaker's windows.

"Hello, George. How are you? How was your trip? Can I get you anything?" Her words rushed out in short breaths, as if she'd been running for a train or something.

"Hello, Doris." Daddy's voice was louder when he spoke to my mother. He sounded as if he were trying hard at something, doing chin-ups, maybe. Perhaps he was pretending he was as big and strong as his voice, I thought. I looked at the special hand brakes on his car. Then I looked at my father's lifeless legs. "I'll take a big glass of water," he told her. My mother went back into the house and returned quickly with the water. When she handed my father the glass their hands didn't touch.

Nana and Mommy loaded the trunk of my father's car, the two of them struggling with my big old suitcase, while Michael quietly watched. Nana put the chicken and the cake in a bag on the backseat, along with a pillow and a blanket for when I got sleepy. Michael hung back a little, folding his arms across his chest and not talking at all, until Nana gave him a little push, tellng him, "Give Bebe a kiss. She's getting ready to go and you won't see her till September. Go on now. Don't take all day."

Michael kissed me quickly on my cheek. "You gonna write me?" he asked. His voice was soft and strange and I knew instinctively that he felt left out. I was going off with my daddy and he was staying at home with the women. Michael's daddy never came to take him anywhere. I felt sorry for my abandoned cousin.

"I'll write you some good letters," I promised him. Michael's eyes were still downcast.

Nana and Mommy kissed me good-bye about fifty million times before it was finally the last, truly last kiss.

"Be good," my mother admonished me.

"You drive safely," Nana said to my father. Her voice was like a stern teacher's when she said that.

"I will," he promised her.

"WE'LL JUST GO HOLLER AT EDDIE AND THEM RIGHT QUICK, OKAY, chickadee?" my father said as he rounded the corner, heading for my Uncle Eddie's grocery store. I nodded. Daddy steered with his left hand; his right arm was around my shoulder. I played with his fingers.

My Uncle Eddie's store was full of people, as usual. Nobody paid me much attention at first as I stood silently in the doorway. Then Aunt Marie saw me. "Well, look who's here," she said to Uncle Eddie, who was grinding up some steak for an old man with a thin swatch of hair in the middle of his head and just enough teeth to make me wonder, Was he gonna chew that meat or just suck the juice? With my Uncle Eddie, work always came first. He never stopped what he was doing, just looked up quickly and smiled at me, a fast, lopsided grin, then said to his customer, "My niece. She's a smart one." I showed every tooth in my mouth when Uncle Eddie said that. The man looked at me and started laughing, "Huyahuyahuya." When the man had paid for his hamburger, Uncle Eddie turned his attention to me. "Say, there, Be Be. You on your way down home, huh? See, ole Uncle Eddie knows where you goin'. Don't even hafta tell me."

I giggled. "My daddy said for you to give us two bottles of soda. Grape and cream."

"Soda, huh? He give you some soda money? I ain't in the giveaway business."

I held out a dollar. Uncle Eddie took it and handed me the sodas and some change. "Where's your ole big-head daddy any-way?"

I laughed again, feeling good that Uncle Eddie was teasing me and that I could see his lopsided grin. "He's outside."

When Uncle Eddie went outside I chatted with my aunt for a while and then with my Uncle William, my Aunt Edith's husband, who worked part-time at the store. Presently Uncle Eddie returned. "Your daddy said for you to come on if you want to go see Grandma." He held out his hands. There were bloodstains from the meat on some of his fingers. His hands smelled like fish and raw meat and . . . sweet things. Good ole Uncle Eddie. Now it was my turn to grin. There was a Baby Ruth in one hand and a lemon Tastykake pie in the other. "Which you want?"

"That one," I said, pointing to the candy bar.

Aunt Marie called from behind the counter. "Tell him you want both of them." She was laughing.

Uncle Eddie handed me the candy bar, then he gave me the pie. "There. Don't ever tell nobody Uncle Eddie didn't give you anything." When Aunt Marie started laughing again, louder this time, I did too.

"Whatcha wanna do this summer?" Daddy asked as I got back in the car.

"Eat crabs!" I said solemnly.

"That's what we gonna do."

Out of the window long stretches of rowhouses went by in a blur until we were no longer in the city. When we reached the highway Daddy opened our windows all the way and the breeze whipped between us so loudly we could barely hear ourselves speak. He drove very fast. I wasn't afraid. I could tell that my daddy liked feeling the power of his car sailing across the highway. I knew he claimed that power, attached himself to it somehow.

My daddy was powerful too. The summer before, we had been careening down the highway when we swerved a little and started bumping. "Damn!" Daddy said, sucking his teeth hard. He looked at my startled face. Daddy didn't usually cuss around me. " 'Scuse me, baby." He pulled the car to the side of the road and stopped.

It was dark outside. I was scared. "Whatsa matter?"

"Flat tire."

I could hear the crickets as soon as Daddy opened the car door. There was a full moon. Daddy leaned into his wheel, reached behind him and grabbed his chair from the back, and yanked it through the front door. He opened the chair, pulled it close to him, then hopped into the seat without bothering to put the pillow down. He rolled around to the trunk and took out the jack, a spare and a flashlight.

"You can stay there," he said, when I started to get out. I squealed as the car started jerking up, up, up. It was hard to watch him from where I was sitting, but I could see his thick arms, his muscles flexing in the moonlight. Sweat was dripping behind his ears.

He changed that tire in five minutes. A car slowed down, but he waved it on. That surprised me. When he got back in the car I said, "Daddy, you changed that tire all by yourself."

Daddy said, "Sure. Whatcha think?"

I was halfway grown before I realized it was my father's determination to see himself as strong and capable that had him changing tires in the night. He wanted me to see him that way too.

We drove for hours, eating chicken wings and thighs, nibbling on the cake and the Baby Ruth and drinking cold sodas as well as the lemonade in the thermos Nana had packed. After a while I took off my shoes and socks and tossed them onto the floor in the back. Daddy unbuttoned his top two shirt buttons, pulled a rag from behind his seat and began swiping at his damp neck. I read aloud to Daddy from *The Story of Harriet Tubman,* and then we listened to the radio until the station started crackling like dried-up fall leaves. As the day wore on, the June breeze turned silky; it was like a gentle pat across our faces. All the while we drove, Daddy and I had our hands on each other. My daddy's arm rested on my shoulder; I held his wrist. We were on the edge of summer.

It was almost dusk when we reached Route 17. I could smell summer on that road. The lush, heavy oak trees on either side of the one-lane highway grew so thick their branches stretched across the road to each other in an embrace, making a dark, leafy tunnel of the road. "Look, Daddy, the trees are kissing," I said. He laughed. To our far right, beyond the dense leaves and branches, the murky waters of Dismal Swamp lay still and foreboding. Grandma once told me that before the Civil War slaves swam across the swamp to escape north, and I thought of the runaways as the stronger night breeze whistled and rattled against our windows. Maybe their ghosts came out at night, as haunting as the Turtle Lady, the green phantom who lurked in North Philly looking for children to eat. But I didn't see any ghosts, just water. The night air held a chill and Daddy and I rolled our windows all the way up. The trees loomed alongside us as tall as dark giants. All of a sudden I saw fading daylight again as the kissing trees thinned out. There in the clearing the words "Welcome to North Carolina" and below that, in smaller letters, "The Tar Heel State" blazed out in blue and red. Almost summer. My bladder filled immediately.

"I gotta, I have to go to the bathroom."

"Can't you wait? We'll be there in fifteen or twenty minutes."

"I gotta go now, Daddy."

The car slowed and he pulled over to the side of the road near a deserted picnic table surrounded by a grove of pine trees. "Look-ahere. Go duck behind that first tree. And Bebe, uh, uh, you better pull your shorts, I mean your panties, else you're gonna wet yourself." He laughed a little. His eyes crinkled up. From the prickly, thin sound of his laughter I knew he was embarrassed. I went behind a tree, about twenty feet away from the car. I heard Daddy yelling. "Lookahere. Watch where you step. Might be a snake in there." I peed fast. When I got back to the car I could hear a trickling sound. He was emptying his urine duct. "Might as well go too," he said.

The sky turned inky and crickets began to sing their brittle nighttime lullaby. Route 17 went right into Route 58, the heart of South Mills. The town was a collection of a few houses, a post office and a justice of the peace. My cousin Ruby, Aunt Lela's daughter, and her family lived there. We stopped at her house for a split second, long enough for my plump, pretty cousin to hug me and for Daddy to shoot the breeze with her husband, Snood-lum, and drink a great big glass of water while I raced around the yard in the dark with their two sons, Johnny and Jimmy. Then we had to go, because I was getting antsy. Summer was up the road apiece, waiting for me.

From Ruby's I could have walked to Grandma's blindfolded, the land around me was so familiar. I could have followed the smell of the country night air so weighted with watermelons, roses and the potent stench from the hog pens. We crossed the bridge running over the canal that bordered South Mills. A sign an-nounced that we had entered Pasquotank County. On either side of us, spread out like an open fan, were fields of corn, soybeans, peanuts and melons. White and brick frame houses broke up the landscape. Some belonged to white folks, some to colored. We reached Morgan's Corner and my stomach started quivering. It was where I bought my Baby Ruths and comic books! As my father's car slowed, my eyes scanned the fields of corn and soy-beans for the opening to Grandma's. There it was! The car nearly stopped and we slowly turned into the narrow dirt lane. We jostled and bounced over the muddy ruts, the motor churning and sput-tering as the tires attempted to plod through waterlogged ditches, a result of the last rain. Daddy drove slowly and carefully. "Sure don't wanna get stuck up this lane," he muttered. My stomach was churning just as desperately as the wheels on my father's Pontiac. We lurched out of a deep gulley and glided into the front yard. Finally it was summer.

Grandma Mary was sitting on the porch waiting for us, as I knew she would be. She could outwait anybody. She told me having babies gave you patience. Grandma had had twelve children; one baby died at birth. "You have to wait for the pains to start, then wait for them to go, all that waiting with nothing but a rag to bite down on," she said. She stood up when we drove into the yard. "Hey," she called, walking toward us. My father had barely parked before I was scrambling out of the car and Grandma caught me up in her fat ole arms, hugging and squeezing me. She had a smell, deep in her bosom, like biscuits and flowers and I don't know what all else. That's what washed over me. I turned around to see my daddy pulling his wheelchair out of the back of the car and placing it between his open car door and his seat. He gave a huge lunge and hopped from the driver's seat into the chair. Then he pulled out the pillow he sat on, hoisted up his body and stuffed the pillow under his behind. He rolled over to the ramp in front of the house, pulled himself up and went inside, yelling, "Hey," to Mr. Abe, Grandma's second husband, and "Hey there, girl," to Bunnie, my Aunt Susie's teenage daughter; Aunt Susie had died a few years earlier. I heard Mr. Abe answering back. Mr. Abe had been singing, some old gospel song that only he sang and nobody else. I hadn't heard that song in a year, a whole year. As soon as he answered my father, he started up with his song again. I stood on the porch with Grandma, soaking up Mr. Abe's song, trying to hear it not as last year's song, but as a song of this summer. I stood on Grandma's porch and listened hard. Mr. Abe's song was my bridge; if I could cross that bridge I was back home. I started humming.

# CHAPTER 3

Feathers flying, wings beating hard, squawking like a wild banshee, the chicken streaked past Grandma's outstretched hands, away from the back porch and across the barnyard. Whooosh! Grandma slammed the door real fast, trapping the remaining two birds inside the rickety coop. Slowly she stood up. She let her arms hang loose next to her body for a moment and made a faint, wordless sound, not even a sigh. A summoning. Then she slowly lumbered past the pump, into the small wooden shed that served as the smokehouse, picked up a large ax hanging on the wall and plodded after the feathered escapee. I trailed right behind her.

Grandma had been fattening the three hens for several weeks, isolating them from the other chickens who had the run of the henhouse and the yard. She fed the birds nothing but corn kernels and water. "You gotsta clean out chickens, 'cause no tellin' what all nasty stuff they be eatin'," is what Grandma told me the day she snatched the three unsuspecting chickens—bip, bam, bip— lightning fast; before they could even squawk they were in the cage. Now the three birds were plump and ready for the frying pan. But first Grandma would have to catch them.

Her large, bare feet dragged through the dirt as she tracked the chicken across the yard. Grandma never wore shoes unless she was going out of the lane, which most weeks meant only Sundays. The soles of her feet were as tough and hard as leather. She was a big woman, very wide and sturdy. She reached in one of the pockets of her dress, pulled out a handkerchief, wiped at her nose, then put the handkerchief away. Thin lines crisscrossed her high cheekbones, her forehead and under her eyes, reflecting her almost seventy years. As she walked her long, silky braid dangled down her back.

"You gonna get 'em, Grandma?" I asked, excitedly watching the frantic chicken race across the yard in the direction of Grandma's vegetable garden.

"You sure you wanna see this, Bebe? Gone be bloody and I don't want you gettin' scared and hoopin' and hollerin' and havin' nightmares and all."

"I'm not gonna be scared, Grandma. It's gonna be fun."

"That's what you call it, huh?"

Sure it was fun! The only chickens I saw in Philly were the frozen fryers Nana brought back from the A&P. Scared? Not me! Boy oh boy! I couldn't wait to write Michael about this!

It was only a little after six o'clock in the morning; the ole rooster was blaring away from his perch atop the henhouse. Already I could feel the beginnings of a steamy day. The whole week had been wet and hot, full of mosquitoes and weak winds. The sun and rain had worked their magic on the earth. Grandma's front yard was full of red, yellow, pink and orange zinnias and red and yellow roses. White and yellow daisies made a trail right in front of the porch. Bumblebees and hummingbirds circled the flowers then zoomed in for the nectar. The white two-story clapboard house seemed even more stark behind such dazzling colors. At the end of the yard where the lane started, a full, pretty tree was bursting with tiny hard green balls. I called it the ammo tree, because the little green balls stung when I hit Jimmy and Johnny on their smooth, round heads with them (they always hit me on my bare legs). Behind the house to the side of the barnyard, Grandma's vegetable garden was crammed with little shoots: green beans, butter beans, tomatoes, cucumbers, watermelons and squash, and the tiny heads of the collards and turnips were just beginning to show. Beyond the vegetable garden on one side were rows and rows of hard, low plants that would soon bloom into cotton. On the other side of the house going toward the lane, I saw stalks of corn with tiny ears poking out. Near where Daddy parked his car, the pear and fig trees had already flowered and were loaded with fruit. Before I left in August, Grandma would begin preserving and canning the fruits and vegetables that were growing all around her. But today was going to be more exciting than just cooking up some dumb ole pears and figs. Today she was going to kill the chickens. Just as soon as she caught them.

The frenzied chicken skidded on its tiny bird legs, reversed its direction and headed toward the pigpen. Big Boy, Grandma's fattest hog, lolled in the mud, barely grunting as the hen neared. Grandma plodded behind the chicken. She wasn't walking fast. She wasn't breathing heavily. She just kept coming. The squawking bird, spying Grandma, turned and raced back toward the vegetable garden, almost crashing into Frosty, the white mule, who stood placidly, his eyes flickering as he watched the chase. The rest of the hens, about thirty of them, lined up along the edge of the yard, clucking and observing their sister's misery with growing excitement. Everywhere the chicken went Grandma followed, a little slower, but steady. Finally the bird just seemed to give up. Backed itself up against the fence that bordered the garden. Stood there frozen and terrified as Grandma swept down and plucked it up by its feet.

I was right behind Grandma, so eager for the slaughter to begin that I almost stepped on her heels. I didn't want to miss one bloody minute. This was better than sitting through three monster movies at the Senate. This was gonna be gooood! The bird's body slapped against Grandma's thighs as she trudged several yards to the mountainous pile of wood next to the smokehouse. Grandma slammed the hen down on the chopping block; the bird let out a screech that probably woke up all the Moores lying in the family graveyard way beyond the cotton field. In the same instant, Grandma came down on the little neck with one lightning swoop of the ax. Whackorooni! The small head hit the ground with a soft thud, landing right at my foot, sprinkling blood on the toe of my white sneakers. I froze. I stared at the red blood on my white sneakers and had my first conniption right there. I felt the blood dripping down into my shoe and dribbling against my foot, and I jumped into the air so high and so fast that Frosty brayed at the sight. When I came down I was screaming as loudly as the decapitated chicken. Blood! On my leg! Ugh! Ugh! Ugh! I was scared of blood, and the sight of that twitching head dripping blood and guts from its beak and neck was worse than any nightmare I'd ever had. *It was gonna get me!* I dashed around, wild as the headless chicken, looking for safety. Grandma! She'd protect me. I grabbed Grandma Mary's dress and a good hunk of her as well. My grandmother wouldn't let the Headless Chicken get me. As long as I held onto Grandma Mary, I was safe. As I clung to the folds of her blue dress a hush went over the barnyard. The little head at my feet was motionless. Now the rest of the dismembered bird went into a death dance, wailing and pitching its headless body across the yard, leaving a trail of blood and feathers behind. I was riveted by fear and revulsion, watching the chicken die. Then the Headless Chicken whipped its mortally wounded body around and commenced dancing my way. I raced toward the woodpile. Only I didn't let go of my grandmother, who stolidly held her ground. Not only didn't I manage to get away, I tumbled right into the path of the Headless Chicken. The creature's shrieks pierced the air. So did mine. *"It's gonna get me! It's gonna get me!"* As the bloody hen inched closer I wrapped myself around Grandma Mary's leg and hid my eyes in her flesh. If I was going to be eaten alive and drenched in chicken blood I didn't necessarily want to see it.

"Get up, baby," Grandma commanded, but I only clung to her more tightly. All I could envision was the Headless Chicken jumping on me and taking my head off. The only safe spot in the world was Grandma's leg and I wasn't moving.

"Get up, now. It's done gone."

There wasn't a sound in the whole barnyard. I lifted my head just a little and managed one tiny peek. I didn't see the chicken.

"There it is yonder," Grandma said.

I turned my head around. Dragging itself to the center of the yard, the Headless Chicken was in the last stages of collapse. Several of the hens that had stood back to watch suddenly rushed forward, pecking at the body.

"Ugh! Ugh! Ugh!" I said.

"Shooo-ooo!" Grandma shouted, and the chickens scattered like dust in a windstorm.

"Shooo-ooo!" A little distance had made me bold and boda-cious. I imitated my grandmother, chasing the hens to the far corner of the yard. The Headless Chicken lay in a bloody heap in the center of the yard. It wasn't moving.

"You loves your chicken fried or baked?" Grandma asked me after she beheaded the three chickens, carried them back to the house and plunged each one into a pot of boiling water to loosen up the feathers. We were sitting on the back porch. The air still carried the odor of scalded flesh. Grandma was in a hard-back chair, her two front feet caked with dust and stretched open to a wide V in front of her. Rhythmically she pulled handfuls of feathers out of the chickens' bodies and threw them into a big paper bag on the floor by her feet.

"Fried. Both."

"Which, Miss Lady?"

"Fried the best."

"Okay. Grandmama gone fry you some chicken."

"My daddy told me he likes chicken and dumplings."

"Your daddy likes food," Grandma said, laughing. "Eatin'est man I ever did see. He eats more'n any one of my youngins."

"More than Uncle Johnny?" Uncle Johnny was tall and husky. He smoked cigars, told funny stories and ate with gusto.

"Your daddy's my eatin'est chile," Grandma repeated. "And he's cut back some, because he don't want to get too big in that chair. Before he got hurt . . ." I moved in close when my grandmother spoke those words, ignoring the raw odor of fresh death clinging to her apron.

"How did my daddy get in the accident?"

Grandma looked at me, then she looked down at the chicken in her lap. She spoke slowly, her words falling into the rhythm of her plucking. "Well, you know, when your daddy got hurt, he was doing just fine. Just fine. He finished college. He put hisself through that school up in Greensboro. What's the name of that place?"

"A and T. North Carolina Agriculture and Technical College."

"You right smart. You know your grandfather was a contractor. He hired out men to work in the logging woods. And he put George to work for him. George told him, said, 'Daddy, this ain't for me. I'm gone to school.' And that's what he done." Grandma nodded her head toward me. "When your daddy puts his mind on something, he does it. Did you know that?"

"Yep." I smiled.

"Anyway, he got that book learning. He was the county farm agent." Grandma looked at me quizzically. "Your mama tell you that?" she asked sharply. I nodded. "Humph! Anyway, he was the one that would tell the farmers what to plant and how to do they crops and all. That's an important job." Grandma stopped and straightened up a little. "The white people called him Moore. And I don't know, him and your mother had this little house and they'd opened up a restaurant with some of they friends. Fried chicken and fish. Sandwiches. Your daddy was always thinking about making money. And George, he got him this car. He liked cars. That's natural for men to like pretty cars. Ain't nothing wrong with that," Grandma said, her voice suddenly tight and defiant. "I don't have no bad youngins. But what I mean to say is that your daddy was fixin' to be rich and important. That's what he wanted to be. And just when things was going just right, well then, out of nowhere, he, he got hurt. It was like somebody just scrambled up his body like you see me scrambling up a mess of eggs in a fry pan. That's how his body was. Doctors say spinal cord injury. That's what makes you walk." Grandma sighed heavily. "Sometimes people, they just don't judge right."

Grandma was being too kind to the evil person who hurt my father, cut him down right when he was beginning to be rich and powerful. "Some people shouldn't be allowed to drive a car at all," I said rather sharply. Grandma looked at me, squinting behind her glasses. She jerked the last handful of feathers out of the hen and placed the bird in the pan with the other two. She stood up, brushing off the bits of feathers that clung to her apron. Then she spoke magic. Her words came out in a soft rush.

"I believe George is gone walk again. Because if he wasn't, his legs would have done shriveled all up. And his legs ain't shriveled. They smooth and healthy-lookin'. I believe your daddy is gone walk someday."

I looked at Grandma. Her eyes were closed and her head was bowed. "You do?" I couldn't breathe.

"Yup."

Grandma Mary took the pan of chickens into the kitchen. I heard her start cooking breakfast. I was rooted to the chair I sat in; everything around me was a dizzying array of dancing lights and shadows, wiggly lines; only my heart stood still. I moved toward that light, fast and sure. I melded into that light instantly, without question, wrapped my seven-year-old heart around it and began to dream. Yes. Yes. Yes. Something wonderful was going to happen. My father was going to walk again. Grandma Mary said so.

That night my father and I lay side by side in his wide bed. Outside the window, the moon was a golden arc illuminating our conversation: night talks, my daddy called them.

"Daddy, were those chickens still alive after Grandma cut off their heads?"

"Life was leaving them. They were half dead and half alive."

"Daddy, when did they stop feeling pain?"

"As soon as they were all the way dead."

"Well, Daddy, how come the other chickens started pecking at them, huh?"

"I don't know. Chickens are kind of like scavengers . . ."

"What's a scavenger, Daddy?"

". . . Meaning they eat any ole thing, even dead things, so maybe that's why. Or maybe they're just mean, like some people. Taking advantage of somebody who's down."

"Daddy . . ."

"Yes."

"If I fell in Dismal Swamp and started drowning, could you save me?"

"Yup."

"You could!?" I was incredulous and overjoyed at the same time.

"I can still swim. That's funny to think of, but it's true. You ain't planning on drowning, are you?" He laughed. I liked my daddy's nighttime laugh, so close to my ear it could float down inside me.

"Unh unh."

"Daddy . . ."

"Yes?"

"You know those things in your closet that help you to walk?" Should I tell him, I wondered. Should I tell him the wonderful thing that was going to happen?

"Those old braces?"

"Yeah. How come you don't ever wear them?"

"They don't do any good, baby. With my condition, they don't really help."

"Well, you should practice in them."

"Practice what?"

I didn't want to say, "Practice walking." I decided right then I would keep my secret, so I didn't answer.

We heard the drone of a mosquito. "Shhhhhh," Daddy said. He cocked his head to one side. The sound grew louder, closer. All of a sudden my father slapped his big hands together and the sound stopped. "Got 'im," Daddy said. He leaned over the side of the bed and got a tissue from off his nightstand. I put my thumb in my mouth and felt myself floating. I wanted to rub my father's ears, but I was too shy to ask his permission. Besides, I wanted him to think I was a big girl, not a baby. So I turned on my side, my back to him, and began pulling my own ears and sucking my thumb.

"Bebe."

"Uh huh."

"You sucking your thumb?"

52

I snatched my thumb out of my mouth and hid it under my pillow.

Daddy laughed. "Girl, you gone have teeth like Bugs Bunny if you don't stop."

"Okay, Daddy."

"Don't you wanna have pretty teeth like your ole man?"

I giggled. "Uh huh."

"Guess I'm gonna hafta put some hot sauce on that thumb, so it won't taste so good."

"Oh no, Daddy. Don't do that." Ugh! Hot sauce on my thumb!

"Well, what should I do to make you stop?"

I was quiet for a second. Then, "You should give me a reward?"

"A reward for what?"

"A reward for every day I don't suck my thumb. Every day I don't suck my thumb you should give me a dime."

"A dime, huh?"

"Uh huh." I slipped my thumb back in my mouth, grabbed my ear and listened to a chorus of crickets chirping until I couldn't hear anything but my daddy's soft chuckles, his faint voice saying, "Naw, girl. You ain't taking me for no dimes."

My father and I crammed July with togetherness: short trips to Elizabeth City, long rides past Dismal Swamp. We went visiting every day. We cruised along to our journeys at full speed in my father's dark green Pontiac, taking curves audaciously. I was never afraid. I sensed it was important to him to fly down the road as if he owned the highway. Inside the car I sprawled in the back if we were going far, chomping down hard on Double Bubble, languidly flipping through *Archie, L'il Dot,* and *Millie the Model.* The breeze flicked softly against my thighs and between my toes. I stretched out as if I were on a sofa and let the motion of the car lull me to sleep. His legs, my father called his car.

I got to see Jimmy and Johnny at least twice a week. Sometimes I carried the hard green balls in my pocket and soon as I saw them I'd pitch my ammo at their heads. Ruby would say, "Now stop that, Bebe," but she'd be laughing too. When Miss

Rosie, who lived in the only other house down the lane, had her nieces and great-nieces visiting her from Baltimore, I skipped to her house to play.

My father took me to meet a little girl named Eugenia, so light and curly-headed she almost looked white. Her father was a doctor and her beautiful mother was a schoolteacher who never rose from her lawn chair the whole time we were there. She told my daddy that I was very bright. Their house looked prettier than the one Wally and Beaver lived in, and Eugenia's room was pink, white, frilly enough for a princess. She was a princess. Eugenia attended boarding school because, she told me in a lilting, sniffing voice that could belong only to a princess, "the schools around here aren't good enough."

Daddy seemed proud of knowing Eugenia's father. "Her daddy's a doctor," he told me several times. "Good friend of mine," he crowed. I detected something in his voice that said he felt important claiming Eugenia's daddy as his good friend. I couldn't look at him when he was telling me how much Eugenia's daddy liked him.

One July day we were sitting in Grandma's front yard. I was sitting under the ammo tree, reading a comic book. Daddy wasn't doing anything except rolling his chair back and forth. I looked up at him; his face was all screwed up. Suddenly he swiveled his chair around and headed out the gate toward his car. "C'mon, Bebe," he called over his shoulder, "let's go someplace." My father wasn't good at doing nothing.

We drove to Chesapeake and visited my cousin Eula. When Daddy pulled into her yard and honked his horn, Eula's youngest daughter, LaVerne, who was my age, came flying out of the house and gave my daddy a big kiss and a hug. I didn't say anything, just watched. I was used to little girls and even boys hugging on my daddy.

Daddy and I always returned to Grandma's from our journeys just before the sun went down. On the floor of Daddy's green Pontiac, crammed in a paper bag, were the remnants of a junk feast that would be absolutely forbidden in Philadelphia. There were empty potato chip bags and soda bottles, candy wrappers and half-full packages of chewing gum. My father made me throw everything away when we got to Grandma's. He liked his car to be spotless at all times. "A clean car rides better," he told me.

At night Daddy, Grandma, Bunnie and I watched the large black-and-white Philco television that was in a corner of the living room. While the television was on, Mr. Abe sat in the dining room reading from a large book of children's Bible stories. We could hear him in the next room, because he always read aloud. We heard him muttering through *Death Valley Days* and *Lassie*, and even when Nat King Cole was singing on *The Ed Sullivan Show*, Mr. Abe sat right there in the dining room reading his book. When he tired of reading, he'd lean back in his chair and sing. Mr. Abe's reading wasn't so hot, but his singing was better than any television show. The music eased out of his half-parted lips effortlessly. Mr. Abe moaned hymns so old and handed-down, so syncopated by human rhythms that there was a clink of chains in each verse. His voice made chills dance on my back.

Most nights Bunnie and I took our bath together. I adored my big cousin and loved being with her, but our bathing together wasn't so much for companionship as for convenience. Taking a bath in the country was a big job. The bathroom had been added on after my father's accident, but there was no hot water and sometimes the cold tap didn't work. One night Bunnie built a fire in the wood stove and then went outside to pump several buckets of water to heat for our bath. We lowered our bodies into the steaming water, and went limp as two-day-old roses as we sat in the tub. Then Bunnie's face brightened. "You want a bubble bath, Bebe?" I nodded eagerly. Bunnie got up, sneaked across the back porch dripping water every whichaway, went into the kitchen and brought back the bottle of Lux dishwashing detergent that Grandma kept near the sink. Bunnie squirted Lux into the water and started paddling her hands. I squealed with delight.

"What y'all doin' in there?" Grandma hollered.

"Nothin'," Bunnie and I yelled back.

When the original bubbles faded, Bunnie raked her hand across the water and made more. My big cousin washed me until I squeaked, and then she rinsed us both off with a remaining pail of warm water.

"On the seventh day he rested" was taken literally in Grandma Mary's house. Grandma cooked Sunday dinner on Saturday and the one time I asked her if I could iron a blouse on the Sabbath her eyes told me no before she could fix her lips to say the word. "Sunday's the Lord's day," was all she said. On Sunday mornings the household met in the living room at six o'clock for family prayer. Mr. Abe prayed the same old rambling, mumbling words every single Sunday, although it took me years to realize this, because I fell asleep as soon as I got down on my knees. "And Lord, we want to thank you for the flowers and the beautiful birds." That was the verse I finally began to recognize.

Church in Pasquotank County was the same as in Philadelphia—an all-day affair. Some of Daddy's men friends lifted him up the cement steps that led to the church. Daddy sat in the back, so he could get out of everybody's way quickly when the service was over. The Sunday after Grandma killed the chickens one of my Sunday-school friends and I slipped out of services, ostensibly to go to the bathroom; instead we ran around to the back of the building and played hide-and-seek in the thick woods that bordered the church. We caught a frog jumping in the tall grass. It felt cool and slimy as I carried it carefully in my hands. Only, when we got back in church the frog slipped between my fingers and went hopping down the aisles. I was scared that somebody saw me. I thought Miss Rosie saw me but she didn't say anything, so I thought I got away with it, until later on, at home, when I was plucking out the ingrown hairs on Daddy's chin with a tweezer, he said to me, "I didn't know you liked frogs so much, Bebe." It was maybe the first time that I remember my father catching me doing something bad. Kinda bad. And I sort of drew in a quick breath, not knowing what he would do or say. But he didn't say a word. He started swiveling around in his chair acting antsy. "Let's go get us some watermelon," he said. I ran to the car.

That night, long after my daddy's snores started rocking the house, I crept out of bed. The moon lit up the room in a soft haze. I went to the closet and opened the door. I quietly pulled out my father's braces. I touched the smooth brown leather harness and put my hands around the hard metal strips. I pressed the trusses with my fingers. When, I thought. When?

This was the summer of my seventh year. A warm, flowery place, thick with family, chickens, car rides and a growing dream.

# CHAPTER 4

"Bebe! Comehererightquick." When Daddy wanted me "right quick" it meant he needed my help. I liked helping my father. I ran into his room. "Yes, Daddy."

He was in his wheelchair bending over to tie his shoes. When he straightened up I could see that his shirt hung outside his pants.

"I want you to help ole Daddy get his shirt tucked in." He looked at me and gave me one of his "help me" smiles. They were special. Not so much tooth. Mostly eyes that said: Well, you know I can do this by myself, but I like having you do it. "Lookahere. When I raise up, you just pull up the back of my pants over my shirt. Okay. Here we go." Daddy stood up in his chair, bearing down on the armrests with his hands. I grabbed a handful of pants, but just as I was about to pull up his pants, Daddy fell back in the chair.

"I didn't get it."

"You didn't?" Daddy laughed. "Okay. let's try again. Here we go!"

Daddy jerked himself up, holding onto the handrails of his chair. His short-sleeved shirt revealed hard muscles that seemed to dance a little as he strained to hold himself up. I snatched up his pants in my two hands and pulled up as hard as I could. In the yard I could hear the hens clucking and Big Boy grunting in the pigpen. In a few weeks he'd be reunion barbecue.

"Okayokayokay. That's good." Daddy fumbled around with his pants, pushing his shirt inside, zipping up his zipper while I pretended to be looking out the window. "Thank you, baby," Daddy said. "Couldn't make it without you."

Summer was racing by. It was August. In a few weeks I'd be going home. I missed Mommy, Nana and Michael, but I didn't want to think about leaving my father. "Daddy, is there a library anywhere near here?"

"Whatsa matter, you done read all those books you brought already?"

"I only brought six. I wanted to go to the library and get some more books."

"Well, uh"—Daddy looked at the floor—"this is the country, Bebe. And even Elizabeth City isn't real big. What kind of books you want?"

"I don't know. Books about kids. I like Little Eddie books and Ramona books. You know about those books, Daddy?"

"I don't think so." My father looked a little nervous.

"Well, they have them at the library."

"Well, Bebe, the library, that's a little complicated, but, uh . . ."

"George and Bebe!" Grandma called to us from the kitchen in a loud, booming voice.

"Ma'am?" Daddy called back to her.

"Y'all come eat breakfast."

"We're coming," Daddy yelled. To me he said, "We'll get you some books, all right?"

Grandma had fixed a breakfast fit for stevedores, chain gangs. My grandmother, Bunnie and my father heaped their plates with fried fish, fried potatoes, sausage, scrambled eggs, hot bread and preserves. They poured themselves glasses of orange juice and milk, cups of coffee with cream and sugar. I ate only cold cereal, which was always a point of conversation with Grandma. "That all your mama feed you up there in Phillydelphia? Post Toasties. Humph!" Phillydelphia was suspect.

"That's what she likes, Mama," my father said, his mouth full of sausage and biscuits. He winked at me.

"Humph," Grandma said again, then poured herself another cup of coffee.

After breakfast Daddy and I took off. The lane was a muddy mess from all the rains, so Daddy had to inch his way out, carefully maneuvering around slushy puddles and patches of earth that sank like quicksand. We waved to Miss Rosie and to Mr. Abe, who was out in the field stripping the leaves of the corn for fodder for Frosty and the pigs. He had been up since way before dawn, and when we passed and I shouted, "Hey, Mr. Abe," he looked startled but waved at us.

We drove to my cousin Belinda's house. I called it Belinda's house, but actually the house belonged to Cousin Emily, her grandmother. Cousin Emily's father and Daddy's father were brothers. Belinda had lived in New York with her mother for a while, but she didn't like the crowded city. I wanted to walk to Cousin Emily's by myself, but Daddy told me I was too young. Cousin Emily was a midwife and had delivered many of the babies between New Land, South Mills and Mill Pond, the tiny black communities that dotted the landscape around Grandma's house. I loved visiting Belinda. Her grandmother's house was right behind the sawmill, where most of the black men in Pasquotank County worked; at noon I could hear the whistle that signaled their lunch break. It was a big house with a wide porch that swung around from the front to the back. And it stood up off the ground at least two feet. Belinda and I played games under there sometimes, but mostly we dressed up in the old dresses that Cousin Emily kept in a dark trunk in her room.

Belinda was sitting on the porch, but she jumped up when we drove into her yard. Her braids bounced as she ran to the car on my daddy's side. She leaned inside and kissed his cheek. They smiled at each other.

"Well, Miss Belinda. Hey there," Daddy said, hugging her back.

"Ma-ma," Belinda called to Cousin Emily, "Cou'n George

and Bebe out here." Like mine, Belinda's speech had slipped into the softer cadences of the South. New York and Philadelphia were overpowered by Pasquotank County rhythms. The *n* was dropped, the *s* was slurred, and the verb *to be* helped all the others do their work.

A door slammed and Cousin Emily burst into the yard, smiling and making comments as she strode toward us. Cousin Emily was maybe in her early sixties, a loud, outspoken woman, a widow of many years.

"Hey there, George. Hey, Be Be." Cousin Emily beamed at me. "That girl sho' do favor you, George, and that's the truth. Right long in here," she said, drawing a swift line up and down the bridge of her nose with her thumb and index finger pressed together. "And y'all got the same smiles. 'Zactly the same," Cousin Emily exclaimed as she walked over to the car.

My daddy grabbed me when she said that and the sound of his laughter bounced from my ears into my bones and marrow. My daddy's laugh was an explosion. He laughed from his gut. Belinda came around to my side of the car and opened my door. "Hey," she said, staring at me.

"Hey," I said, staring back. Even though we had played together almost every week since the summer started, we always had an initial shyness whenever we got together.

"You wanna play?"

"Uh huh."

"Whatchu wanna play?" Belinda was an agreeable girl. I knew that whatever I wanted to do was all right with her.

"Dress-up."

"Come on." She took my hand.

I turned to my father. "Daddy . . ."

"Go 'head. Go 'head. I'm gonna talk to Cousin Emily then I'm fixin' to go off for a little bit. I'll come back and get you in a couple of hours."

"Leave her here long as you want," Cousin Emily said.

Belinda and I ran to Cousin Emily's bedroom and pushed out the trunk she kept behind her door. A treasure chest. We opened it and pulled out old dresses—blue, green, lavender; silk, satin, wool—and shoes, blouses, skirts, and ancient hats with exuberant plumes in the crown, and pocket books: everything we needed to create a brand-new world. We put the costumes on right over our shorts and blouses. The transformation was immediate. Marilyn! Liz! Lena! We were no longer two ordinary colored girls. We were queens, empresses, movie stars! We paraded inside and outside in fine old dresses that swept the floor as we walked, "cutting butter" just as hard as we could with our scrawny little hineys. Our high heels clicked as we strutted around Cousin Emily's room.

"What y'all doin?" June Bug, one of Belinda's Pasquotank County cousins, and one of mine, poked his little peanut head inside our castle. He was only six, a rusty-kneed little barefoot pest who thought my name was Huhbebe with a question mark.

"Playin'," I said in my best "why don't you get lost" tone.

"Playin' what? Huhbebe?"

"Dress-up."

"Y'all look so funny."

"Boy, go head on away from here. You gettin' on our nerves now," said a clearly exasperated Belinda.

June Bug only snickered and settled himself on the floor, his bony back pressed against the lumpy iron bed. "Y'all look so funny," he repeated. Belinda gave me the eye; we would ignore him.

"Whatchu gone be when you get grown, Bebe?" Belinda asked me in an adult tone of voice.

"A social worker."

"Huhbebe, a what?" June Bug asked.

"A social worker. That's the person who helps children who don't have parents find a home," I said, disdain dripping from my voice.

"How you get to be that, Huhbebe?" June Bug wondered.

This stupid, pesky boy. "You hafta go to college and get a degree."

This worldly information dazzled June Bug, who could barely contain his awe. "What are you gonna be?" I asked June Bug.

"Awww, everything I wanna be colored people can't be," June Bug said nonchalantly. He flopped himself on the floor and began picking at his baby toe, which must have been the single ashiest piece of flesh on the planet.

His answer puzzled me. "What do you mean? What do you want to be?"

"I wants to be a policeman or a fireman or the man that drives the train." June Bug rattled off his heart's desires in a dull, matter-of-fact voice, all the while picking at his little gray toe. "But colored people ain't 'lowed to be those things." He pulled a long, thin strand of dead skin from between his toes.

I stared at June Bug incredulously. "Awww, boy, that's a lie," I started to say, but the words sputtered in my mouth. Confusion dazed me. I racked my brain trying to recall seeing a colored policeman or fireman anywhere, but I couldn't remember. I knew about segregation and integration and I knew, of course, from my summers in North Carolina, that there were signs that said "White" and "Colored," signs for restaurants and water fountains. But Grandma and Daddy told me that the white water was hot and nasty. And once when I was on my way back to Philadelphia with Uncle Otto and Aunt Lela, my aunt marched me right into the white ladies' bathroom. She stared everybody down and waited while I was in the stall. So at seven I believed those signs were a mean-spirited nuisance, but that the word *colored* and *white* had no real power in my life. Now here was June Bug telling me those words had killed his dreams.

June Bug asked eagerly, "You from Phillydelphia, Huhbebe? Y'all gots colored policemens and firemens up there, Huhbebe?"

"I don't know. I think we do."

"I seen colored policemen in New York," Belinda said casually.

Then they must have them in Philly, I thought to myself. Philly and New York were both in the North.

"You did? What was they doin'?" June Bug asked eagerly. He had stopped picking his toe. His round, wide eyes blinked excitedly.

"Doin'? Wan't doin' nothin' 'cept walkin' down the street swingin' sticks."

June Bug's laughter was a frenzied war whoop. Without

warning, he leaped up from the floor and sprung into a handstand.

"June Bug, get on down and stop actin' stupid. You know Mama don't want you cuttin' up in her room," Belinda said, her voice quivering with irritation.

"You been on *Bandstand,* Huhbebe?" June Bug asked me when he regained his balance.

"That's for teenagers," I said. What a dummy.

"Colored teenagers be dancing on there, Huhbebe?"

"No." I was absolutely sure of this.

This time June Bug's face fell. "Colored people can't dance on *Bandstand* in Philadelphia?"

Now I was confused again. "I didn't say they couldn't. I just said they don't." But why don't we, I wondered silently. I thought of the *Bandstand* girls with their pageboys and ponytails, their poodle skirts, bobby socks and loafers, and the crew-cut or duck-tailed boys that swung them around and around. When I got to be fifteen or sixteen I'd march right on that show and dance better than anybody. "Those white kids on there can't dance anyway," I said adamantly, as Belinda and June Bug stared at me without speaking. Well, they can't! The words exploded in my mind. When I got on *Bandstand,* I'd show them how to dance. They'd be glad to see me coming!

It was after four o'clock when Daddy picked me up. He had gotten a haircut and tiny pieces of black hair were stuck to his sweaty neck and shirt collar. "Look in the backseat," my father told me, as we pulled out of Cousin Emily's yard. Books. A shopping bag full. I leafed through the pages as we drove home. No Ramona. No Little Eddie books. The books were old and musty. There was no library stamp on them. I realized suddenly that the library had a sign; it was like *Bandstand,* I thought glumly. That's why we couldn't go there. Daddy watched me in the rear-view mirror. I smiled into pages I wasn't reading.

Grandma Mary and Mr. Abe were sitting on the porch, en-joying the faintest sliver of a breeze. Daddy rolled his chair into the middle of the yard, under the ammo tree, and began reading the paper. He looked up at me and said, "These ingrown hairs are killing me." I got up, went inside and returned with alcohol, tweezers and cotton, and placed them in a neat line on a rusty old metal chair that had been in Grandma's yard forever. My father cleared his throat, then rolled his head back, letting his neck go limp. He rested his hands in his lap, occasionally raising one to point to a spot on his face that he felt was particularly inflamed and irritated, that needed my immediate attention. I pretended to search diligently for the curly hairs that had reentered his skin, patting his face softly with my hands as I looked, plucking the rare hairs I came across with a great deal of fanfare and alcohol. I was only seven, but I realized that this ritual of touching had nothing to do with razor bumps at all.

I stood on the bracers of his chair, my arms tightly circling his neck, and looked up in the sky. My daddy put the paper down and looked up too. A great flock of birds flew overhead. Summer was on their wings.

THE WEEK BEFORE I WAS TO RETURN TO PHILLY, GRANDMA MARY AND I stalked the aisles of the girls' section at Belk and Tyler's department store in Elizabeth City, looking for my school clothes. It was an end–of–the–summer ritual.

"Now you go find what you like," Grandma told me as she settled herself in a chair near the saleslady. She was prepared to sit there all day if she had to. Waiting was easy for her. The girls' department wasn't very big, nothing like Wanamaker's or Gimbels, where Mommy and I shopped in Philadelphia. Elizabeth City's entire shopping district was only two or three blocks. From her seat, Grandma could see every garment I chose. I hopped from rack to rack, picking out a red plaid skirt, a plain blue corduroy skirt, a blue plaid jumper and several blouses with collars and buttons. "Don't you need no little dresses?" Grandma asked, frowning slightly. She meant for church. Grandma was always thinking about church. In Pasquotank County everybody and especially little girls got real froufrou for church. Lots of lace and crinolines, special bows and barrettes and little fancy socks with lace at the top. I looked through the dress rack, pushing aside several lacy creations, and picked out a simple dress with pearl buttons and a wide skirt and a satin sash. Grandma smiled and nodded. I knew she was probably thinking I could get into heaven easy wearing that dress. I picked up three others, one a blue and gray plaid, another red with a white collar and a green print. "You love that green?" Grandma asked me in such a way it was clear *she* didn't. I put the green dress back and substituted another green one, with big pockets and a thin belt. "Uh huh. Now that's nice," Grandma said, smiling and touching the replacement fondly. "Pick out a coat," Grandma instructed me. "A good warm one with a hood. Don't you think you need one with a hood? Don't it get cold in Phillydelphia?"

We stayed in the store almost two hours. I tried everything on, then I changed my mind and chose new things and tried them on, slowly appraising myself in the mirror. Grandma Mary roped me in a few times when she questioned my taste, but otherwise she gave me free rein. I liked shopping. Liked standing in front of the mirror, feeling my new dresses against my skin and dreaming of where I could wear my beautiful new clothes. But most of all, I liked knowing that my father was buying me clothes. Liked best hearing my father say early that morning, "Weeeeeelp, Daddy's gotta get his baby some clothes today." It was years before I realized that at the time my father was a poor man, his only earnings a meager Social Security check, augmented by turning his car into a taxi service. I always thought of him as rich and powerful, a man who could buy me whatever I wanted.

When we got home I gave Daddy a fashion show. My father sat in the living room as I sashayed past him, twirling and whirling, strutting and grinning. Daddy leaned forward in his chair every time I entered the room. He was smoking a Winston. Whenever I finished showing him an outfit, he'd hold the cigarette in his mouth, squeeze his eyes almost closed so the smoke wouldn't burn them, and clap. Then he'd take the cigarette out and say, "Sharpsharpsharp. My baby's real sharp." When he clapped and whistled, I tried to think of ways I could show him the same clothes over again and make him think they were new, but I couldn't so I just walked real, real slow, trying to hold onto the last bit of summer.

"You get everything you want?" he asked when I'd shown him the last dress.

"Yep."

"Are you happy?"

"Yep. Thank you, Daddy."

"Oh, you're welcome, sugar. Daddy wants his baby to have everything she wants." I didn't know then just how much he meant those words.

Family reunion was held Labor Day weekend. Friday night Grandma and I lay across different beds in different rooms, looking out windows that faced the lane and the road beyond. We talked to each other through the wall that separated us. We sat up half the night, watching out the window, looking up the lane to see whose car would slip and slide through those muddy ruts. I loved my aunts, but I watched for my father's seven brothers. When I saw two dim headlights from the end of the lane grow brighter and brighter and closer, the truth is, I was waiting for my uncles. What I wanted was for Grandma Mary's house to fill with men's voices.

My uncles' cars rolled slowly up to Grandma's door in shiny splendor. They drove huge Fords, Oldsmobiles and Pontiacs with pearly whitewalls and big, shiny chrome fenders they'd polished the day before they left Camden or Philly or New York. John, Elijah, Eddie, Cleat, Joe, Sammy, Norman. JohnElijahEddie-CleatJoeSammyNorman.

I sneaked peeks of them as they got out of their cars and entered Grandma's house. They were tall, powerfully built men who moved with energy and grace. Grandma's boys had done well, pretty wives, healthy children, good factory jobs that would eventually lead to other possibilities. That was their magic: they all believed in their possibilities.

By Saturday evening everyone had arrived. Grandma moved around her blackened wood stove with more gusto than usual. Bustling in her pantry, she pulled down mason jars full of sticky fruit: pears and peach preserves, pickled watermelon rind, stewed tomatoes, corn. The kitchen smelled sweet. My aunts helped with the cooking. The women swished around the stove, pulled to-

gether like rounded bits of darkened steel under the kitchen's mag-
netic spell. Their voices were soft music, their words like gentle
tinkling. I watched them, smelled their Jergens and cream sachet
and disappeared to find the men.

My uncles were washing their cars under the pear and fig
trees. Bare chests were showing, with hair in thin strands and
some balled up in bunches tight as fists. Sweat was running down
their foreheads and glistening from their faces and backs. They
were talking about baseball and calling each other "man."

"Okay, then. Okay. Who was it had the first colored player,
huh? Answer me that." I took a few steps toward the cars, the
chests, and then stopped.

"Awww, man, we talking about 'fifty-seven. This here is
nineteen fifty-seven. Don't go getting historical on me now."

"Yeah, 'Lijah wants to open up the history books," said Uncle
Norman. He was the baby boy. Only Edith was younger.

"Man, shut up," Uncle Elijah retorted playfully. Slowly I
moved forward, inching my way toward the pear tree.

Norman laughed.

Uncle Joe was leaning against my father's chair. He and Daddy
were smoking cigarettes, the smoke billowing up into their personal cloud. Uncle Johnny was smoking a pipe. A little closer to
the lane, Uncle Eddie and Uncle Cleat were wiping the tops of
their cars, pausing from time to time to take long, generous swigs
of Dr Pepper.

My uncles were handsome magicians. Their words, thick
chests and strong arms pulled me like some strong invisible mag-
net. I wanted to be near them. I stole from the house into the
yard, near their cars, just wanting to be closer, sensing that they
didn't want intruders. Uncle Sammy stood quietly, laughing at
the others. He had only recently gotten out of the Marines and
had just recovered from a bout with spinal meningitis. He was
thin. He saw me and said, "All right now. You all watch your
mouths now. Watch your mouths." And then all my uncles saw
me, leaning against Grandma's fence looking at them.

"Hey, Miss Be Be. You wanna wash this car, girl?"

"*Ole,* Be Be. You growing girl."

"Hey, pretty face. Catch," Sammy said. I held out my hand and caught a gleaming quarter.

Daddy said, "Bebe, you go on in the house. This is menfolk's talk out here."

"I wanna tell Uncle Norman something," I said, walking over to my youngest uncle and pulling him away from his brothers. Uncle Norman bent down and I whispered in his ear. "When I took Cindy to the bathroom she made bright pink dodo." Cindy was Uncle Norman's daughter, a precocious three-year-old.

Norman laughed. "You tell Cindy her daddy said for her not to swallow her bubble gum." I nodded.

As I walked back to the house I could hear Norman, Joe and Sammy talking. They were working at the same knitting mill in Philadelphia. "They're gonna hafta take us off those pressers soon and let us get on some real machines," Sammy was saying in his quiet way.

"You think they're gonna let colored guys get on those machines and pay us that big money?" Joe asked.

"Get me my own factory," Norman said.

I heard my father's voice, low and eager. "Yeahyeahyeah. That's the ticket. Now we could do that."

The next day Mr. Abe killed Big Boy. When the pig was dead, Mr. Abe slit its stomach, scooped out the entrails and put them in a bucket. Uncle Joe and my daddy helped him tie the hog upside down from a pole in the backyard and shave all the hairs off while the blood dripped into a bucket. Uncle Joe, Uncle Eddie and my father yelled at me and the rest of my little cousins not to get too close, because of all the mess, but I kept sneaking closer and closer. My cousin Eddie Jr. was as close as he wanted to be, so why couldn't I stand where I wanted? Finally, Uncle Joe pronounced me a "hardheaded little thing" and nobody said a word when I stood next to Eddie Jr.

We held the reunion at Uncle Cliff's in Chesapeake. I rode in Uncle Johnny's car and sat on Aunt Rena's lap. Uncle Cliff was my father's father's brother and Cousin Eula's father. He was a very old man with dark brown skin and very white hair who smiled and patted my hand when I said hello. At the reunion I played tag and giant steps with cousins I hadn't seen since the year before and some I'd never seen. Cindy sat on Uncle Norman's lap and I heard him tell her, "Don't eat any more bubble gum, hear?" The grown-ups gathered in tight little clumps, talking about things I had seen on the evening news. Some dead boy named Emmett Till. Something called a bus boycott. Segregation. Integration. "Things is fittin' to change in America," said Uncle Cliff. "They fittin' to integrate the schools." Uh huh. Uh huh. Mebbe.

The picnic table in Uncle Cliff's yard was full. Daddy and I fixed our plates and sat under a shade tree together. June Bug wanted me to play, but I waved him away. I pulled my chair so close to my father's that our arms touched when they were resting. Daddy and I ate like yard dogs, tearing into the meat on our plates. I savored each bit of barbecue as though it were my last. My father smiled at me, moved his big hand over my plaits, saying, "BebebebebebebebebebeMoore," until we both were laughing. I started to ask him right then and there, "Daddy, when are you gonna start walking?" I bit my tongue. It would just happen one day, that's all. And when it did happen, my daddy would come to Philly and get me and my mommy. And we'd be together.

The taste of barbecue was still in my mouth when I woke up the next morning. I was going home. At the foot of the bed my summer clothes and my new clothes were packed in two neat suitcases. I had legs full of mosquito bites, a newly acquired Pasquotank County drawl, sun-blessed skin, but not quite enough of my father to get me through the winter. Grandma Mary gave me a powerful hug. I stood on the bracers of my father's wheelchair until Uncle Eddie called me to his car. Then I sat in my father's lap and he pulled me to his chest and held me there, tighter, tighter, tighter.

"C'mon, Bebe. Kiss your Daddy good-bye," Uncle Eddie told me.

I did. A fast kiss on his cheek and one last fast hug.

"I'll see you Thanksgiving," Daddy whispered. His eyes were wet. I nodded.

I got into Aunt Marie and Uncle Eddie's car and headed north.

"C'mon now, Be Be," Uncle Eddie said, looking at me in the rearview mirror, "quit crying. You're gonna see your Daddy again."

But not for a long time, I thought as I sobbed. Not for a long, long time.

MY MOTHER AND NANA HELD OUT THEIR ARMS AS UNCLE EDDIE'S CAR pulled up to the curb in front of our house. As soon as I got out of the car their arms came down on me like a sweet net. Their kisses smelled of Emeraude and Avon cream sachet. I felt their earrings pressing against my cheek. Their breasts were firm against my thin chest.

Mommy and Nana carried my bags upstairs to the room I shared with my mother. I stood in the corner, studying this room, trying to make it mine again. My room. It all came back to me, faster than I expected, faster than I even wanted.

My mosquito bites healed and as September wore on I faded from brown to yellow again, the darkness peeling away under the dimmer Philadelphia sun. I returned to a household where capable and loving women made sure that I had enough culture and Christianity, that I greased my legs and learned the difference between nice children and riffraff, that I was proper. My southern speech evaporated in a swirl of corrections.

"Bebe, don't say 'He be,' " my mother said, frowning.

"Don't talk flat," Nana admonished me.

"Open your mouth when you speak and don't call me ma'am. I hate that. It's so country," Aunt Ruth said irritably.

My North Carolina words needed a softer setting, corn standing tall in the background, roosters, chickens, pigs, people who wore shoes only on Sunday, folks who cured their own headaches by humming them away. Nana and Ruth hated the South. "Atlantic City. That's as far south as I go," Nana said flatly. I thought about the "Colored" and "White" signs and what June Bug had said. And yet it was my Daddy's home and I wanted to like it. I did like it and I didn't want Nana hinting that I shouldn't.

Outside my bedroom window I could hear the sharp click of heels and taps against the concrete pavement. Brakes were screeching as children rushed into the street for balls. I heard the hard slap of double-dutch ropes, turning, turning, turning, as little girls jumped, singing, "I wish I had a nickel, I wish I had a dime, I wish I had a sweetheart to love me all the time." Such a lonely rhyme. On the corner, five teenage boys, with brilliant-colored 'do rags holding their conks in place, harmonized, while down the block their mothers screamed their names.

Summer hadn't been long enough. I tried, but I couldn't crowd into short southern hot spells enough of my father to dilute completely the Wonder Woman potency of my female world. I was a girl and my mother and Nana figured that their love and North Carolina summers were enough.

At night I slept with my mother in a wide double bed. She cuddled me silently in her arms and I lay there comforted, my small hips jutting softly into her groin. I put my thumb in my mouth and stroked my mother's ears, not caring about my dime. My back felt the gentle pressure of her breasts, pressing, pressing.

I was happy to be back home, but a part of me was missing. Summer had run out. I longed for my father's voice, his thick, strong neck, his wonderful, joyful whoop of a laugh. I missed the speed of his highly polished home, his white-walled legs. I missed his yell for me, deep, thick and resonant.

"I want my daddy," I cried.

"You'll see him at Thanksgiving," my mother answered.

"I want my daddy," I screamed.

"Awww, sweetie. Shhhhhhh. Ahhhhhhh. Don't cry. Don't cry."

My mother moved in closer, wrapping me in soft words, soft hands, breasts. I gasped for air. I was drowning in a sea of bosoms.

# CHAPTER 5

The red bricks of 2239 North 16th Street melded into the uniformity of look-alike doors, windows and brownstone-steps. From the outside our rowhouse looked the same as any other. When I was a toddler, the similarity was unsettling. The family story was that my mother and I were out walking on the street one day when panic rumbled through me. "Where's our house? Where's our house?" I cried, grabbing my mother's hand.

My mother walked me to our house, pointed to the numbers painted next to the door. "Twenty-two thirty-nine," she said, slapping the wall. "This is our house."

Much later I learned that the real difference was inside.

In my house there was no morning stubble, no long johns or Fruit of the Loom on the clothesline, no baritone hollering for keys that were sitting on the table. There was no beer in the refrigerator, no ball game on TV, no loud cussing. After dark the snores that emanated from the bedrooms were subtle, ladylike, little moans really.

Growing up, I could have died from overexposure to femininity. Women ruled at 2239. A grandmother, a mother, occasionally an aunt, grown-up girlfriends from at least two generations, all the time rubbing up against me, fixing my food, running my bathwater, telling me to sit still and be good in those grown-up, girly-girl voices. Chanel and Prince Matchabelli wafting through the bedrooms. Bubble bath and Jergens came from the bathroom, scents unbroken by aftershave, macho beer breath, a good he-man funk. I remember a house full of 'do rags and rollers, the soft, sweet allure of Dixie peach and bergamot; brown-skinned queens wearing pastel housecoats and worn-out size six-and-a-half flip-flops that slapped softly against the wood as the royal women climbed the stairs at night carrying their paperbacks to bed.

The outside world offered no retreat. School was taught by stern, old-maid white women with age spots and merciless gray eyes; ballet lessons, piano lessons, Sunday school and choir were all led by colored sisters with a hands-on-their-hips attitude who cajoled and screeched in distaff tongues.

And what did they want from me, these Bosoms? Achievement! This desire had nothing to do with the pittance they collected from the Philadelphia Board of Education or the few dollars my mother paid them. Pushing little colored girls forward was in their blood. They made it clear: a life of white picket fences and teas was for other girls to aspire to. I was to *do* something. And if I didn't climb willingly up their ladder, they'd drag me to the top. Rap my knuckles hard for not practicing. Make me lift my leg until I wanted to die. Stay after school and write "I will listen to the teacher" five hundred times. They were not playing. "Obey them," my mother commanded.

When I entered 2B—the Philadelphia school system divided grades into A and B—in September 1957, I sensed immediately that Miss Bradley was not a woman to be challenged. She looked like one of those evil old spinsters Shirley Temple was always getting shipped off to live with; she was kind of hefty, but so tightly corseted that if she happened to grab you or if you fell against her during recess, it felt as if you were bouncing into a steel wall. In reality she was a sweet lady who was probably a good five years past her retirement age when I wound up in her class. Miss Bradley remained at Logan for one reason and one reason only: she was dedicated. She wanted her students to learn! learn! learn! Miss Bradley was halfway sick, hacking and coughing her lungs out through every lesson, spitting the phlegm into fluffy white tissues from the box on her desk, but she was *never* absent. Each day at three o'clock she kissed each one of her "little pupils" on the cheek, sending a faint scent of Emeraude home with us. Her rules for teaching children seemed to be: Love them; discipline them; reward them; and make sure they are clean.

Every morning she ran a hygiene check on the entire class. She marched down the aisle like a stormtrooper, rummaging through the ears of hapless students, checking for embedded wax. She looked under our fingernails for dirt. Too bad on you if she found any. Once she made David, a stringy-haired white boy who thought Elvis Presley was a living deity and who was the most notorious booger-eater in the entire school, go to the nurse's office to have the dirt cleaned from under his fingernails. Everybody knew that what was under David's fingernails was most likely dried-up boogies and not dirt, but nobody said anything.

If she was death on dirt and earwax, Miss Bradley's specialty was head-lice patrol. Down the aisles she stomped in her black Enna Jettick shoes, stopping at each student to part strands of blond, brown or dark hair, looking for cooties. Miss Bradley would flip through plaits, curls, kinks—the woman was relentless. I always passed inspection. Nana put enough Nu Nile in my hair to suffocate any living creature that had the nerve to come tipping up on my scalp. Nu Nile was the official cootie killer. I was clean, wax-free, bug-free and smart. The folder inside my desk contained a stack of spelling and arithmetic papers with As emblazoned across the top, gold stars in the corner. Miss Bradley always called on me. She sent me to run errands for her too. I was her pet.

When Mrs. Clark, my piano teacher and my mother's good friend, told my mother that Logan Elementary School was accepting children who didn't live in the neighborhood, my mother immediately enrolled Michael and later me. "It's not crowded and it's mixed," she told a nodding, smiling Nana. The fact that Logan was integrated was the main reason Michael and I were sent there. Nana and Mommy, like most upwardly mobile colored women, believed that to have the same education as a white child was the first step up the rocky road to success. This viewpoint was buttressed by the fact that George Washington Carver, my neighborhood school, was severely overcrowded. Logan was just barely integrated, with only a handful of black kids thrown in with hordes of square-jawed, pale-eyed second-generation Ukrainians whose immigrant parents and grandparents populated the neighborhood near the school. There were a few dark-haired Jews and aristocratic-looking WASPs too. My first day in kindergarten it was Nana who enthusiastically grabbed Michael's and my hands, pulling us away from North Philly's stacked-up rowhouses, from the hucksters whose wagons bounced down the streets with trucks full of ripe fruits and vegetables, from the street-corner singers and jitterbugs who filled my block with all-day doo-wahs. It was Nana who resolutely walked me past the early-morning hordes of colored kids heading two blocks away to Carver Elementary School, Nana who pulled me by the hand and led me in another direction.

We went underground at the Susquehanna and Dauphin subway station, leaving behind the unremitting asphalt and bricks and the bits of paper strewn in the streets above us. We emerged at Logan station, where sunlight, brilliant red and pink roses and yellow chrysanthemums, and neatly clipped lawns and clean streets startled me. There were robins and blue jays flying overhead. The only birds in my neighborhood were sparrows and pigeons. Delivering me at the schoolyard, Nana firmly cupped my chin with her hand as she bent down to instruct me. "Your mother's sending you up here to learn, so you do everything your teacher tells you to, okay?" To Michael she turned and said, "You're not up here to be a monkey on a stick." Then to both of us: "Don't talk. Listen. Act like you've got some home training. You've got as much brains as anybody up here. Do you know that? All right now. Make Nana proud of you."

A month after I returned from Pasquotank County, I sat in Miss Bradley's classroom on a rainy Monday watching her write spelling words on the blackboard. The harsh sccurr, sccurr of Miss Bradley's chalk and the tinny sound the rain made against the window took my mind to faraway places. I couldn't get as far away as I wanted. Wallace, the bane of the whole class, had only moments earlier laid the most gigunda fart in history, one in a never-ending series, and the air was just clearing. His farts were silent wonders. Not a hint, not the slightest sound. You could be in the middle of a sentence and then wham! bam! Mystery Funk would knock you down.

Two seats ahead of me was Leonard, a lean colored boy from West Philly who always wore suits and ties to school, waving his hand like a crazy man. A showoff if ever there was one.

I was bored that day. I looked around at the walls. Miss Bradley had decorated the room with pictures of the ABCs in cursive. Portraits of the presidents were hanging in a row on one wall above the blackboard. On the bulletin board there was a display of the Russian satellite, *Sputnik I,* and the American satellite, *Explorer I.* Miss Bradley was satellite-crazy. She thought it was just wonderful that America was in the "space race" and she constantly filled our heads with space fantasies. "Boys and girls," she told us, "one day man will walk on the moon." In the far corner on another bulletin board there was a Thanksgiving scene of turkeys and pilgrims. And stuck in the corner was a picture of Sacajawea. Sacajawea, Indian Woman Guide. I preferred looking at Sacajawea over satellites any day.

Thinking about the bubble gum that lay in my pocket, I decided to sneak a piece, even though gum chewing was strictly forbidden. I rarely broke the rules. Could anyone hear the loud drumming of my heart, I wondered, as I slid my hand into my skirt pocket and felt for the Double Bubble? I peeked cautiously to either side of me. Then I managed to unwrap it without even rustling the paper; I drew my hand to my lips, coughed and popped the gum in my mouth. Ahhh! Miss Bradley's back was to the class. I chomped down hard on the Double Bubble. Miss Bradley turned around. I quickly packed the gum under my tongue. My hands were folded on top of my desk. "Who can give me a sentence for 'birthday'?" Leonard just about went nuts. Miss Bradley ignored him, which she did a lot. "Sandra," Miss Bradley called.

A petite white girl rose obediently. I liked Sandra. She had shared her crayons with me once when I left mine at home. I

remember her drawing: a white house with smoke coming out of
the chimney, a little girl with yellow hair like hers, a mommy,
a daddy, a little boy and a dog standing in front of the house in
a yard full of flowers. Her voice was crystal clear when she spoke.
There were smiles in that voice. She said, "My father made me a
beautiful dollhouse for my birthday."

The lump under my tongue was suddenly a stone and when
I swallowed, the taste was bitter. I coughed into a piece of tablet
paper, spit out the bubble gum, and crumpled up the wad and
pushed it inside my desk. The center of my chest was burning. I
breathed deeply and slowly. Sandra sat down as demurely as a
princess. She crossed her ankles. Her words came back to me in
a rush. "Muuuy fatha made me a bee-yoo-tee-ful dollhouse." Miss
Bradley said, "Very good," and moved on to the next word.
Around me hands were waving, waving. Pick me! Pick me! Behind me I could hear David softly crooning, "You ain't nothin'
but a hound dog, cryin' all the time." Sometimes he would stick
his head inside his desk, sing Elvis songs and pick his boogies at
the same time. Somebody was jabbing pins in my chest. Ping!
Ping! Ping! I wanted to holler, "Yowee! Stop!" as loud as I could,
but I pressed my lips together hard.

"Now who can give me a sentence?" Miss Bradley asked. I
put my head down on my desk and when Miss Bradley asked me
what was wrong I told her that I didn't feel well and that I didn't
want to be chosen. When Leonard collected the homework, I
shoved mine at him so hard all the papers he was carrying fell on
the floor.

Bile was still clogging my throat when Miss Bradley sent me
into the cloakroom to get my lunchbox. The rule was, only one
student in the cloakroom at a time. When the second one came
in, the first one had to leave. I was still rummaging around in my
bookbag when I saw Sandra.

"Miss Bradley said for you to come out," she said. She was
smiling. That dollhouse girl was always smiling. I glared at her.

"Leave when I get ready to," I said, my words full of venom.

Sandra's eyes darted around in confusion. "Miss Bradley

said . . ." she began again, still trying to smile as if she expected somebody to crown her Miss America or something and come take her picture any minute.

In my head a dam broke. Terrible waters rushed out. "I don't care about any Miss Bradley. If she messes with me I'll, I'll . . . I'll take my butcher knife and stab her until she bleeds." What I lacked in props I made up for in drama. My balled-up hand swung menacingly in the air. I aimed the invisible dagger toward Sandra. Her Miss America smile faded instantly. Her eyes grew round and frightened as she blinked rapidly. "Think I won't, huh? Huh?" I whispered, enjoying my meanness, liking the scared look on Sandra's face. Scaredy cat! Scaredy cat! Muuuy fatha made me a bee-yoo-tee-ful dollhouse. "What do you think about that?" I added viciously, looking into her eyes to see the total effect of my daring words.

But Sandra wasn't looking at me. Upon closer inspection, I realized that she was looking *over* me with sudden relief in her face. I turned to see what was so interesting, and my chin jammed smack into the Emeraude-scented iron bosom of Miss Bradley. Even as my mind scrambled for an excuse, I knew I was lost.

Miss Bradley had a look of horror on her face. For a minute she didn't say anything, just stood there looking as though someone had slapped her across the face. Sandra didn't say anything. I didn't move. Finally, "Would you mind repeating what you just said, Bebe."

"I didn't say anything, Miss Bradley." I could feel my dress sticking to my body.

"Sandra, what did Bebe say?"

Sandra was crying softly, little delicate tears streaming down her face. For just a second she paused, giving a tiny shudder. I rubbed my ear vigorously, thinking, "Oh, please . . ."

"She said, she said, if you bothered with her she would cut you with her knife."

"Unh unh, Miss Bradley, I didn't say that. I didn't. I didn't say anything like that."

Miss Bradley's gray eyes penetrated mine. She locked me into her gaze until I looked down at the floor. Then she looked at Sandra.

"Bebe, you and I had better go see the principal."

The floor blurred. The principal!! Jennie G., the students called her with awe and fear. As Miss Bradley wrapped her thick knuckles around my forearm and dutifully steered me from the cloakroom and out the classroom door, I completely lost what little cool I had left. I began to cry, a jerky, hiccuping, snot-filled cry for mercy. "I didn't say it. I didn't say it," I moaned.

Miss Bradley was nonplussed. Dedication and duty overruled compassion. Always. "Too late for that now," she said grimly.

Jennie G.'s office was small, neat and dim. The principal was dwarfed by the large brown desk she sat behind, and when she stood up she wasn't much bigger than I. But she was big enough to make me tremble as I stood in front of her, listening to Miss Bradley recount the sordid details of my downfall. Jennie G. was one of those pale, pale vein-showing white women. She had a vocabulary of about six horrible phrases, designed to send chills of despair down the spine of any young transgressor. Phrases like "We'll just see about that" or "Come with me, young lady," spoken ominously. Her face was impassive as she listened to Miss Bradley. I'd been told that she had a six-foot paddle in her office used solely to beat young transgressors. Suppose she tried to beat me? My heart gave a lurch. I tugged rapidly at my ears. I longed to suck my thumb.

"Well, Bebe, I think we'll have to call your mother."

My mother! I wanted the floor to swallow me up and take me whole. My mother! As Jennie G. dialed the number, I envisioned my mother's face, clouded with disappointment and shame. I started crying again as I listened to the principal telling my mother what had happened. They talked for a pretty long time. When she hung up, ole Jennie G. flipped through some papers on her desk before looking at me sternly.

"You go back to class and watch your mouth, young lady."

As I was closing the door to her office I heard her say to Miss Bradley, "What can you expect?"


"OOOOH, YOU'RE GONNA GET IT, GIRL," IS HOW MICHAEL GREETED me after school. Logan's colored world was small, and news of my demise had blazed its way through hallways and classrooms, via the brown-skinned grapevine. Everyone from North Philly, West Philly and Germantown knew about my crime. The subway ride home was depressing. My fellow commuters kept coming up to me and asking, "Are you gonna get in trouble?" Did they think my mother would give me a reward or something? I stared at the floor for most of the ride, looking up only when the train came to a stop and the doors hissed open. Logan. Wyoming. Hunting Park. Each station drew me closer to my doom, whatever that was going to be. "What can you expect?" I mulled over those words. What did she mean? My mother rarely spanked, although Nana would give Michael or me, usually Michael, a whack across the butt from time to time. My mother's social-worker instincts were too strong for such undignified displays; Doris believed in talking things out, which was sometimes worse than a thousand beatings. As the train drew closer to Susquehanna and Dauphin I thought of how much I hated for my mother to be disappointed in me. And now she would be. "What can you expect?"

Of me? Didn't Jennie G. know that I was riding a subway halfway across town as opposed to walking around the corner to Carver Elementary School, for a reason: the same reason I was dragged away from Saturday cartoons and pulled from museum to museum, to Judimar School of Dance for ballet (art class for Michael), to Mrs. Clark for piano. The Bosoms wanted me to Be Somebody, to be the second generation to live out my life as far away from a mop and scrub brush and Miss Ann's floors as possible.

My mother had won a full scholarship to the University of Pennsylvania. The story of that miracle was a treasured family heirloom. Sometimes Nana told the tale and sometimes my mother described how the old Jewish counselor at William Penn High School approached her and asked why a girl with straight Es (for "excellent") was taking the commercial course. My mother replied that Nana couldn't afford to send her to college, that she planned to become a secretary. "Sweetheart, you switch to academic," the woman told her. "You'll get to college." When her graduation day approached, the counselor pulled her aside. "I have two scholarships for you. One to Cheyney State Teacher's College and the other to the University of Pennsylvania." Cheyney was a small black school outside of Philadelphia. My mother chose Penn. I had been born to a family of hopeful women. One miracle had already taken place. They expected more. And now I'd thrown away my chance. Michael, who was seated next to me on the subway and whose generosity of spirit had lasted a record five subway stops, poked me in my arm. "Bebe," he told me gleefully, "your ass is grass."

Nana took one look at my guilty face, scowled at me and sucked her teeth until they whistled. My mother had called her and told her what happened and now she was possessed by a legion of demons. I had barely entered the room when she exploded. "Don't. Come. In. Here. Crying," Nana said, her voice booming, her lips quivering and puffy with anger. When Nana talked in staccato language she was beyond pissed off. Waaaay beyond. "What. Could. Possess. You. To. Say. Such. A. Thing?" Embarrassingyourmotherlikethatinfrontof *those people!*" Before I could answer she started singing some Dinah Washington song, real loud. Volume all the way up. With every word she sang I sank deeper and deeper into gloom.

Later that evening, when my mother got home and Aunt Ruth, Michael's mother, came to visit, the three women lectured me in unison. The room was full of flying feathers. Three hens clucking away at me, their breasts heaving with emotion. Cluck! Cluck! Cluck! How could I have said such a thing? What on earth was I thinking about? Cluck! Cluck! Cluck! A knife, such a, a *colored* weapon.

"But I didn't do anything," I wailed, the tears that had been trickling all day now falling in full force.

"Umph, umph, umph," Nana said, and started singing. Billie Holiday this time.

"You call threatening somebody with a knife nothing?" Aunt Ruth asked. Ruth was Nana's middle girl. She was the family beauty, as pretty as Dorothy Dandridge or Lena Horne. Now her coral lips were curled up in disdain and her Maybelline eyebrows were raised in judgment against me. "They expect us to act like animals and you have to go and say that. My God."

Animals. Oh. Oh. Oh.

My mother glared at her sister, but I looked at Aunt Ruth in momentary wonder and appreciation. Now I understood. The unspoken rule that I had sensed all of my life was that a colored child had to be on her best behavior whenever she visited the white world. Otherwise, whatever opportunity was being presented would be snatched away. I had broken the rule. I had committed the unpardonable sin of embarrassing my family in front of *them*. Sensing my remorse and shame, Mommy led me out of the kitchen. We sat down on the living room sofa; my mother took my hand. "Bebe, I want you to go to your room and think about what you've done. I don't understand your behavior. It was very hard for me to get you in Logan." She drew a breath. I drew a breath and looked into the eyes of a social worker. "I'm extremely disappointed in you."

I didn't go straight to my room. Instead I sneaked into Michael's room, which overlooked Mole Street, the tiny, one-sided alley of narrow rowhouses that faced the backyards of 16th Street. Michael and I usually played on the "back street." Alone in Michael's room with the window open, I could hear Mr. Watson, our neighbor, hollering at one of his kids. Why had I said what I said? What had possessed me? Then I remembered. "Muuuy fatha made me a bee-yoo-tee-ful dollhouse for muuuuy birthday." Something pinched me inside my chest when I heard those words. Pain oozed from my heart like a tube of toothpaste bursting open, going every whichaway. Blue-eyes kept yapping away with her golden hair and her goofy little smile. Who cared what her fatha did? Who cared? I couldn't help it. When she came into the cloakroom I got mad all over again. When I said I had a knife, she looked just like Grandma Mary's chickens. Scared. And my chest stopped hurting. Just stopped.

Mr. Watson's baritone voice was a seismic rumble echoing with the threat of upheaval, violence. His words floated over Mole Street and into the bedroom window. Whoever was in trouble over there was really gonna get it. None of this "go to your room" stuff. None of this corny "I'm disappointed in you" stuff. Mr. Watson was getting ready to beat somebody's ass.

Adam's. He was the youngest and one of my playmates. I could tell by his pleading voice. "Please, Daddy. I won't do it anymore, Daddy. I'm sorry, Daddy."

Michael came into the room. "What are you doing?" he whispered.

"Shhh. Adam's getting a whipping."

"You better go to your room before Aunt Doris comes upstairs."

"Shhhh."

My playmate's misery took my mind off my own. His father's exotic yelling hypnotized me. From downstairs I could hear the hens, still clucking away. Michael and I sat quietly, not making a sound. Mr. Watson's voice sounded so foreign coming into our house. For a moment I pretended that his anger was emanating from Michael's bedroom, and I remembered how only last year he got mad and ran after all of us kids—Jackie, Jane and Adam, his own three, and me. His face was covered with shaving cream and he held a razor in one hand and a thick leather belt in the other. I don't recall what we had done, but I remember him chasing us and yelling ferociously, "This belt's got your name on it too, Miss Bebe!" And I recall that I was thrilled when the leather grazed my hiney with the vengeance of a father's wrath.

My mind drifted back a few years. The memory was vague and fuzzy. When I was four or five I was playing on Mole Street when my ten-year-old neighbor, a boy named Buddy, asked me to come inside his yard. He was sitting on an old soda crate. "Come closer," he told me. "Wanna play doctor?"

"Uh huh."

"You can examine me."

I told my mother, prattling on about the "game" I had played. She sat me down on her bed. "Did he touch your private parts?"

"Nope." Why was Mommy's face so serious?

"Did you touch his?"

"I touched his zipper." Had I done something wrong?

Nana went into hysterics, singing and screeching like a wild woman. "Mother, just calm down," Mommy told her.

Mommy was cool, every inch the social worker; she took my hand and we walked down the street to Buddy's house. He was in his yard making a scooter out of the crate. "Buddy," my mother said softly. When he saw the two of us, he dropped his hammer. "Buddy, I want to talk with you."

My mother questioned him. Calmly put the fear of God in him. Warned him of penalties for a repeat performance. And that was that. Not quite. Weeks, maybe months later, my father came to visit me, one of his pop-in, no-real-occasion visits. My mother, my father and I were sitting in his car and she told him about my playing doctor. His leg shot out in wild, uncontrollable spasms. His face became contorted and he started yelling. Nana's screeching paled in contrast. This was rage that my mother and Nana could not even begin to muster. And it was in my honor. This energy was for my avengement, my protection. Or should have been. But the sound of his fury frightened me. I remember angling away from my father, this man who was yelling like an animal in pain. I leaned toward my mother, and she put one arm around me and with her other hand tried to pat my father's shoulder, only he snatched away. He leaned forward and started reaching for his chair. "I may not be able to walk, goddammit, but I can tear that little son of a bitch's ass up."

My mother kept talking very softly, saying, "No, no, no. It's all right. He's just a kid. I took care of it. It's okay." I leaned away from my father's anger, his determination. He frightened me. But the rage was fascinating too. And after a while, when my father was shouting only a little, I moved closer to him. I wanted to see the natural progression of his hot words. If he snatched his wheelchair out of the backseat and rolled up to Buddy's house, what would he do? What would he do in my honor?

My mother calmed my father. His shouting subsided. I was relieved. I was disappointed.

"Hey"—I suddenly heard Michael's persistent voice—"ain't you glad Mr. Watson ain't your father?" I felt Michael's hands, shaking my shoulder. "Ain't you?"

I didn't answer. I was thinking about Miss Bradley, Jennie G., Aunt Ruth, Nana and Mommy. All these women with power over me. I could hear Mrs. Watson telling her husband that enough was enough and then the baritone telling her he knew when to stop and Adam letting out another feeble little yelp. "Muuuy fatha made me a bee-yoo-tee-ful dollhouse." Maybe my mother would write my daddy and tell him how bad I had been. Maybe he would get so mad he would get into his car and drive all the way to Philly just to whip my behind. Or tell me he was disappointed in me. Either one.

THE BOSOMS DECIDED TO FORGIVE ME. MY MOTHER WOKE ME UP WITH a kiss and a snuggle and then a crisp, "All right, Bebe. It's a brand-new day. Forget about yesterday." When I went to get a bowl of cereal that morning, my Aunt Ruth was sitting in the kitchen drinking coffee and reading the newspaper. She had spent the night. "Did you comb your hair?" she asked me.

I nodded.

"That's not what I call combed. Go get me the comb and brush."

She combed out my hair and braided it all over again. This time there were no wispy little ends sticking out. "Now you look nice," she said. "Now you look like a pretty girl, and when you go to school today, act like a pretty girl. All right?"

I nodded.

Last night Nana had hissed at me between her teeth. "If you want to behave like a little *heathen,* if you want go up there acting like a, a . . . *monkey on a stick . . . well,* thenyoucangotoschoolrightaroundthecornerandI'llwalkyouthereandI'llwalkyoubackhomeandI'llcomeandgetyouforlunchnowyou*behave*yourself!" But today she was sanguine, even jovial, as she fixed my lunch. She kissed me when I left for school.

On my way out the door my mother handed me two elegant letters, one to Miss Bradley and the other to Jennie G., assuring them that I had an overactive imagination, that I had no access to butcher knives or weapons of any kind, that she had spoken to me at length about my unfortunate outburst and that henceforth my behavior would be exemplary. These letters were written on her very best personalized stationery. The paper was light pink and had "D.C.M." in embossed letters across the top. Doris C. knew lots of big words and she had used every single one of them in those letters. I knew that all of her *i*s were dotted and all of her *t*s were crossed. I knew the letters were extremely dignified. My mother was very big on personal dignity. Anyone who messed with her dignity was in serious trouble.

I was only five when an unfortunate teller at her bank called her by her first name loud enough for the other customers to hear. My mother's body stiffened when she heard, "Doris, oh Doris," coming from a girl almost young enough to be her child.

"Are you talking to *me,* dear?" Her English was so clipped, her words so razor sharp she could have taken one, stabbed the teller and drawn blood. The girl nodded, her speckled green eyes wide and gaping, aware that something was going on, not quite sure what, and speechless because she was no match at all for this imperious little brown-skinned woman. "The people in *my* office all call me *Mrs. Moore.*"

And she grabbed me by the hand and we swept out of the bank. Me and Bette Davis. Me and Claudia McNeil. People stepped aside to let us pass.

So I knew my mother's letters not only would impress Miss Bradley and Jennie G. but also would go a long way toward redeeming me. After Miss Bradley read the note she told me I had a very nice mother and let me know that if I was willing to be exemplary she would let bygones be bygones and I could get back into her good graces. She was, after all, a dedicated teacher. And I had learned my lesson.

My mother wrote my father about the knife incident. I waited anxiously to hear from him. Would he suddenly appear? I searched the street in front of the school every afternoon. At home I jumped up nervously whenever I heard a horn beep. Finally, a letter from my dad arrived—one page of southpaw scribble.

*Dear Bebe,*
*Your mother told me what happened in school about the knife.*
*That wasn't a good thing to say. I think maybe you were*
*joking. Remember, a lot of times white people don't understand*
*how colored people joke, so you have to be careful what you*
*say around them. Be a good girl.*

> *Lots of love,*
> *Daddy.*

The crumpled letter hit the edge of the wastepaper basket in my mother's room and landed in front of her bureau. I picked it up and slammed it into the basket, hitting my hand in the process. I flung myself across the bed, buried my face into my pillow and howled with pain, rage and sadness. "It's not fair," I wailed. Ole Blondie had her dollhouse-making daddy whenever she wanted him. "Muuuy fatha . . ." Jackie, Jane and Adam had their wild, ass-whipping daddy. All they had to do was walk outside their house, look under a car, and there he was, tinkering away. Ole ugly grease-monkey man. Why couldn't I have my daddy all the time too? I didn't want a letter signed "Lots of love," I wanted my father to come and yell at me for acting like a monkey on a stick. I wanted him to come and beat my butt or shake his finger in my face, or tell me that what I did wasn't so bad after all. Anything. I just wanted him to come.

# CHAPTER 6

"Hurry up, girl," Michael said as we ran down the front steps. We wanted to get to school early so we could play. Running down 16th Street, we waved to Mr. Crawford, who was on his way to work, and to Mrs. Lewis's teenage son, Charles, who was slowly lumbering down the street struggling with a huge tuba case.

When we raced around the corner we could see that Susquehanna Avenue was already crowded with children scurrying to school and adults on their way to work. The street was full of cars and people laughing and shouting at one another. Rosen's, the jewelry store, and Green's Drug Store hadn't opened yet. But men with lunchpails were coming out of Willie Jacks' Good Home cooking carrying freshly baked doughnuts and Styrofoam cups filled with steaming coffee. The odor of coffee and doughnuts wafted through the air. As we rushed past Pagejo's, we could see that it was already full of children buying a day's supply of Mary Janes, Double Bubble, and Good and Plenty. The door was open and we got a peek of Old Lady Pagejo running all over the place, her wild gray hair streaming down her back, yelling at kids to get out once they got their candy. Her blind dog, Sallie, was lying in her usual corner, fat old belly heaving in and out real fast. The dog and Old Lady Pagejo had the same colorless eyes, not blue or gray, just kind of clear and see-through. Strange eyes. We looked in Junior's Shoe Shine Parlor and Barber Shop, where the ancient retirees assembled in the early morning to drink their coffee and shoot the breeze, to see if Pete was getting his shoes shined. Anne and Pete rented the third-floor apartment of our house and sometimes on our way to school we'd meet Pete, whom Michael and I both adored, coming out of the shoeshine parlor, and he'd walk us to the subway. But Pete wasn't at Junior's this morning.

We were almost out of breath when we reached Broad Street. As we descended the steps to the subway, a sudden gust of cool wind sent the front of my skirt flaring up into my face; we knew the train was coming even before we heard it. Michael laughed and grabbed my bookbag. "C'mon," he said. Pressing my skirt down with one hand, my lunchbox bouncing against my thigh, I ran with Michael, breathing in the dampness of the underground tunnel. When we got to the toll booth, we quickly dropped our PTC tokens into the box, rushed through the turnstile and jumped on the train just as the doors were about to close.

As soon as we felt the rocking motion of the train zooming out of Susquehanna and Dauphin, Michael raced off to the other end of the car. His was soon the loudest voice among a chorus of rowdy preteens all headed for Logan. That was all right with me; I pulled out a Little Eddie book and became so immersed that I was startled when Michael yelled at me that we were at Logan.

The early birds were congregating in the yard, playing a fast game of ball, jumping rope, doing whatever they could do to have fun until the bell rang. I was standing in the yard, looking for my friends. Carol and Linda and I had planned to jump rope before school. Lately when I wasn't doing anything but thinking about a lot of different junk, Jennie G.'s voice would come into my head. "What can you expect?" That's what I heard as I was standing in the yard. I shook my head to chase away the thought, when I saw Sandra walking across the schoolyard. It had been only a few weeks since the knife incident. I should have known better, but when she looked at me I kind of rolled my eyes and did a snake-neck grit at her for about five seconds, first making sure there

were no witnesses, just to get a little piece of revenge. After all,
she had told on me. Then I looked the other way. But not before
I saw that same scaredy-cat expression she wore the day I mentioned the knife to her. I was instantly sorry and felt guilty, but
Sandra ran off before I could apologize.

I was feeling sorry about everything as I walked down to the
big poplar tree at the end of the schoolyard, where Linda and
Carol were already waiting for me. Sorry I had ever heard about
Sandra's dollhouse. Sorry I had made up the knife. Sorry I had
gotten in trouble. And I was sorry my daddy had sent me only a
scribbly letter, when what I really wanted was for him to come
and be with me.

"C'mon! Hurry up, girl!" Linda and Carol were yelling.
"Let's jump rope!" I ran toward the tree, forgetting everything.
Double dutch was our passion, our drug, and right now I needed
a fix to wipe out my sorry feeling.

The bell was going to ring soon. We could maybe get in a
few sets of double dutch if we hurried. Carol had brought her
rope, a thin cord that burned our legs if it slapped against them.
Carol jumped while Linda and I turned the ropes faster and faster,
whipping up the air with our speed. Clipclipclipclip. The ropes
kept up a fierce rhythm as they smacked against the pavement.
We sang loudly, "Miss Mary Mack, Mack, Mack . . . all dressed
in black, black, black . . . with silver buttons, buttons, buttons
. . . all down her back, back, back. . . ."

"Can we jump with youse?"

Martha and Iris, two girls from the Ukrainian section of
Logan, stood in front of us smiling. They had patches of rose on
their cheeks and on the tips of their noses. We smiled back at them
faintly, tightening our grip on the ends. Most of the white girls
played together at the other end of the schoolyard and jumped
single ropes. Carol, Linda and I looked at the girls and then at
each other. We were thinking the same thing: Oh brother.

"Y'all just stand right there and watch for a minute, okay?"
I said, jumping into the ropes, feeling the wind in my face lifting
my braids. Maybe they would go away. Why did they want to
play with *us* anyway?

Linda took her turn and then Carol went again. I was about
to jump again when Martha asked, "Is it our turn yet?" Carol,
Linda and I rolled our eyes. Why wouldn't these girls go back to
the other part of the yard where they came from?

"Okay. All right," Carol said, "how about if y'all turn first.
Let's see you turn."

Martha and Iris took the ends and wrapped the ropes around
their hands. Then they started turning. Clipaclop . . . clipaclop
. . . clipaclop. Carol groaned softly. They were double-handed!
Hopelessly double-handed. Carol got behind Iris. I stood behind
Martha. We took their hands in ours and guided them. Clipclipclipclip. Then we let go. Clipaclop . . . clipaclop . . . Carol shook
her head.

"We're gonna help y'all, okay?" Carol said. Martha and Iris
nodded happily. We put our hands over theirs. Clipclipclipclip.
"Linda, take your turn," I yelled.

While Linda jumped, Carol and I kept the ropes clipclipclip-
ping at a rapid pace. From time to time we would let go of our
charges' hands to see if they were catching on, but immediately
we heard the clipaclop . . . clipaclop . . . and we'd cover their
little double-handed fingers with our own steady hands. Clipclipclipclip.

"When is it our turn? We want to jump," Iris called out.

"Okay, you can have a turn," Carol said, sighing, as she took
the ends from her. I shot my friend a dirty look, which she ignored.
"Go ahead. Jump."

Iris stood there facing the ropes as if she were afraid of them.
"How do youse get in?"

"Run in," I said, trying to keep the disgust from my voice.
"Do your arms like this, like you're pumping yourself," I said,
flailing my arms behind my back as though I were pushing off.

Iris charged into the rope and promptly got smacked in the
face. A bright red welt rose up on her cheek.

"Let her stand in," Linda said patiently. Let them take their
hineys on out of here, I felt like saying.

We parted the ropes so that Iris could stand in the middle.

When she nodded that she was ready, we began turning. She missed. We started again. She missed.

"Running in is better," Carol declared. We made Iris run into the turning ropes. She missed. Linda, Carol and I looked at each other; we rolled our eyes to Canada and back. The bell rang.

"Daaaaaaaaaag," Linda, Carol and I said in unison.

Iris and Martha were grinning from ear to ear. "Can we jump with youse again at recess?"

"We're not jumping," Carol said quickly.

"Yeah. Yeah," I added, "sometimes we just sit around and, uh . . ."

"Talk," Linda chimed in, smiling.

Martha and Iris looked at each other. We heard a sharp, piercing whistle. Miss Tracy, a thin teacher with the face and disposition of Frankenstein, was waving at us to hurry into class. Carol snatched up the ropes and we all began to run.

For a few days after the knife incident Miss Bradley gave me the business. When I raised my hand, she'd look the other way, just as she did with Leonard. And sometimes when she saw me looking at her she'd shake her head as if to say, "How could you have done such a thing?" Which was just as bad as my mother's "I'm so disappointed in you." When Miss Bradley looked at me with her watery gray eyes I'd feel ashamed all over again. It was as if I had done something to her personally. As if I'd really pulled a knife on her or something. When she shook her head at me I wouldn't even try to concentrate on the lesson. Either I'd stare out the window or I'd look at Sacajawea. Sacajawea was always friendly.

"Is there anything else that is happening in the news?" Miss Bradley asked one day after we had finished discussing what it would mean for the United States to have Alaska in the union. The whole class was excited about Alaska becoming a state, especially when Miss Bradley told us that we might get some Eskimo pen pals. Leonard was waving his hand like a madman. "Leonard," Miss Bradley said, which shocked everybody.

Leonard stood up. He pulled at his dopey tie. "Some colored

teenagers are trying to go to school with the white people in some place called Rock something down south. . . ." When we heard the words "white" and "colored" we all became quiet; everybody sat up. No one had ever used those words in our classroom before, at least not in reference to people. "And the white people are mad, because they don't want to go to school with colored people. And the white people started beating up the colored kids. President Eisenhower had to send some soldiers, a whole bunch of Army men!" Leonard's voice was a runaway train that crashed through stop signs. We could hear Miss Bradley gently put the chalk down.

Linda, Carol, Leonard, Wallace the farter and I looked at each other. Miss Bradley was looking at us too, as was the rest of the class. Her face blanched then turned very rosy. No matter what she was feeling, Miss Bradley wasn't going to let an opportunity for a spontaneous geography lesson go by. She was too dedicated for that. "Well," she said slowly, "the place you are talking about is called Little Rock. That is a city in the state of—who knows the state?"

"Mississippi."

"No."

"Alabama."

"No."

"Missouri."

"No."

"North Carolina."

"No."

"South Carolina."

"No."

"California."

"No."

"Poland."

"Now, now, now. Calm down, boys and girls." But everybody was screaming with laughter.

"Arkansas." This finally from Jeffrey, a huge boy with three or four chins who knew just about as much as God.

"Right. In some states like Arkansas, uh, Negroes and, uh, white people aren't allowed to go to school together. That was the law. But now the law is changing," Miss Bradley paused, a little unsure of her words. She looked puzzled. She took a deep breath and tried to sound happy and peppy. I could feel her straining. "Children, aren't we glad that in the Philadelphia public school system, all boys and girls can learn together?"

"Yes, Miss Bradley," everybody said, but Linda, Carol, Wallace, Leonard and I instantly raised our hands, our faces pinched up in perplexity and eagerness. I was waving my hand, because I wanted to ask Miss Bradley who was closing up the schools and how could they do that. And how come white and colored kids couldn't go to school together in Little Rock in the first place? Behind me I could hear Wallace saying, "Oooh, Miss Bradley. Ooooh, oooooh, oooooh, Miss Bradley." And I thought, please pick him or he'll fart us into kingdom come. But Miss Bradley didn't pick Wallace. Carol and Linda were waving their hands and I knew they wanted to ask the same questions I had. But our teacher clapped her hands and said in a loud booming voice that there would be no more questions, because it was time for arithmetic, that we had to move on. So I just looked at Sacajawea.

Gradually Miss Bradley stopped giving me the business. A week or two after the incident, when she was checking everybody's nails she told me to stand up and said my fingernails were the cleanest in the class. Also my ears. The good ole days had returned. In a matter of weeks I became her pet once again. Whenever I raised my hand she called on me. In front of the whole class one day, she said I read with beautiful expression. And I did. I was the one Miss Bradley sent to the nurse's office to get the honey-and-lemon mixture for the chronic cough she had. She let me erase the blackboard and clap out the erasers. When the school sponsored a special class for creative writers, she sent me. Sandra and I even made up: that is, after a couple of weeks I could tell that she wasn't afraid of me anymore, and we said hello to each other and everything, which was about all we'd ever said to each other anyway. All in all, it was as if nothing had ever happened. Even better.

When Jennie G. asked Miss Bradley to choose two students

to represent the school on an educational television show for children, Miss Bradley picked Susan, a little red-haired girl, and me.

The evening I was to go to the television station, the Bosoms crowded around me, chattering away. Aunt Ruth had bought me a beautiful blue dress to wear. "Now you'll look like a television star," she said. She was excited, as if it were she who was going instead of me. Nana brushed my hair until every strand was lying down. And my mother hovered around me, saying, "Now don't forget to speak loudly and to enunciate. Say! your! words! clearly!" My mother thought the only prerequisite for heaven was good grammar.

Mommy and I took a bus to the TV station. We rode for a long time, way past North Philly and downtown. The studio was kind of dingy until the bright lights were turned on. There was a space for the audience and that's where Susan's parents and my mother sat. The show was broadcast live, and the host, who wore a bow tie, told us not to be nervous. I sat next to Susan; she smelled like Ivory soap. Every time the host spoke I could smell the spaghetti he must have eaten for dinner. He asked Susan and me questions about arithmetic and spelling and stuff like that. He kept making little corny jokes and laughing a lot. Susan and I laughed too. Then the man did a science experiment with a straw and water and we helped. When the experiment was over, he asked us what we were going to be when we grew up. Susan said she was going to be a mommy and I said I was going to be a social worker. And the man said, "Ladies and gentlemen, aren't they wonderful?" And that was the end of the show.

After the man shook our hands and we said good-bye and thank you, my mother took me to get a soda at Horn & Hardart. When we got home, Nana kissed my neck and whispered, "Now see, now see how they act when you act nice?"

I said, "Uh huh," but later I wanted to qualify my response. I wanted to be good for Miss Bradley, but this "they" Nana was talking about I wasn't so sure of.

I wrote my daddy to tell him about my being on television. His response came back quickly. It was a short, sloppy letter.

*Dear Bebe:*
*I am fine. Hope all is fine with you. I saw your cousin Belinda*
*last weekend. That was great, you being on television and*
*answering all those questions. That was very fine. I'm so very*
*proud of my little girl.*

> *Lots of love,*
> *Daddy*

I left the letter on my mother's bureau, unfolded. I read it six
times, and every time I got to the "I'm so very proud" part I
smiled.


"HEY, BOY, YOU GOT LIPS LIKE CHEETAH'S MAMA!"

"And you smell like Cheetah's great-grandaddy!"

Linda and Carol pitched their comments to a dark comet who
flashed a sliver of a grin as he circled the three of us, grazing each
of our behinds with his open palm. We stamped our feet and
screamed our rage in unison.

"Quit feeling us, you black, ugly, apehead monkey," I
shrieked as our tormentor sped off in another direction.

William paused in mid-stride, turned his head and called out,
"You yella, ringworm-head . . ." Then he was gone. The missing
epithet—"dukey butt," maybe—would be repeated tomorrow.

"You got more ringworms than hair!" Carol shouted.

"Aha! We screamed you," I yelled, happy that we had gotten
in the last word.

Grown-ups had death and taxes as sure plagues. Linda, Carol
and I had William. We battled relentlessly with him for the prime
real estate under the poplar tree. Besides that, William was just a
fresh little pest who was always trying to put his hands where our
mothers told us no boy's hands should go. For the moment,
though, we were satisfied that we had chased off our enemy. We
placed our black-and-white speckled copybooks on the ground
and sat down on them.

"Did you bring the magazine?" I asked Carol eagerly, looking around to see if anyone was watching us.

She shook her head. "My sister hid it."

Gloom momentarily settled over us. Carol had two teenage sisters who were avid readers of *True Confessions*. When they discarded the magazines, Carol usually brought them to school and we read them together under our tree, haltingly piecing together the difficult words.

"But I remember one story." Linda and I leaned in closer so we wouldn't miss a single word. "It was about this lady. And she was reallll pretty. But her boyfriend was very mean. He was very jealous, and anytime they went out to a party or a nightclub, if any other man even looked at his girlfriend, he was always ready to fight. So, anyway, the lady . . ."

"Is that the one about Jill and Bobby and Ron?" I asked, interrupting. "And the two men start fighting over the lady. And she ends up marrying Ron. And they live in a pretty house and they have two children and then Bobby comes around bothering Jill?" We loved that story with its dashing hero, its beautiful, helpless female and, most of all, the happily-ever-after ending. Carol nodded. "We heard that already," I said, feeling cheated.

"Is that the story where the man brings the lady flowers and takes her to the nightclub?" Linda asked. Her voice and eyes got warm and dreamy and I knew she was about to ask Carol to tell it again. I didn't like hearing the same old stories over and over.

"That's the same one," I said. "Don't you know any other stories?" I asked Carol hopefully. She shook her head.

"Wanna play rope?" Carol asked us.

"Nah," Linda answered. I shook my head.

Carol, Linda and I were best friends, blood sisters with the elbow scars to prove it. We looked alike, three small girls with beribboned braids that bounced when we jumped double dutch or did cartwheels. Our lives were intertwined by more than blood. We had the same teacher. We sat together at lunchtime. We all hated William and we all loved cute, cute, cute Robby. The latter we chased around the schoolyard with relentless passion; the former we ran away from as fast as our skinny little legs could carry us. And we all thought that if we could just look like Cheryl, a paperbag-brown girl with thick black curly hair that hung down her back and framed her eyes in silky spikes, life would withhold nothing from us. We were smart and talented. We were in the first reading group. Carol could draw. Linda could sing. And I could write stories. We were wedded by looks, brilliance, talent, coincidence and secret longings, but what made us soulmates was this: we were daddy's girls without daddies. The pain of their absence was our greatest bond.

Sometimes after we had tired of double dutch and monkey bars, when we had finally escaped from William and "screamed" on his family origins and chimpanzee lips for the ten-millionth time, we'd gather under the huge poplar tree at the end of the schoolyard and press our little bodies against the trunk, and melancholia would drip from us like sap. The shade from the wide arch of limbs and leaves covered us like a shadow. We missed our dads. The greatest comfort we found in each other was that under our tree we could share our precious memories of our fathers.

"One time, one time, when I was a baby," Linda said, breaking the silence and stopping to laugh a little as she related her story, "when I was real little, well, one time my father was throwing me up and down and making me laugh and he threw me up and when he caught me I had dodoed and he got it all over his hands."

Carol and I said, "Ugh." Linda started laughing and we joined in, feeling as she felt, once again like that infant who was loved and protected in a father's strong hands. Linda smiled at us as if to say, "See? See how much my father loved me?" I smiled too and felt my own daddy lifting me, kissing me under my chin, tossing me high into the air for no reason other than to delight me.

"Did he drop you?" Carol wanted to know. She was the first to stop laughing. Carol's voice was often that of an adult in a child's body. She didn't mention her father as much as Linda and I did, and when she talked about him, she seemed to be speaking of things she'd been told about the man, rather than experienced for herself.

"No, of course he didn't drop me!" Linda said disgustedly, her voice almost a squeak. She was a tiny needle of a girl whose speaking voice went into high soprano whenever she got excited.

"One time my daddy came to see me, and my mommy told him he couldn't take me out," said Carol, lowering her voice to a conspiratorial whisper. Carol was the only one of us who had bangs, and as she spoke she took her two pointing fingers and rolled her bangs with them as if they were curling irons. She wore her plait to the side with an elaborate ribbon; that style gave Carol an air of sophistication, as did the mole above her lip that was so perfect it seemed to be the work of an eyebrow pencil. "And my daddy got really mad. He was yelling and when he started all that hollering, I started crying. And my mom said to him, 'See there. See there. See what you did.' "

"But why didn't your mother want your father to see you?" I asked. I had never seen my mother and father argue. When they sat in my daddy's car they did not touch, but they agreed on everything concerning me. Certainly my mother and father never argued about when my daddy could see me.

Carol shrugged. "He must not've paid my mommy the money."

"What money?" Linda and I asked. We looked at each other.

Carol gave us both an exasperated glance, and the mole above her lip began to quiver. "The fathers are spozed to pay money to the mothers to help take care of the children. Otherwise they can't come see the children. My daddy was spozed to buy me some Easter clothes and he didn't," she said indignantly.

Linda and I stared at Carol. She had her hand on her hip and her bottom lip was sticking out. The outline of her taut little body was more like that of a miniature woman than that of a child. An angry little woman.

"But suppose your daddy didn't have any money?" Linda had found a cause. Her voice was way in the upper registers.

"Yeah," I said, agreeing with Linda. We knew that fathers should take care of their children, but not to be allowed to see their own kids just because they didn't always have money, this was unfair to the daddies.

"My daddy has plenty of money!" Carol said with a sudden, almost proud ferocity that caused Linda and me to jump. "He just bought a new car."

Linda was speechless. She was the baby of the group, in both age and outlook. I could see the disbelief in her eyes. Had the money and spent it on himself and didn't give his child anything? What kind of daddy was that? I felt sorry for Carol, but I wasn't as shocked as Linda. I knew a man just like Carol's father. Linda and I eyed each other again and in a single, silent blink we agreed: Carol's father was a bad man.

Carol saw our knowing glances. She put her other hand on her hip and looked away from us as she spoke, "Anyway, I'm gonna get me another daddy."

"Is your mother getting married again?" Linda asked.

"Maybe." Carol leaned in and we drew a tighter circle. "She told me to call her boyfriend Daddy. He buys me lots of things."

Carol's words disturbed me. You just couldn't pick a new daddy because he bought you stuff. Buying stuff didn't make a man your daddy. You got only one real daddy, I reasoned, and if he was not good, then you were just out of luck. I wasn't out of luck. Even if my father didn't come every time I wanted him to, we had North Carolina summers; we had midnight rides down Route 17. My daddy would save me if I was drowning.

"My father," I said proudly, "my father can't walk. He has to be in a wheelchair."

"How come he can't walk?" Carol asked.

"Because a car accident hurt him."

"Oh," Linda and Carol murmured.

"I get to push his wheelchair and when I get tired I step on the back of the bracers and my daddy takes me for a ride."

"One of my mommy's friends fell asleep driving his car and when he woke up his car was in a ditch and he had a broken leg. It got better, though," Carol said casually.

My father wasn't stupid enough to fall asleep while he was driving! He didn't do crazy things like that. "It wasn't my father's fault," I said coldly.

Carol shrugged. "I didn't say it was."

Didn't she know that my father was a royal king, plowed down by an enemy in the heat of the battle? Didn't she realize that he was good, completely good, and that his survival was a testimony to his nobility and fortitude? Hadn't she guessed that I was the daughter of a special man and was therefore special too? I frowned at my friend, who placidly looked me in the eye as if she hadn't the faintest notion of what had caused my rancor. My father's accident had happened to him; he hadn't caused it.

"Sometimes something goes wrong with cars," Linda said carefully. I smiled at her gratefully.

I didn't tell Linda and Carol that my father was going to walk again. Didn't explain that his legs hadn't shriveled, that they were only still and waiting. That as we sat below the poplar tree his legs were getting stronger and stronger, and any day I'd look up and there he'd be, standing right beside me. That was a secret I shared with no one.

We talked about our daddies, but never why we weren't with them. Maybe our mothers had shielded us too well from the pain that had cut our families apart. What we knew was this: our fathers were visitors in our lives and we in theirs. Whether our fathers had beaten our mothers or run around with other women or not worked hard enough to support our families, we had no idea. We weren't old enough even to imagine or wonder about these things, let alone assume guilt or innocence. It would take years before our curiosity welled up and became insatiable. We would have our own bosoms, thick hair under our arms and between our legs by the time we sat our mothers down on the edge of their beds, persisting in the face of their evasive sighs, their shifting eyes, and pulled the story from them. For now we couldn't imagine what those stories would be. For now we had the comfort of the shade of our poplar tree, of double-dutch ropes, turning, turning, turning. We had mothers we loved and daddies we longed for. We had each other. It would be years before we chose sides.

# CHAPTER 7

It was the end of October, a radiant Indian-summer day full of sunshine and soft winds. Frankie Lymon and the Teenagers were wailing rock-and-roll love into our tiny backyard from the radio Michael had propped up in the open kitchen window. The sweet ooh-wahs of the tenor transformed the small square of harsh gray asphalt. Even the chrysanthemums Nana had planted in the three dirt-filled old car tires that sat in the middle of the yard seemed to be bouncing to the beat. Inside the house Nana was frying Chinese-style pork chops for dinner. The pungent odor of the meat floated out the same window as the music. In the center of the yard Michael and I were dancing, or rather, I was attempting to dance, and Michael, my nine-year-old instructor, was critiquing my performance.

"Unh unh. No. Move your feet more and shake your head a little. Twist your butt," Michael commanded.

Anxious to please, I shook my head with such vigor that my pink barrette popped off and hit the ground. One of my three plaits immediately came undone and my hair billowed down one side of my neck. I didn't miss a step. If Michael said my slop wasn't correct, then the whole world could be tumbling down around me and I would be finger popping and foot stomping till he said I had it right or the oceans swept me under, whichever came first. I looked up at Michael, who was still shaking his head in disapproval. My cousin crouched down in front of me, grabbed one of my feet and moved it back and forth. I could smell the Brylcreem Michael used on his hair and see the shiny stocking-cap waves. When he stood up he was a whole head taller than I. He grabbed my thigh and guided it in the right direction. Then he let go, stood back and watched me, his feet patting the whole time. The music was blaring away, inside me as well as out. This time I knew I had it. I was slopping for real.

"Yeah, yeah, yeah. You got it," Michael said, walking around me, his hands in his pockets, just a-grinning, as if he were some fat-cat impresario auditioning me for a lineup at the Apollo or something. He was really pleased that I was such an apt student. "Now you won't be jive," he said. Michael was learning that people were divided into two categories: cool and jive. He felt duty-bound to impart this wisdom to me, his most loyal follower. To be jive was to be out; to be cool was to be in. Michael considered himself the coolest of the cool and he certainly didn't want to be associated with anyone who wasn't and he definitely didn't want any jive relatives. That would have been embarrassing.

"This is how the cool people dance," Michael told me, joining me in the slop now that I was a worthy partner. I mimicked him, tilting my head a little, leaning my body sideward, putting my right hand into my pocket.

"Am I cool?" I asked hopefully. I sure didn't want to be jive by myself.

"Yeah, you're cool," Michael said reassuringly. Then to show me just how cool he was, Michael put one hand in his pocket, bent at his waist a little and walked around the yard with one foot dragging behind the other. Michael was doing the hoodlum stroll to perfection. He looked me up and down as I slopped. "You need to learn some steps," he said, suddenly spinning away from me. "You have to know how to squirrel people."

"Squirrel people?"

"Outdance them," he said in a condescending tone. "Watch me." Michael's feet slid across the ground. He rotated his hips and shook his shoulders wildly. He tugged at his blue jeans and pulled them above his ankles, revealing the red and blue argyle socks Nana had bought him. Then he did a series of rapid-fire hops and skips up and down the yard while I stood back and watched him admiringly. Michael was as handsome as his mother was beautiful. And he was a born dancer. He moved like oil flowing from a bottle. Looking at Michael I knew I'd never have the fluidity and grace he had, but at least now I knew some of his moves. But then Michael was always my predecessor, dragging me down paths he'd already crossed.

ONE YEAR EARLIER, WEEKS BEFORE CHRISTMAS, MICHAEL HAD GRABBED me by the hand and pulled me to the basement closet. "See," he said, opening the door and revealing Betsy Wetsy in all her blue-eyed glory. I was flabbergasted, so stunned I couldn't speak. There were the roller skates I wanted. And the clothes!

"I told you wasn't no Santa Claus, " Michael said jubilantly. "Your mother is Santa Claus! There ain't no man in a red suit bouncing down the chimney going 'Ho ho ho.' That's just some stuff they made up so we'd be good. Aww, don't cry," Michael said, noticing my forlorn stare, my sadness at seeing a beloved dream suddenly die without warning. I was sniffling and snuffling up a storm, unable to prevent the small river that was flowing down my face. Michael grabbed me by my sweater and pulled me toward the closet. "Hey. Hey. C'mon now, stop." He shook me a little, but I only cried harder. "Bebe, lissen. Lissen. You can play with your doll every day until Christmas."

I peered up into the closet. Betsy Wetsy stared back at me. Michael pulled a chair inside the door, climbed up on it, pulled down the baby doll and whacked her on the back. She really could cry! I wiped my eyes with the back of my balled-up hands. Michael handed me the doll. Leave it to my cousin to show me the rewards of being a realist.

"If Michael told you to jump off a building would you do it?" my mother asked me when she discovered the doll out of her box.

Well. Maybe.

In the end I didn't even get to keep my doll. When Nana saw it she pulled me aside and asked, "Don't you want a pretty brown doll?"

I wasn't sure I did. I thought Betsy Wetsy was pretty. But Nana convinced me that she would find me a better doll. The day after Christmas Betsy disappeared, and in her place Nana handed me a colored, no-name baby doll who didn't cry or pee. I was *too* upset.

"I don't want that! I want Betsy Wetsy," I wailed.

"Oh, go on and play with her," Nana said sweetly. She placed the doll in my arms and told me to rock her.

Miss Colored No-Name went right under the bed. I wanted me a doll that could *pee*. The following year Betsy Wetsy appeared on my Christmas list once again.

For my unswerving loyalty my cousin rewarded me with merciless teasing and ruthless tattletaling. For Michael, getting me in trouble and going to the movies were one and the same: a good afternoon's entertainment. But that was Michael. To love him didn't necessarily mean you'd get loved back in quite the same way. Michael didn't promise devotion; he promised excitement.

My cousin was a showoff and his mouth always got him into trouble. He talked back to teachers at Logan and at Sunday school. Every well-brought-up colored child in Philadelphia knew that you were supposed to sit nicely on the subway during the ride to and from school. You were supposed to read a book or talk quietly or do nothing. On the subway Michael raced from car to car, jumping across the open spaces while the train jerked back and forth speeding to the next station. When he wasn't switching cars, he threw spitballs and yanked the dangling braids of any of the girls he knew, including me. Michael was bad, bad as he could be.

Irreverence was his signature. One Sunday morning, Miss Smith, our Sunday-school teacher, went to get my mother because Michael wouldn't stop talking like Kingfish from *Amos and Andy*. Miss Smith had passed out pamphlets about Miriam finding the baby Moses in the bulrushes. Michael had his pamphlet on his lap and he was whispering in a really loud voice, "Oh, And-ee. Ooooooh, And-ee. Dey done found de baby. Where Sapphire? Where Sapphire? Ho-leee mackel. Ho-leee mackel."

Little girls with cotton gloves and crisply ruffled dresses, little boys with dark suits and bow ties, whose parents had admonished them to be on their best behavior, were falling on the floor in uncontrollable giggles. I was laughing so much I thought I was going to throw up. One pudgy kid had slipped off his chair and was howling so vigorously he couldn't get back up. Michael said, "He'p me, Andee. I's fallin'."

Nobody actually saw my mother come in. It was as if all of a sudden everybody felt a force and looked at the door and there was Control, Presence and Dignity coming right at us. There was Doris C. Moore, so mad it hurt your eyes to look at her. She clapped her hands smartly and said slowly, "This is a disgrace!"

Michael froze right in the middle of his sentence. He said, "Ho-lee mack . . ." and just stopped. He didn't move a muscle. Michael would talk back to everybody else in the world, but not my mother. My mother could be one scary sister. She gave a long, cold stare that took in the entire class. Children scrambled to their seats as if they were playing musical chairs and the music had just stopped. The room was almost silent when the pudgy boy let out one last helpless giggle. My mother turned to look at him and it was as if rays of kryptonite came shooting out of her eyes. The boy choked on the laugh. We all folded our hands and began studying our pamphlets.

Then Mommy's eyes settled on Michael. Quietly, she said, "Michael." My cousin raised his eyes balefully. "Behave yourself. And don't let me have to come back in here."

Later at home, she was less imposing when she confronted him. "Why are you so . . . so . . ." Mommy's professional training prohibited her from using the word "bad." "Why are you so disruptive?" she finally asked.

"Awww, Aunt Doris," Michael said, sidling up to my mother and putting his arm around her shoulder, "the other kids were talking first." With Michael it was always the other kids. "You don't fuss at Bebe when she talks in class." Michael's integrity vanished whenever he found a convenient scapegoat. And I was the most convenient of all.

"Bebe doesn't act like you and you know it," my mother retorted. "Michael," she said, her face softening, but clouded with worry and concern, "please try to . . . to . . . do the right thing. I just want you to do your best, okay?"

"Okay, Aunt Doris."

But he never did. He would do anything for attention. Michael acted up at piano lessons, at art class, at day camp and at Nicetown Boys' Club. The blue-haired spinsters who taught us at Logan wouldn't tolerate Michael's mimicry and monkeyshines. His grades reflected their displeasure. They gave him Ds and Fs in conduct and work habits and scrawled their frustration in the tiny rectangle reserved for their comments, along with a conference date and time written in red ink and circled. My mother would read this and press her lips together, making of her mouth one razor-thin line. Aunt Ruth never attended Michael's conferences and rarely signed his report cards. What she did was give Nana money for Michael's clothes and food, and say, "He did?" with a blasé wave of one hand when Nana told her about Michael's grades. My mother visited Michael's teachers and wrote her name at the bottom of his dismal report cards and in parentheses next to it the word "guardian."

Michael got Mr. Singer in fourth grade, and he was the only teacher Michael every really obeyed. Mr. Singer was the only male teacher at Logan. Michael was crazy about him. He loved Mr. Singer's dirty drawers; he did whatever that man told him to do.

Carol, Linda and I were under our tree one spring day when I spotted Michael's class having physical education. The girls were on one side of the yard and the boys were on the other. I heard Mr. Singer say, "All right, Michael, you lead the men and form your squadron. All right, you guys, line up behind Michael. Michael, lead your men in exercise."

Michael's face was sunshine city. He was so happy moving the boys in a straight line. He was wearing a blue corduroy jacket and black pants, and he'd gotten a haircut over the weekend. Even from the tree I could see how handsome he looked marching around the yard. I stood up to get a better view. Linda said, "What are you smiling about?" She looked. "It's only goony ole Michael."

Yes, but this Michael wasn't silly and disobedient. This Michael was purposeful and manly. Redeemed. I couldn't help smiling. If Nana and Mommy had seen Michael in the schoolyard with his men they would never have stopped smiling.

In his own way Michael claimed me more ferociously than I ever claimed him. In the schoolyard, at church, on Mole Street, Michael told everyone I was his sister. The assertion wasn't usually challenged, unless people knew the truth. We looked alike. Except for our noses, we looked as though we could have had the same parents. Michael's nose was small, with tiny, delicate nostrils. Such little teeny-weeny nostrils. Nana used to tease him. "How do you breathe with that little tiny nose? Hope you can get through life with those nostrils." My nose was broad, with wide nostrils. The first time Michael called me Bullet Nostrils I cried and ran inside and put one of Nana's hair clips right down the center of my nose, because Linda told me her mother had pinched her nose when she was a baby and that's why it was narrow. The hair clip left a long red welt. When I went downstairs to the kitchen Nana looked at me hard. "What's the matter with your nose?" she asked.

"Uh . . ."

"What did you do to yourself? Did you put something on your nose?"

"I'm trying to make it smaller. Michael said I had big bullet nostrils, so I put one of your hair clips on it."

Nana started laughing. "Sometimes you act like you don't have the brains God gave a flea." Then she hollered, "Michael, come here!" When he appeared she said, "Why are you calling her Bullet Nose?"

Michael started laughing. "I didn't call her that."

"Yes, you did, you little liar," I screamed.

"Don't call her names. And you," she said, turning to me, "why do you believe everything this boy tells you?" Nana asked me this in exasperation. I shrugged. I didn't know, maybe because some part of me knew he needed that kind of blind devotion. Even as a child I recognized that Michael needed from me a relationship that was closer than cousins, something more substantial, more sustaining. It took me years before I realized why.

JUST AS MICHAEL AND I WERE SLOPPING OUR HARDEST WE HEARD someone banging on our gate. We knew who it was: Jackie, Jane and Adam. We opened the gate and there they stood: our closest pals and our worst enemies.

We lived on stately 16th Street; they lived on dinky ole Mole Street. They went to the neighborhood school; we went to Logan. They were kinda dark; we were kinda light. They had a father and a mother. We had only the Bosoms guarding our lives.

We felt our differences keenly. They would build up inside us and every once in a while we'd feel the pressure and declare war. The last great war had occurred when Michael called Jackie, Jane and Adam's father a grease monkey. Michael's mouth started a whole bunch of wars.

We were sitting on the Watsons' steps eating Popsicles. We each had a different-color Popsicle. I was eating a blue one and Michael was sucking on a white one. Everybody was kind of quiet—it was after dinner and we'd been playing hard since after school. Jackie had just joined us; her mother had washed and straightened her hair after school. Jane said she had to get her hair straightened the next day, which was Saturday.

Michael said, "If I was a girl I wouldn't let anybody straighten my hair. Think I'd let somebody stick a hot comb in my head and burn me up? Unh unh. Nope."

When he said that, I thought, "Uh oh."

"So what would you do, never get your hair washed?" Jane asked sarcastically.

Shut up, Michael. Shut up.

"Every girl who gets her hair washed doesn't get it straightened, dummy. Bebe doesn't get her hair straightened. We have good hair." He said this casually, as if it weren't the least bit important. I held my breath and felt my belly explode in tingles.

Jane stood up, her chest heaving in and out. "Yeah, where'd y'all get your good hair from, huh? Your invisible daddies."

"At least our fathers ain't no grease monkeys!" Michael said loudly.

We all stood up then. Jackie said quietly, "We declare war."

We had ten minutes to build our courage as well as an arsenal of sticks and stones. Michael and I fled to the security of our yard. Jackie, Jane and Adam fought from Mole Street. We hurled our guerrilla missiles through the air and screamed vile insults at each other over the fence.

"Your whole family's so ugly they gotta sneak up on a glass of water."

"Your mama!"

"Your grandmama!"

"Your whole generation!"

"Ya ugly yellow lemons!"

"Ya black tar-babies!"

"Ya mama!"

"Ya daddy!"

"Least we got one!"

When Adam tried to climb over into our yard, Michael and I beat his fingers with a stick until he retreated. When Jackie tried to climb over we threw a cup of water on her hair. She screamed so loud we froze; we thought we had killed her. We heard a door open and Mrs. Watson saying, "What are you children doing? Get in this house. Get in here." Then, *What happened to your hair!!*"

Jackie screamed, "We're gonna get you tomorrow, Michael and Bebe!"

But the next day, after eyeing each other balefully from our respective sides of the street, we made up. The truth was, we had no one else to play with. After we called a truce, we organized one of the many clubs we always started after a war. This one was called the Busy Bee Club. Some of the others had been the Doll Club, the Saturday Movies Club, the Club to Collect Money to Buy Fried Seafood. We had all kinds of clubs.

"What are y'all doing?" Jane asked curiously when we opened the gate. Michael and I didn't usually play together inside our yard unless we were feuding with the Watsons, and currently peace was reigning.

"Dancing," I answered proudly.

"What kind of dancing?" Jackie asked suspiciously. She was twelve, the oldest of the three, and had been to dancing parties. She was reluctant to share her glory.

"The slop," Michael proclaimed with an air of nonchalance.

"Y'all babies can't do no slop," Jackie said derisively. She started laughing and Jane and Adam joined in. Michael and I looked at each other in instant, mutual anger. We hated the way Jackie, Jane and Adam always seemed so united, how they always seemed stronger than we were. It wasn't even the fact that there were three of them. It was as if they had some invisible support that gave them a kind of sureness and strength we could never attain. Here the girl was calling us jive; *that* wasn't to be tolerated. Michael reached over to the radio and turned the volume all the way up. He grabbed my hand. Sam Cooke was having a party.

Michael and I slopped from one end of our concrete-paved yard to the other. Michael slopped all the way down to the ground, got back up, spun around, did a split, got back up and slopped some more. The clickety-clickety of his taps echoed throughout the yard. My maneuvers were considerably less gymnastic, but I was *cool*. When the song ended, sweat was pouring down Michael's face and I could feel my shirt sticking to my back.

Jackie blinked away every trace of admiration and envy from her eyes and said mildly, "Uh huh. Y'all almost got it."

"We can do it better than you can!" Michael retorted defiantly. "Let's see you do it."

Jackie's legs and feet began trembling as if an earthquake were rumbling up and down her bones. She slid around our yard, shaking her behind and moving her feet. The girl could dance. But we were better.

"Aww, girl, we squirreled you," Michael said, laughing. Michael and Jackie looked at each other defiantly and for a moment it looked like war. Then Jackie said, "Shoot. Let's make leaf houses. Can y'all come out?"

Halfway down the street, a huckster's open fruit truck was

backing out of Mole Street. The smell of apples, tangerines and bananas filled the tiny alley. From the end of the block we heard the fruit seller shouting something in rapid Italian. A dog barked. Two houses down from Jackie, Jane and Adam, the Woo Woo Lady, a deaf-mute Nana had not unkindly nicknamed because of the noises she made, was throwing bread crumbs to a flock of greedy pigeons. Her small grandson rushed into the throng and for a moment all we could hear was the flapping of wings.

We began collecting and arranging the huge piles of red and gold poplar leaves that had fallen from the tree outside our fence. Then we fashioned the leaves into kitchens and living rooms.

"Do come in and have some tea, darling," I told Jane in my Bette Davis voice as I held an invisible cup in the air. My mother was big on Bette Davis and watched all of her old movies on television. When my mother was watching Bette Davis you had to either be quiet or leave the room. Usually I would join her on the sofa and she would put her arms around me and we'd watch Bette together. Bette Davis was culture. And when my mother wanted to get some culture or wanted somebody else to get some, you didn't speak or cut any monkeyshines. You just watched silently and let your body absorb the betterment. And when it was over you were an improved person. Or at least you could say "Oh, darling" with an elegant air. Michael, of course, never stood still long enough to absorb the right kind of culture.

"Dis here de bar and grill, An-dee. Want some whiskey?" Michael asked from the Red Leaf Tavern. Jackie drank greedily from a pretend glass. When everybody laughed, Michael said, "Ho-lee mackel. Ho-ooo-oo-leee mackel, An-dee. Sapphire drinking all de whiskey."

Our leaf houses had turned into the projects and stretched past three of the 16th Street backyards when Mrs. Watson called our friends inside. "Y'all better watch out for the Turtle Lady," Adam warned us ominously after his mother had called three times and he and his sisters knew they couldn't dally any longer.

"That's right, the Turtle Lady's back, y'all," Jackie said, echoing her brother with a solemn nod of her head.

I shuddered. The very thought of being grabbed by the

infamous green woman with the head of a turtle and the body of a woman who had a penchant for eating children alive gave me the shivers. Every year or so the Turtle Lady made her grim appearance in North Philly and now she was back. What if she did come down Mole Street? What if she tried to get Michael and me? What would the two of us do?

"How come the Turtle Lady only comes down Mole Street when y'all hafta go in the house and we can stay outside and play, huh?" Michael asked, his lips twitching with sarcasm. "Maybe the Turtle Lady's in your backyard right now," Michael said jeeringly as he plunged into a deep pile of poplar leaves.

"Turtle Lady gonna get you, Michael," Adam bellowed as he closed his front door behind him and his sisters.

Michael and I ran from one leaf dwelling to the next, pretending to live in each. Finally, when we were exhausted from playing house, we began to throw the leaves at each other. In the midst of the frenzy we heard a door slam. We didn't even look up until Barry was right beside us.

Sprinkled in among the predominantly black population of Mole Street were a few white families. The Woo Woo Lady and her family were Irish. Next door to them were the McCowans, another huge Irish clan of at least ten, including mother, father, grandmother and children, all wedged into a tiny two-bedroom brick rowhouse. At the end of the street that spilled into Susquehanna Avenue there was a black man married to a German woman and their frizzy-haired, stuck-up daughter, Helena, who was jive with a capital J. Whenever I or any of the other colored kids tried to talk to her, the ole snob would respond to us in German. Like we didn't know she spoke English all day long at school. And there was Barry, whose Jewish mother and Italian father screamed ethnic slurs at each other in fights that reverberated from their bedroom window to the listening street below. There were one or two white families on 16th Street, but most of the whites had moved out of the area when black people began moving in. The ones on Mole Street couldn't afford to leave. They knew it and so did we.

I was close enough to see that Mole Street was the great

equalizer. Mommy's "they" couldn't be this pitiful lot of freckle-faced people who couldn't even afford to move away from an alley. This couldn't be the they who went around tacking up signs that said "Colored Women," "White Ladies." Had to be somebody else.

So we struck a truce: the white people on Mole Street wouldn't act superior and the colored people wouldn't look down on them. For the most part, the two groups were polite to each other. Black and white mothers would sometimes shoot the breeze as they bought their fruit from the huckster, but they didn't get too close.

Nana told Michael and me not to play with Barry or any of his four younger siblings. "I ain't seen poor white trash like that since I left Virginia." When Nana left Virginia, she wasn't even walking, but she loved to act as if she had lived a whole life "down South."

My mother was mortified that Nana had made such a mean comment in front of us. As a social worker, my mother believed in the equality of all people. "Mother, don't say that," she said, wrinkling up her nose as if she smelled a dead rat.

"P.W.T., honey," Nana repeated, and my mother gave her a look full of icicles.

But Nana really didn't have to warn us away from Barry and his brothers and sisters. They were mean, perpetually angry, and they struck out at anyone in their way for no apparent reason and completely without warning. Barry particularly liked to pick on Michael and had been trying to goad him into a fight for months. We kept our distance.

So when I looked up and saw Barry looming over us, my heart dropped into my shoe. Barry was maybe twelve or so, but he seemed much older. He was a husky boy and from our position on the ground he looked even bigger and more intimidating. He was standing so close to us that I could see the tiny hairs on his upper lip and others sprouting on his chin. He began kicking our leaves. And then, without even looking at him, he kicked Michael. Michael hesitated. He looked at me for a moment and I could detect the fright in his eyes. He must have seen the same in mine because I knew Michael couldn't fight and the thought of him getting hurt made me frantic. He sold aplenty wolf tickets, but behind the bark there was no muscle. Michael slowly got up. What was he going to do, I wondered. I looked toward our yard. Maybe we could run in and slam the door in Barry's face. But what if Barry knocked the door in or jumped over the wall? Where was Nana or my mother? But what could they do? I felt hopeless and helpless.

Michael turned to Barry and said, "Hey, boy, you better watch where you're putting your feet." I had to admire Michael. He was going to mouth off to the very end. You woulda thought he was Sugar Ray Robinson or something, the way he sounded. But words just weren't enough.

"Yeah, punk, whatcha gonna do about it?"

I could taste Michael's fear in my own throat. What was he gonna do? Maybe, I thought frantically, maybe Michael could fight. Maybe he would magically light up the sky with a blaze of fisticuffs and pummel Barry into the ground. Maybe that's how boys learned to fight. They just all of a sudden, out of the blue, kicked somebody's ass one day.

Barry moved toward Michael. When Michael instinctively backed up I knew my fantasy was just that. He kept shuffling backward until Barry had him up against the big poplar tree. "I said, Whatcha gonna do about it, sissy?"

I started crying. The thought that my beloved cousin was about to get beat up right before my very eyes was too much for me. "Leave him alone," I screamed to Barry, who totally ignored me.

"Get your stinking breath out of my face," Michael said, trying to shove Barry, who was leaning into his chest. "Your breath smells like ten toilets. I guess your family can't afford toothbrushes, huh?"

"Who you think you're talking to, sissy?"

"I'm talking to you."

Barry punched Michael in the chest. Bam! Michael hesitated and then weakly shoved Barry. Barry knocked Michael down and jumped on top of him. They were rolling around in what had once been our leaf projects. I screamed as Barry walloped Michael in the face and stomach again and again. Bam! Bam! I picked up a small rock and slammed it down on Barry's head. A thin trickle of blood began dripping down his neck. He turned around and looked at me as though I were a pesky little puppy yapping at his legs, and continued to flail away at Michael. I started screaming so loudly I got dizzy. Doors began opening. All of Mole Street came out. Old Mrs. McCowan and three of her grandchildren stood in the doorway and watched. The Woo Woo Lady, who had been sitting on the steps, began making loud noises and gesticulating wildly toward Barry. I ran into the house and brought Nana out. She looked bewildered for a second when she saw Barry on top of Michael, punching his face.

"Hey, you. Stop that," she yelled faintly. Barry ignored her.

"Go get his father," she told me.

"Yo, Barry, get offa that ked. Leave him be." Barry's father's voice was like car tires driving slowly over gravel. He didn't tell Barry; he commanded. Barry got up, leaving Michael on the ground crying and clutching his bloody nose.

"Barry started it. Barry started it," I wailed in the direction of Barry's father. "We weren't doing anything but playing and he came out and started picking on Michael for no reason."

"Look, boys fight," Barry's father said wearily and without a trace of sympathy. "Your brother ought to learn to fight." He was a short, squat man. He wasn't wearing a shirt. Thick dark hair carpeted his chest and back. He gave Barry a shove toward his steps. "Get in there, you."

Barry went with his father up the steps. "Lissen, you, how many times do I hafta tell you to leave that kellurd ked alone, huh? Huh?" His short, wide palm smacked the back of Barry's head. "How many times, huh?" Smack. Smack.

Barry's father waited for him at their open front door. He stood in the doorway, shaking his head at Barry, a grin slowly spreading across his face. "Ya big knucklehead," he said. Then he flung his arm around his son and pulled him inside the house.

Watching them I felt a slow burning sensation in my chest. I began to cry as I followed Nana and Michael toward the house. Nana turned and looked at me. "Don't cry. It's all right."

But it wasn't all right. I watched as Michael wiped the blood away from his fragile nostrils. Him and his little teeny nose, I thought, suddenly angry. Why couldn't he fight? Other boys knew how to fight! Big sissy!

I closed my eyes and there he was. Tall. Powerful. Strong. He was bending over Michael. He was saying, "Come here, son. Now hold your chin down. Bring your hands up. Higher. Good. Okay, now hit me. Hit me hard, son. Aww, c'mon, you can hit harder than that. Good. Good!" When I opened my eyes there was nothing, just piles of red and gold leaves dancing in the wind.

# CHAPTER 8

On a Saturday morning not long after the fight I sat on the edge of our bathtub, watching Michael brush his teeth. Michael had awakened me so early that morning it felt like Christmas. He had tiptoed into my mother's room even before cartoons came on (just as on Christmas) and he shook me a little until I half opened one eye. Then he whispered, "Get up. C'mon, get up."

I was feeling groggy, but I rolled out of bed. Mommy sat up and said, "Michael? What are you kids up to?" but she lay back down without hearing our answer. I got up and bumped into Michael, and he said, "Come into the bathroom and talk to me." So I followed him down the hall and it wasn't until I felt that cold porcelain on my bottom that I remembered that of course it wasn't Christmas. But the day was special all the same, because Michael's father was coming to take him out to buy him some shoes.

I propped both my bare feet along the edge of the bathtub and hugged my knees as though I were a trapeze artist taking a break on the high wire, all the while trying to remember what my Uncle Kenneth looked like. I couldn't see his face, no matter how hard I scrunched up my eyes and concentrated. It had been a long, long time since Michael or I had seen his father. Years.

Michael stared at his smile in the medicine cabinet mirror and lifted his top lip with his fingers; he flicked his toothbrush carefully over each one of his teeth. Then he rinsed his mouth three times with the strong, cheap red mouthwash that Nana bought, making the whole bathroom smell like the dentist's office. When Michael looked at his smile again his lips and tongue were red. He filled the yellow plastic cup with plain cold water and gargled with it over and over, trying to make the tint disappear. He kept smiling and examining himself in the mirror.

"You look nice," I said. "The red is gone." It was mostly gone.

Michael sort of grunted and pulled at his yellow-and-black-striped polo shirt, tucking it into his black corduroy pants for the thousandth time that morning. He took off his stocking cap and began to brush his hair carefully, so as not to muss the glorious waves that had been set in place overnight. He and I had shined his black shoes to glossy perfection the night before, but he bent down and wiped at them with a balled-up piece of toilet paper.

"You look very nice," I repeated, sensing that my cousin needed reassurance. My behind felt cold and stiff from the icy porcelain; I stood up to stretch and rubbed my bottom through my flannel pajamas.

Michael never talked about his father. He was good at pretending not to care that Kenneth wasn't around. Real good. When Nana announced at dinner that his father was coming on Saturday and was going to buy him some shoes and spend the day with him, he just said, "Oh, yeah?" as if it were no big deal, as if it happened every single day instead of once every blue moon. He never said he missed his father or wanted to see him. Never threw himself on the kitchen floor, kicking and screaming and scuffing up the light-colored linoleum with his hard brown school shoes as he yelled, "Why doesn't he come! Why doesn't he come!" and when Jackie, Jane and Adam started in with, "Y'all must not have no daddies," sometimes Michael said simply, "So what? So what if we don't," so unabashedly that they could derive no joy whatsoever from his confession. But that quick, slippery "So what?"

was just on the surface, something Michael tossed out for myopic suckers. I was closer; I could see deeper. I observed his longing when my daddy came to get me. When I ran to my father's car and waved back at Mommy, Nana and Michael, he always had a hungry look in his eyes, as if he'd seen a giant sweet potato pie, only he couldn't get close enough to eat any. So what? So everything.

When Michael was seven, my mother, with her social worker's intuition, asked my father if my cousin could spend a summer in North Carolina. Asked pointedly if my father would "spend some time with Michael." I was happy enough to share my daddy and the pleasures of the country with my cousin, but Michael wasn't used to Pasquotank County ways. "Where's the phone? Where's the hot water?" he wanted to know. Michael didn't know how to say "Yes, ma'am" and "No, ma'am." He teased Grandma's frisky yard dog, threw corn husks at Frosty, the dingy white mule, chased Grandma's chickens from morning till night and even talked back to Grandma.

One night after dinner, before the mosquitoes had come out, my father, Michael and I were in the front yard. Daddy had just finished smoking a cigarette, had thrown the butt in the grass and rolled over it with his chair. He had his head turned up looking at the sky when all of a sudden he said, "Okay, Mike. See what you can do." He pulled a baseball out of the side of his chair and tossed it at Michael, who was grinning excitedly, almost feverishly. He caught the ball and threw it back to my father. The next one was higher. Michael leaped and the ball just fell into his cupped hand. They must have thrown twenty or thirty good clean catches back and forth, over and under, one right after the other. Michael had small wet circles underneath his arms and little drops were beading up and dripping down from my father's hairline. They were egging each other on and teasing, saying, "You call that a throw?" "You call that a catch?" They were laughing as they threw the balls, laughing and sweating and having a good time. Then Michael tossed one back for my dad; it went way over his head. Daddy said, "Go get it, Mike. You know I'm not going in a ditch after any ball." When Michael brought him the ball, Daddy said, "Well, I'm tuckered out now, Mike. We'll play some more to-morrow maybe."

Michael, panting a little from getting the ball, said eagerly, "Okay. Okay. Tomorrow." He asked me to play with him for a little while, but quit after he got fed up with my terrible pitching and catching.

When Grandma called us in for bed that night I said, "Good night, Daddy." And Michael said, "Good night, Daddy—I mean, Uncle George." He was a little embarrassed, but not really. Daddy patted Michael on the head and said, "Good night, man." Michael went to bed grinning.

So maybe my mother's plan worked a little, but not all the way. When Daddy and Michael weren't throwing the ball together, it was me standing on the bracers of my father's wheelchair with my hands around his neck and Michael throwing green balls from off the ammo tree into the lane. At the end of the summer, when my daddy took me shopping for clothes, Michael didn't get any. When the next summer rolled around, Michael said he didn't want to go to North Carolina because there was nothing to do. He never came again.

MICHAEL AND I WERE EATING BREAKFAST WHEN THE DOORBELL RANG. We gave each other startled glances from across the table and quickly choked down the rest of our Cheerios and milk. I stood up and looked at Michael expectantly, but then neither of us moved. We could hear Nana at the door with Kenneth. I felt Michael's hand gripping my arm. I turned around. His pink smile was gone and his eyes were staring straight ahead. What was he scared of, I wondered.

Heh. Heh. Heh. We heard the laughter from the vestibule as we crept into the living room. The door separating the living room from the tiny entrance was closed to keep the heat in, so the sound was muted. "I swear, Betty, you just get better-looking as the years go by. Heh. Heh. Heh." Then in a louder voice he cried, "Where's my boy? Heh. Heh. Heh." Kenneth's voice suddenly boomed into the living room as Nana opened the door. Michael swallowed. We both looked up.

Our house wasn't big enough to hold Kenneth's beauty. Everywhere he walked the place seemed lit up. Such elegance belonged on a Hollywood screen or in front of a microphone as he crooned to screaming throngs of women, not in an ordinary living room in a mediocre house in North Philly. Kenneth was tall, slender and resplendent in a pale gray sharkskin suit and gray shoes so shiny I could see my face in them. His nails were polished and his silky Cab Calloway hair was smooth and fragrant. There was a cigarette stuck in the corner of his mouth and Uncle Kenneth closed his eyes a little as the smoke curled up. I was so dazzled I couldn't speak. Michael was mesmerized.

Kenneth seemed to glide into the living room, a brilliant smile set in cement on his face. "Hey there, big fella. Heh. Heh. Heh," he said, grabbing Michael around his waist. He squeezed Michael hard and closed his eyes, then pulled Michael away from him and held onto his arms tightly, just looking at him as if searching for something, all the while with a pleading look on his face. Please. Please. Please. That is what the look said. Then Uncle Kenneth let Michael's arms go. He brushed off the front of his suit and straightened his tie. "Heh. Heh. Heh," he said toward Nana, who seemed not to be dazzled at all. She was standing away from him with her back against the vestibule door, looking at him with no real expression at all, except that her lips were twitching, which is what happened right before she was about to sing "Unforgettable" real fast.

"Pretty little Bebe," he said quickly, noticing me for the first time. He bent down to kiss me on the cheek and I breathed in his aftershave. It was strong and spicy and made me dizzy. I stepped away from Kenneth.

Michael seemed small standing next to his father. They looked alike. Michael wasn't as light as his father and his hair wasn't anywhere near as straight, but anyone could see he was his child. And Ruth's. He looked like both of his gorgeous parents. I could imagine Ruth, Kenneth and Michael together, walking down 16th Street as people stared and traffic stopped. Ruth and Kenneth taking Michael to the doctor's and all the patients just gazing at them dumbfounded. I could see Ruth and Kenneth in the Calypso Lounge, the bar stools swiveling and squeaking as patrons turned to watch them take their seats. The beautiful couple must have staggered under the weight of their beauty. Was that why they couldn't take care of Michael, because they were overburdened with their own good looks?

"Well, let's go, big fella. Heh. Heh. Heh." Kenneth put his hand on Michael's shoulder and steered him toward the door.

Nana bent down and gave Michael a quick kiss. "Be good," she told him.

As he walked up 16th Street with his father, Michael looked back at Nana and me and waved. He was smiling. When he passed Mr. Crawford he said hello and sort of stuck his chin out a little. From the front door we could still hear Kenneth's "Heh. Heh. Heh." Nana said, "Umph," and closed the door.

I was watching *Heckle and Jeckle* and Nana was dusting the furniture around me when, less than an hour later, the doorbell rang. Nana frowned; putting her dust rag in her apron pocket, she walked to the vestibule and opened the front door. It was Michael, alone and empty-handed. He barreled into Nana's chest and clung to her. She pulled him away. "What happened? Where's your father? Where are the shoes?" Nana demanded, her voice growing loud and harsh, her eyes narrowing, her lower lip beginning to vibrate.

Michael looked at the floor. He explained to the floor. Slowly. Carefully. His eyes seemed weighted down, as though he might fall asleep in the middle of his next sentence. "We went to that store where you bought my last pair of shoes," Michael began.

"Buster Browns?" Nana asked.

"Uh huh. And that man, that fat man with the red face, was waiting on us. He measured my feet. I wear a five and a half medium. And he showed me . . . all . . . these shoes," Michael said, pausing to wipe his eyes. "And I saw a pair I liked and I asked him," Michael wailed, "I asked my . . . faaaather if I could get them and he said yeah. Only, when it was time to pay, he kept feeling around and he couldn't find his wallet. So he told the man he couldn't get the shoes. Then he said, 'Come on, champ. We hafta go.' And when we got outside he said he'd hafta take me to the park another day. He asked me if I knew my way home and then he just, he just, juuuust left me." Michael was sobbing.

Nana veered crazily, like the needle of a racing speedometer. She bolted through the vestibule, and we heard ". . . of a bitch" as the front door slammed behind her. Michael's arms were folded tightly around his body as though he were trying to keep all his insides from falling out. He looked at me and his luminous eyes were empty for a moment, then suddenly full.

It was worse than when Barry beat him up. Then, I had run to the refrigerator to get ice. I had opened up the medicine cabinet in the bathroom, found the Mercurochrome for Nana and watched as she dipped a swab into the orangey medicine and gently dabbed the end of Michael's little delicate nostrils. Then I helped her put the ice cubes into a damp washcloth and held it under Michael's eye. This time I could see no bruises; I could touch no wounds. Michael didn't say a word, just flopped down on the floor and sobbed, his whole chest heaving in and out. He wiped his face several times and tried to get up, but then he started crying again. I watched him for a few minutes, unable to move. I looked toward the vestibule for Nana or my mother, but neither of them came. Finally I put my arm around his shoulder and pulled his head onto my chest. While I was patting Michael's shoulder, while I was telling him not to cry and feeling the slick trickle of my own tears, I was thinking: him and his shiny shoes, him and his dumb laugh. Rat! He was bad and awful and I hoped he fell down dead in the street. Ugly rat! Why couldn't he be good, like my father?

I was taking my bath that night when I heard Nana talking with my mother. ". . . High yella, slick-haired bum. Told Ruth he wasn't worth two cents, but she wouldn't listen to me."

"Has she ever?" my mother asked with a sigh.

Nana's voice rose, flew away. "Won't even take care of his own child! Men! I remember after I left your father . . . Your father! That . . ."

"Now, Mother . . ." Mommy's voice was smooth as cherry-flavored cough syrup.

" 'Now, Mother' nothing!" Nana snarled. "All these god-damn men do is make a baby, zip up their pants and walk off into the sunset." Her words sputtered and sizzled like water tossed into a hot frying pan. Nana hissed like a rattler. "You know what he told her when she asked him for support for Michael. He said, 'Get money from the man you're . . .' " Nana's voice became muffled. I couldn't hear. I didn't understand. Get money from the man you're what? What?

There it was again, I thought, leaning my head back against the rim of the tub, flicking my big toes against the second ones so I could make a tiny splatter in the water. Money. Were my friend Carol and Nana right? Was it not paying money that made a man a bad father? Was Kenneth bad just because he didn't buy Michael shoes?

"Does my father pay for me?" I asked my mother when I snuggled next to her in bed.

"Pay for you? What do you mean?"

"Send you money to buy me things. Food. Clothes. All that kind of stuff."

"He buys you your clothes, Bebe. You know that."

"Yeah, but does he send you money?" I clenched my toes, squeezing them hard against my feet.

"Yes. Of course he does."

I sighed with relief as my toes went limp. Carol's father was bad. Michael's father was bad. But my father was good. Good.

IT WAS ANOTHER YEAR, MAYBE MORE, BEFORE WE SAW KENNETH AGAIN. One Saturday, Michael, Jackie, Jane, Adam and I were sitting in the Senate Movies, which was our usual Saturday-afternoon haunt. For thirty-five cents we sat as long as we liked in that dark, magical place, soaking in the odor of popcorn and hot dogs while we rooted for John Wayne, Rory Calhoun and Kirk Douglas to beat the bad guys to the trigger, and screamed for Marilyn Monroe, Jane Russell and Jayne Mansfield as they slithered and pouted from reel to reel. This day Tarzan was triumphing over stamped-ing elephants, marauding lions, ivory pirates and African chieftains

as almost two hundred colored children screamed encouragement.
I added my voice to the throng in between stuffing Raisinets and
Jordan almonds in my mouth.

During intermission a woman's voice came over the loud-
speaker; she called Michael's name. The voice sounded proper and
official as it instructed Michael to come to the refreshment stand.
Jackie, Jane, Adam and I trooped dutifully behind him.

I caught up with Michael and saw Kenneth before he did. I
started to warn him with a quick "It's your father," but by the
time I was ready to open my mouth, Michael had seen him too.
I could tell that by the way Michael's eyes darted all over the place,
as though he were looking for a place to run, to hide. He bit down
on his lip and started swaggering like a jitterbug.

Kenneth was standing in front of the popcorn display drinking
a soda. With his coat slung over his shoulder and his head cocked
a little to the side, he looked as cool as the ice cubes in his drink.
Maybe colder. I could feel a hotness shaking up from inside my
stomach as I stood there watching him drink his soda. Michael
stopped moving when he got maybe five feet away from his father,
and I did too. The Watsons collided into our backs.

"Hey there, tiger," Uncle Kenneth said. Michael mumbled
his hello, looking down at his feet the whole time he spoke. He
acted afraid to look his father in the face, as though Kenneth were
a sun that would burn out his eyeballs.

"Who is that?" Jackie demanded, whispering loudly. "Is that
Michael's father, Bebe?" And then in a lower, more excited voice,
"Is he white?"

"No, he's not white!" I sucked my teeth in annoyance.

"Puerto Rican or something?"

"Why don't you just shut up?"

But our playmates from Mole Street had never seen anything
as exotic as Kenneth and they insisted on some sort of classification.
"Is that his real hair or do he have a process?" This from Jane.

"Is he from Cuba?" Adam demanded. He pronounced it
"Cooba."

Michael kept his distance, mostly looking down at his
sneakers, eyeing his father warily.

"Heh. Heh. Heh." Kenneth laughed to himself as he folded his raincoat carefully over his arm. Noticing me for the first time, he grinned widely, but when I didn't smile back he looked serious for a moment. Then he grinned again, not so wide, not so sure. "Well, hello there, Bebe." Seeing the other kids boldly gawking at him, Kenneth asked Michael, "Hey, aren't you going to introduce me to your friends, champ?" Michael's skin immediately paled and his eyes started racing around, looking for corners, open doors, anywhere to run. Without waiting for Michael, Kenneth smiled again and said, "Hello there. I'm Michael's father. Say, can I buy you kids something?"

He bought popcorn for everybody. When he handed me mine, he pinched me on the cheek and told me I was getting prettier and prettier. I snatched my face away and barely mumbled "Thank you" for the popcorn. It was a trick, his popcorn and smiles, that much I knew. He wanted Michael and me to forget the mean things he'd done before and the good things he hadn't done. He wasn't good for anything but being handsome. The way he looked, he should have been a king, acted like a king, but he was just what Nana said: a bum. He wanted us to forget about the money. Well, I wasn't ever going to forget. And I wasn't the only one. Jackie, Jane and Adam were stuffing the popcorn in their mouths; Michael just held his box stiffly at his side.

"So, uh, how's school, champ?" Uncle Kenneth asked. His voice sounded cheerful, but his words came out as if someone were pushing them out.

"It's okay," Michael said softly.

"Yeah, well, you get your lessons, hear?" Kenneth twirled the gold signet ring he wore on his pinkie.

"Okay."

Kenneth looked down at his nails and kept moving his ring around and around. Michael was still staring at the floor and hadn't moved any closer to his father. He squeezed the unopened box of popcorn. The salesgirl reached across the refreshment counter in front of Michael and handed Kenneth his change. She had on bright red lipstick and golden earrings that jangled against her neck as she walked. Kenneth took a quick look over his shoulder at us kids, then he caught the girl's hand as she was about to turn away and he whispered something to her and laughed. There was something hiding in the sound. "That's not very nice," the girl said, but you could tell that whatever Kenneth had said, she liked it. Michael looked as though someone had slapped him.

As the salesgirl watched, Kenneth pulled out his wallet and opened it. It was thick with green bills. He peeled off a twenty-dollar bill and handed it to Michael. "Tell your mother to get you some shoes."

Michael muttered, "Thank you," and put the money into his pocket. He didn't budge.

"Don't you have a hug for your daddy?"

Michael stared at him. There was absolutely nothing in his eyes: no love, no hate, no anger, no sadness. His eyes were empty. When he saw that look, Kenneth's shoulders sagged just a little. His voice came out raw and heavy, like that of an old man with a bad cold. "Well, okay, killer. You take it easy now. See you the next time." Michael and I watched him until we couldn't see him anymore.

On the way back to our seats, Michael dumped the popcorn into the trashcan. "What you do that for, boy?" Adam cried, his face scrunched up with astonishment. "I coulda ate that."

Michael and I didn't walk home with our friends. We took the long way home and ended up at the North Philly railroad station, standing near a cement balcony that overlooked the trains. We watched the trains come and go for almost an hour, staring in silence at the gleaming steel tracks below us. As we were getting ready to leave, Michael reached into his pocket and pulled out the money Kenneth had given him. He crumpled the bill and threw it on the sidewalk.

"Boy, are you crazy?" I rushed to retrieve the money.

"Leave it there," Michael barked at me, walking faster.

I picked up the bill and put it in my pocket. I was too much Nana's granddaughter to leave money lying in the street. Besides, we could put the money to good use. "Wanna go to Pagejo's?"

The scent of chocolate assailed us when we entered the store. Pagejo's was a dilapidated shop with no order to its arrangement of Mary Janes, Baby Ruths and Almond Joys. There weren't any customers when Michael and I went in. Old Lady Pagejo was sitting in a beat-up chair behind the counter, eating a tuna sandwich and listening to the radio. The blind old German shepherd was in the corner. "What do youse want?" she asked us in an almost surly tone of voice.

"We haven't decided," Michael said firmly.

We wandered quickly through the cluttered store, considering the possibilities. I bought an Almond Joy, because that was my favorite candy. Michael bought potato chips, a Snickers, a Milky Way, ten pieces of Double Bubble, a large box of Good and Plenty, a bottle of grape soda and some cookies. "Daaaag, you gonna eat all that?" I asked, looking in amazement at Michael's storehouse of goodies.

"Yep," he answered solemnly. And he did. We sat on the back steps in our yard and I ate my Almond Joy and Michael ate everything he bought. All in one sitting. Michael just kept packing the food in and swallowing. After a while I don't think he was even tasting the food, just packing it in and swallowing. We stayed out in the yard until it started to get dark and really cold, and I said we ought to go inside before the Turtle Lady caught us, because Jackie had told me earlier that the Turtle Lady was back in town and had eaten a boy in North Philly. And when I said that Michael laughed a little and said, "Turtle Lady. Yeah. Right," in this strange man's voice.

One afternoon weeks later, we came home from school and heard laughter and radio music coming from the kitchen. Nana and a man we didn't know were sitting at the table drinking coffee and eating cake.

"Do you know who this is, Michael?" Nana asked, smiling.

Michael looked at the stranger and a sudden shyness came over him. "No," he said, casting his eyes downward.

"This is your Uncle Bobby, your father's brother." Nana paused, waiting for Michael to speak. When he didn't, she gently prodded. "Say hello."

"Hello."

"That's Bebe, Doris's daughter," Nana told Bobby. I mumbled my hello and then I looked at Uncle Bobby, liking what I saw and felt: cocoa-brown skin, hair so nappy it could cut any fingers even attempting to run through it, a striped cap splattered with paint, big rough hands, large feet in brogans. I liked the way Bobby laughed. When he smiled at me I smiled back.

"Come here, Mike," Uncle Bobby said. "Let me get a good look at my nephew. Well, you're a good-looking boy. Got some of Mama and Daddy too. Are you smart?"

"Too smart," Nana said, chuckling a little.

"You like ice cream sodas?"

Michael nodded warily, as though he didn't quite trust this dark stranger.

"Betty," Uncle Bobby said to my grandmother, "we're going to take us a little spin and maybe get us some ice cream. Bebe, we'll bring you back some. We'll be back before dinner."

After they left I went out back. The Woo Woo Lady was scrubbing her steps and I could smell the harsh ammonia she used. There was no sign of the Watsons; their father's raggedy Chevy was gone. The only child on the street was ole stuck-up Helena walking down the street in her Catholic school uniform, trying her best to act as if she didn't see me. Bunk that girl! I didn't even want to play with that frizzy-haired thing. I looked up and down the street and began feeling a little anxious. All by myself I'd be easy for the Turtle Lady to catch.

Inside the house I flickered on the television. *Bandstand* was on. The dark-haired girl I liked who wore the scarf around her neck wasn't there, and her partner, the blond boy, was dancing with somebody else, a thin washed-out-looking girl who was moving stiffly back and forth, back and forth. She was waaaay out of step. Where did Dick Clark get those no-dancing people from, anyway? Boy, if Michael and I went on *Bandstand,* we'd squirrel everybody in the place. They would feel so bad looking at us, knowing they couldn't do our steps if they practiced for a million zillion years. We'd do so many steps that everybody would gather around us and clap and whistle when we got finished.

Michael came home smiling. "Uncle Bobby took me for a ride," he told me. After dinner, when Michael and I were sprawled across our pillows watching television, he let me feel his ears for a little while and he didn't even tell my mother I was sucking my thumb.

I wanted Uncle Bobby to take Michael more places, to teach him how to laugh with a deep voice and fix cars and kick Barry's ass. I wanted Uncle Bobby to be what Carol was talking about that time under the tree: a new daddy. Maybe one day Michael and I would look out the door and there our new daddies would be. Taking out the garbage. Fixing the car. Walking us to the candy store. This would happen for me when my daddy walked again, as Grandma said he would. It would happen. Until then, though, I would have to make do with summers, with a chilly winter holiday, a weekend in spring when I stepped out of school and heard a car horn honking. Until then I had to make do with letters. Dearest Bebe. Lots of love, Daddy.

One day I would have my father all the time, but until then I needed a way to fill in his absences. I reasoned that I might wander through days and weeks and months before I saw my father again. Sometimes to bring him closer I carried the sum-mertime around in my head. If I concentrated I could hear the crabs he caught in the Chesapeake Bay crawling around in the back of his trunk. I could taste the cream-of-tartar and water concoction he mixed up and made me drink, telling me it would take the itch out of my insect bites.

I tried, but I couldn't crowd into short southern hot spells enough of my father to dilute completely the Wonder Woman potency of my female world.

In the morning my mother hugged me before she went to work. The cloying smells of cream sachet and Jergens that filled my nostrils were sweetly oppressive. I kissed her back quickly and turned away. I had a sharp, sudden hunger for other scents. And so I began to learn, in the fall and the winter, how to make do.

# CHAPTER 9

The Sunday after Uncle Bobby visited us, I sat in the end seat of the fifth pew on the left-hand side of Faith Tabernacle Baptist Church; Michael sat next to me. We were both wedged into the corner by my mother's Playtex-coated hips. There is no give to a Playtex-coated behind, no leniency. Mommy's Sunday hips weren't cutting us any slack. Those hips told us to sit still, be good, listen to the preacher—a message wasted on Michael. After he finished poking me, imitating the minister and laughing at Miss Hat (so dubbed in honor of the feather creations she wore) getting happy, Michael promptly fell asleep.

I followed my mother's instructions to the letter. I adored Reverend Lewis. He was the most important man I knew, the steel thread that held almost a thousand people together. After service, small groups would sometimes gather, speaking his name with the deference reserved for kings and presidents: "Reverend Lewis has decided . . ." "Reverend Lewis said . . ." Jackie Wilson was on tour; Floyd Patterson was in training. There in the pulpit, only a shout away, stood Reverend Lewis. He had star quality. The pastor had his detractors, of course, those who grumbled that he was supposed to be a minister, not an emperor. Only a few months before, half the trustees had been in an uproar, because he wanted to open an ice cream parlor in the church basement. "Never heard of such a thing!" members of the opposition muttered. I hadn't heard of such a thing either, but ice cream in church sounded like a great idea to me.

At the business meeting, Reverend Lewis's opponents were forceful. They quoted scripture, prayed, and muttered and mumbled about how Jesus had thrown the money changers out of God's house.

But the pastor exerted fatherly control. "The Lord never said Christians couldn't make money," he said quietly.

My mother sat in the front of the auditorium with Mr. and Mrs. Harris. Mr. Harris was an usher and the father of one of my Sunday-school friends. I sat in the back with the children.

Reverend Lewis always emphasized racial pride. "And besides," my minister continued, "those of us who are colored need to spend our money with each other." There was a soft murmur of approval. I rooted silently for vanilla, chocolate and butter pecan.

The minister strode down the center of the basement until he was standing next to my row. He pointed at me. "Stand up, Bebe," he commanded. I rose obediently, pleased that he had singled me out. He put his hand on my shoulder. "Now when this child wants an ice cream cone, why should she have to leave the church to get it?"

Nobody said a word as he returned to the front of the room. "The Lord wants colored people to be independent," Reverend Lewis declared. He got a few strong amens on that. The tide was turning in his favor. "Do we need any more discussion?" he asked.

". . . andandand when you ride with Jesus, there ain't no back of the bus. I'm talking about a man from Galilee who's got front seats for *everybody* . . . *for alla God's children* . . . ."

I watched as the nurses fanned Miss Hat, who had gotten happy right on cue. She was barely struggling against them, succumbing at last to the pressure of the two dark hands that held her in her seat. The soft bursts of cool air against her face were calming her down, but what had stirred her up in the first place? Nana said that folks who got happy were just putting on a show.

That's why Nana didn't go to church. Nana always went out dancing on Saturday night and she never came home until Sunday. She had sashayed out the night before wearing a bright green taffeta dress, leaning on the arm of Mr. Robby, her date. "See you when I see you," she called over her shoulder. Nana went to the Brotherhood, a nightclub she frequented because it featured the hot mambo music she liked. Nana said she didn't want to spend Sunday morning watching crazy folks whooping and hollering, acting as if they were so sanctified and holy when all they were doing was showing off. Was Miss Hat showing off or was there really something inside her that could come out only in a shout? I hadn't lived long or hard enough to know.

Reverend Lewis stood in front of the pulpit holding his arms straight out, signaling that his sermon had ended and that the next important piece of business was about to begin. I leaned forward in my seat. Stolid men in suits marched down the aisles, with one hand behind their slightly bent backs, offering velvet-lined baskets for all the dollars, quarters, dimes and nickels the worshippers could afford. Mr. Harris stood only two aisles away from me. I began patting my feet much faster than the organist was playing. When I looked again, Mr. Harris was standing right next to me. He winked when I put in my dime, which is what he did every Sunday. I winked back.

After church Mommy, Michael and I went up to shake Reverend Lewis's hand. Shyness caught me up like a web when I finally stood in front of my glorious pastor. He pulled me deeply into the folds of his robe. "Well, Miss Bebe! How are you, darling?"

"Fine." I looked up shyly at him. He was beaming and patting my arm.

"And when can we expect another Paul Laurence Dunbar poem?" he asked, smiling. "I really enjoyed that last rendition. What was that one called?"

" 'In the Morning,' " I said quickly.

" 'In the Morning!' " he repeated. He turned to my mother. "You know, I think you have a budding little actress. Yes. This girl's got talent. No doubt about it." I moved closer to my beloved pastor. Praise from a deep voice was something I craved. He snapped his fingers and turned back to me. "Say, you know we're having a program next month when the visiting ministers are in Philadelphia. I'd like you to entertain us with a poetic rendition. Would you do that for me?"

Did birds fly? Was there rice in China? Did Eartha Kitt have hips? I could only nod. To have Reverend Lewis personally request me to do anything was an honor. If it brought me recognition and praise from my minister, I would recite a hundred poems.

"Reverend Lewis asked you a question, Bebe," Mommy said.

"Oh, yes. I'd like to say a poem." I grinned at my mother.

"All right. I'll expect it," he said, turning to shake hands with the woman behind us in line.

On the way out the door Mr. Harris spotted us. He stuck out his arm so I couldn't get past. "Where you goin', girlfriend?" he asked, putting his arm around me. My mother and I laughed. Mr. Harris and I played this game every Sunday.

"Now, you gonna be a good girl this week?"

"Uh huh."

"You gonna get all your lessons and mind your teachers and your mama?"

"Yes."

"You not getting married on Wednesday, are you?"

"Nobody wants to marry her," Michael blurted out.

"I do," Mr. Harris said jovially, winking at me. "We're getting married this Thursday, isn't that right?" He nudged me.

I said, "Uh huh," and everybody laughed. Then I said proudly, "I'm going to say another poem at church when the visiting ministers come."

"Are you gonna say it as nice as you did the other one?"

I nodded.

"Well, I'm coming to that, 'cause you laid that other poem out. Yes, indeed. You really said that poem." He patted my arm, then said to Mommy, "This is a real smart little girl you got here. I believe she's gonna be a teacher!"

That a girl child was bright enough to be delivered from mops and buckets and the factory line was high praise indeed, at least the highest Mr. Harris could muster. I smiled appreciatively at the compliment.

Mommy, Michael and I went downstairs and bought ice cream cones, and then walked the six blocks to our house, the wind whipping against our winter coats. My cousin and I skipped ahead and peered into the windows of some of the closed stores along Diamond Avenue and looked over the back fences of the houses we passed. When we finally turned up 16th Street, we saw Nana getting out of Mr. Robby's old blue Ford. We broke into a run, the heels of our slick Sunday shoes clicking against the sidewalk.

"Hello, sweeties," Nana exclaimed gaily when she saw us. She held out her arms and we flew right into them, breathing in Chanel No. 5 and the faint odor of scotch. Her green taffeta dress had wilted somewhat and her henna-colored curls weren't as bouncy as they'd been the night before, but Saturday night's glamour still clung to her. Robby held the door and we all trooped into the house.

Michael immediately ran upstairs to change his clothes so he could go out back and play before dinner. I stayed in my church dress and followed Nana and Mr. Robby into the kitchen. Mr. Robby was from Bermuda and I thought his voice sounded like music. I loved to hear him sing the song he made of my name. I sat down at the kitchen table with him while Nana made them both some coffee and toast.

"Bebe, what you been doing, child?" That sounded like "Baybe, whut you bin doin', chile?" Was there any way to prolong the beauty of Mr. Robby's words?

"Huh?"

He smiled at me and his teeth were as pretty as his musical voice. "I say, chile, how you been?"

"Fine." I smiled back.

Nana placed the coffee in front of Mr. Robby. "Go change your clothes, dollin'," she said to me lightly. Dag. Nana was forever getting rid of me whenever one of her boyfriends was around.

"See you, Mr. Robby," I said, hoping against hope that he'd say my name again in his singsong island voice.

But he said only, "See you," as he slurped his coffee.

I stopped at the kitchen door and turned back toward Mr. Robby. "I'm going to say a poem at church."

"Oh, yeah?" Nana said, sitting down at the kitchen table and drinking her coffee.

"You gonna come?"

"I might can put it on my schedule," Nana said, smiling.

"Will you come, Mr. Robby?"

"You get your Nana to tell me when, okay, Bebe? I come for sure to hear you."

My mother was watching television in the living room. I looked at the screen. A painted woman with narrow eyes and straight hair piled high in a bun was groveling along the floor at the feet of a white man in a naval officer's uniform, and piercing high notes were flying out of her mouth. Culture. I had to get out fast. "Come sit with me," my mother said. Too late.

"What are you watching?" I asked, steady moving toward the stairs.

"This is an opera called *Madame Butterfly*."

"Don't you want to play checkers?" I asked hopefully.

"Come watch this. You'll like it."

"I have to do something," I said, and tore up the steps. I was wondering how I would fill the afternoon, since it was obvious that Mommy wasn't taking us to the main library or the Franklin Museum as she usually did every Sunday after church. I heard the door that connected our house to the third-floor apartment opening. Pete came clattering down the stairs. I was grinning before I even saw him. Anne and Pete were our tenants. Anne could pop gum louder than any female on earth and that quality alone endeared her to me. But it was to Pete that I gravitated. He was big, a tall man with skin the color of a Snickers bar. He had just the beginnings of a belly and his substantial chuckles seemed to come from the bottom of it. Pete laughed all the time.

"There's my girl," he said, scooping me up and hugging me hard around my waist. "Hey, who wants ice cream?"

"Me!" I cried loudly. I looked at my mother.

"You just had ice cream!"

"Aww, let her have some more ice cream," Pete said with a grin. "Never too cold for ice cream, Doris."

"Mommy, can I go? Please."

"What did you say?"

"May I go?"

My mother smiled.

"Where's Mike?" Pete asked.

"Out back."

"Go get him."

Michael and I walked down 16th Street on either side of Pete, kicking at the few brown leaves in our path. "So how was school this week, Mike?" Pete always asked us about school.

"Fine."

"Girlfriend, you doing okay?"

"Uh huh. I got an A on my spelling test and I got a gold star for doing all my homework. And I'm going to say a poem at church."

"Very good. I'll hafta come hear that."

"You will?"

"Sure."

Pete set kids up to ice cream the same way he'd set up his partners at the bar, and for the same reason: kids were a good time to him. Michael liked Pete too, but Anne said Pete was partial to little girls. I moved toward him instinctively.

Pete liked to gamble, and there was an aura about him, a kind of loose and easy charm and self-confidence that perhaps came from his ability to read a stranger in an instant. From time to time he'd come home late on Friday with an empty pay envelope and a long story. Anne, a Florida girl with aplenty sense and a wide streak of Sapphire in her, didn't play that. One time after he lost his wages, Anne made him a sandwich of bread and paper for lunch. At work with all his friends around, he bit down into the sandwich, only to spit it out. On the paper she'd written: "No money, no meat."

Pete took me for rides and walks to the store. He didn't

assume my intelligence and was duly impressed when I read, "In Philadelphia, nearly everyone reads the *Bulletin*" as we passed the newsstands. Pete was always around for special occasions that punctuated my early childhood. I didn't have to ask him; he sought me out. He sat in the front row watching me pirouette around the stage. He beamed as I easy-versioned my way through "The Moonlight Sonata." He assured me my recital dress was pretty, my Shirley Temple curls gorgeous, that I was adorable.

My mother quietly observed his influence, trusted and used it. "I'm going to tell Pete how ugly you're acting," she told me once when I was right in the middle of a bratty outburst. I shut my mouth.

The year before, my mother had taught me a variety of "feminine skills," among them knitting, crocheting and embroidery. She was acting as a kind of big sister/mentor to a "deprived" girl from the neighborhood and she taught both of us at the same time. I didn't like sharing my mother, even to uplift the race, but I didn't protest. The three of us sat on the living room sofa one Saturday afternoon. My mother watched quietly as the girl and I knit one, purled two. Sometimes her fingers gently guided mine around the silver knitting needles and the thick skein of wool. "Now that you've got the hang of it, what are you going to make?" my mother asked me several days later.

I didn't even have to think twice. Ran to the five-and-dime on Broad Street, looking for wool, special wool to protect and comfort. When the saleslady asked me if she could help I told her no, I'd find it myself. What I wanted was soft and just the right color. The maroon caught my eye and stayed there. I paid the saleslady, then ran all the way home to the sofa and the knitting needles. For weeks there was school, church, the sofa and the knitting needles, clicking into the night, and the soft chain of maroon wool, growing longer and longer as Christmas approached.

"My baby sure can knit," Pete said when I handed him the scarf. It was two inches wide and six feet long. The scarf circled Pete's neck at least five times, like a long, warm hug. "Yes, indeed," he said, grabbing me up in a ferocious squeeze, "my baby sure can knit. Thank you, sweetheart."

In my young life, most of the voices that I heard bounced off bosoms. My mother called me Bebe. Nana called me Sweetie and her Little Pumpkin Seed. My father's voice seemed so distant sometimes, so far away and out of hearing range that his tone reverberated against my foggy memory only like a hazy echo. "BebebebebebebeMoore." I grabbed for the echo and like smoke rings it disappeared. But Pete was in front of me, wrapping the scarf around his neck, letting the long ends hang over his shoulders. "My baby sure can knit," he said. Pete's hug captured my breath; his words took hold of me like a strong grip.

Pete bought us double dips; my ice cream cone weighed more than I did. By the time we got back home, my face was sticky and frozen with the remnants of strawberry and chocolate. Pete walked me to the kitchen, where Nana and Mr. Robby were still talking. Pete wet a napkin and wiped the goo from around my poked-out lips. I held out my hands and he wiped them off too.

"Now look at you," Nana admonished me, "acting like a little three-year-old."

"That's all right," Pete retorted, "she's my big baby."

Later that night, under the covers, I was steady practicing for Reverend Lewis. For Mr. Harris. For Mr. Robby. For Pete. " 'Lias! 'Lias! Bless de Lawd! . . ."

# CHAPTER 10

If Sundays gave me a dependable supply of prayerful men, then during the week men were a piecemeal affair, a patchwork quilt I stitched together from whatever brilliant scraps of biceps and aftershave I could find. It was during the week that I needed men the most. Especially the week leading up to the church program, the week my mother went officially berserk. Crazy. Demented. She stalked me from the time she got in from work until I lay my weary head on my pillow. Woman was getting on my nerves. My very last little nine-year-old nerve.

"Bebe," she said cheerfully after dinner on Tuesday, "let's hear your poems."

So I said them. All three of them. I really wanted to say only the two shorter ones, but Mommy kept telling me, "Now Bebe, why don't you learn the longer one? That will be a lovely challenge for you. Life is full of challenges."

So what could I say? I knew she was just going to bug me forever if I didn't do three poems, so I learned "A Cabin Tale," which had about five zillion stanzas. I stood in front of the bedroom mirror and said all three perfectly without forgetting one single word. And then Mommy said, "This time let's have a liiiittle more expression." And I knew then it was going to be a loooooong week.

The closer we got to Sunday, the crazier she got. She became a driven woman. "Now when you say 'When Malindy Sings,' really draw that name out. Say 'Muh-lin-dee,' " she said, her eyes bright and eager from behind her glasses.

"Muh-lin-dee."

"Again."

"Muh-lin-dee."

"One more time."

I should have known. Culture did this to her. "Muh-lin-dee."

"Good."

Jesus, please save me from this woman.

School was no escape from distaff perfection. From my desk in room 14 I watched the snowflakes softly disappearing into the dried-up grass on the school lawn. Miss Lesches, my 4A teacher, was giving out the short stories we had turned in earlier that week. She handed me my paper. Big red A. I was very happy until . . . "This is a good paper, but you could have had an A plus, young lady," Miss Lesches said tersely. "You are one of my most capable students and this grade should have been an A plus. All you needed was a liiiittle more enthusiasm!"

As soon as Miss Lesches walked away I turned around, and Wallace, whose farts and mischief had followed me to the fifth grade, grinned at me. I scowled and looked past his little squinched-up face to Linda and Carol, who sat on either side of him. I drew a quick A in the air. My girlfriends smiled.

A liiiittle more enthusiasm, I thought, as the subway left Logan station. A liiiiittle more expression, I said to myself as the train pulled into Susquehanna and Dauphin. How about a liiiiittle less of these Bosoms crowding around me, trying to make me perfect? How about that? When I got home I changed my clothes and went up to the third floor and knocked on Anne and Pete's door. Sometimes Pete got home early, depending on his shift, and we would watch *Bandstand*. There was no answer, so with a sigh I headed downstairs and turned on the television. The dark-haired girl was back. She was wearing a wide skirt that came almost to her ankles, saddle shoes and a pale short-sleeved sweater. Her ponytail was bouncing all around as the blond boy swung her from side to side. They could not dance. At all. Never even heard of rhythm. But I watched them anyway until the show ended, then I went out back. I sat on Jackie, Jane and Adam's steps waiting for them to come out. Where was their father, I wondered. Many times he was home during the day. Where was their crazy, ass-whipping daddy who knew how to shoot the breeze with kids and be funny and loose and just let folks be? But before Mr. Watson or his kids appeared, Nana called me in to practice my poems. I had to say them in the kitchen while she cut up onions at the sink. Nana kept interrupting me with, "Say it louder, I can't hear you. Don't mumble."

Daaag.

Aunt Ruth came home; she was living with us again. I could smell the Toujours Moi she always wore (which I thought smelled like essence of skunk) and hear her chiming in with Billie Holiday as she sang "No More." Aunt Ruth would turn on Billie Holiday or Dinah Washington as soon as she came home. She was always singing a no-good-man song in a dolorous voice. She held the notes even longer than Lady Day, and for the three weeks since she had appeared at our door with a black eye and several suitcases, the house had been filled with blues and jazz. One thing I liked about Aunt Ruth: she wasn't culture-crazy. She didn't care if I said "Muh-lin-dee" or not. I went in the living room and sat down on the sofa beside her. Aunt Ruth's fingernails were perfectly oval and shone with clear polish. She was holding her hands straight out in front of her as she sang. She hardly noticed me. She was in her own little world of lonesome blues. I raced up the stairs and slammed the bedroom door shut. I was tired of the blues.

I was going over my poems one night, softly mumbling the words as I stretched out across the pillow. I had one of Nana's long silver hair clips pinching my nose shut. I wanted my nose to be thin even if Nana called me a knucklehead. Linda's nose was thin, I thought with a sigh. She said her mother had pinched it when she was a baby. Well, if my mother hadn't had enough sense to pinch my nose when I was a baby and make it nice and narrow, then I'd do it myself, even if Nana's hair clip was making my Negro dialect sound a little nasal. When I said "When Malindy Sings," I sounded like a telephone operator from Brooklyn. Mommy poked her head in the bedroom and I snatched the hair clip off and stuck it under the pillow.

"Are you practicing, sweetie?" As if she had to ask.

"Uh huh."

"Good." She closed the door.

I put the book of poems away and pulled out my A paper. I tore out a sheet of paper from my copybook.

> Dear Daddy,
> I can't wait until summer. What are you doing? What are you doing right this minute; it is almost 8:30 on Wednesday. Here's a little story for you. Once there was a girl named Eleanor Marie who had a dog named Simon. One day as Eleanor Marie was taking Simon for a walk, Simon spied a huge, orange cat who was hissing and sticking her tongue out at him. Quick as a wink, Simon pulled away from Eleanor Marie and ran after the cat. . . . .

As I copied from my paper I expanded the tale. Put a bunch of enthusiasm in it. Some of everything happened to poor Eleanor Marie as she raced around the corner looking for Simon. She got chased into a swamp by monsters. A wicked witch held her prisoner for three years. She got eaten alive by a dinosaur. I ended that first installment with a juicy cliffhanger:

> Daddy, should Eleanor Marie follow Simon down a sewey hole filled with alligators? If you want to find out what happened, you have to write me a letter as soon as you get mine and not take forever like you always do!
>
> Love,
> Bebe

I needed a male voice to penetrate this crazy wilderness of Bosoms gone berserk.

Five days later I got Daddy's response. "Well, Doll Baby, that sure was a good story and I can hardly wait to find out what is going to happen to Eleanor Marie. . . ." He rambled on and on about my story and the weather. "I saw Cousin Eula last week," he wrote. "We sat in the car and talked a long time." About what, I thought, sitting up to fold his letter carefully into its envelope and then flinging myself back onto my bed in exasperation.

The grassy plot next to my cousin's dark green house was vivid enough and I could see the outlines of the older woman and my father sitting in the Pontiac, but nothing else would come to me. Not what clothes they were wearing or how they smelled or whether my father was puffing away on a Winston. And not Cousin Eula's daughter, LaVerne, bringing him the big glass of water he would have surely requested after driving the thirty miles from Pasquotank County. Not LaVerne handing my daddy the water and him playfully thumping her on the head, saying to her, "Girl, you're getting big. Now you better watch out for these little hardheads, hear me?" Not any of that. My imagination refused to create a stage for his fatherhood in which I had no part and certainly not one in which I was replaced. When summer drew to a close and Daddy put me in the back of Uncle Eddie and Aunt Marie's station wagon, in my mind he became suspended in animation until we were together again. My world chugged along without him. Letting other men fill in for my absent father was an unconscious act.

SAMMY, MY MARINE UNCLE, CAME BY ONE WEEKDAY EVENING WITH-out any warning whatsoever. It was still early and I was outside playing. Next door to the Watsons', Old Mrs. McCowan was throwing bread crumbs onto the street and a flock of half-frozen pigeons were feeding greedily and cooing. I was inching my behind as far away from the pigeons as I could without falling off the steps. Ever since the Headless Chicken had come after me, birds weren't too cool with me. With our woolen hats pulled way down over our ears, we were all huddled together on the Watsons' steps having a club meeting. The daily Mole Street Club meeting took place through rain, sleet and hail. Adam's teeth were chattering in my ear and we could all see our breath in the January air. In front of us on wooden blocks was Mr. Watson's newest acquisition, a wreck of a car that he swore he could restore to full glory. It didn't matter how cold or hot it was, every Saturday and part of Sunday would find him under some beat-up old car, trying to make it run. Only the weekend before, Jackie, Jane and I had jumped double dutch beside his newest jalopy. Mr. Watson emerged from under the car from time to time, his dark face even darker with grease and oil stains. "Jackie, go inside da house and brang me my udda wrench," he said, or rather yelled. When Mr. Watson was working on a car, every request was a yell. Jackie dropped the ropes and ran inside. Mr. Watson looked at Jane, then me. "Y'all play too much rope. Gone jump your brains out." I started laughing, then looked at Jane, who was smiling a little. On the curb Mr. Watson had lined up two empty beer cans. "See now, your brains is definitely gone jump out. Keep on jumping." Jane laughed. When Jackie came back and handed her father the wrench, he looked at Jane and me and winked. "Now huh brains jumped out three years ago. Never know it, would you?"

I sat with one part of my behind on the step and the other part hanging in midair. The Woo Woo Lady was putting out her trash when Mommy came outside and called to me, "Bebe, you have a visitor." Everybody got up at the same time and started walking toward my house. "Y'all ain't got no visitor. I got a visitor," I said in a playful way, knowing I'd have been heading toward the Watsons' house if their mother had come looking for them. When I got to the yard, my mother got right up in my face and said, "Did I hear you say, 'Y'all ain't got no visitor'?"

The woman must have had ears all over her body. "Who, me?" I replied.

My mother pressed her lips together and shook her head. She gave me a modified-dignity stare, but I didn't look directly at her. She wasn't zapping me! "Your Uncle Sammy is here," she said finally.

Right away my heart starting thumping hard. "I gotta go in. My uncle is here!" I yelled over the back fence to Jackie, Jane and Adam, who were hovering near our yard with their nosey-butt selves, trying to figure out what was going on. I ran into the house, letting the door slam behind me.

Uncle Sammy was standing in the living room looking at the big tapestry of an old English couple that hung above the console television set. The tapestry was about five feet by three feet and it was very old and expensive. One of the women Nana used to clean house for had given it to her. When Uncle Sammy saw me, he said, "Whatcha know, kiddo?" and gave me a hug.

Sammy was like the Marine uniform he used to wear: clean, crisp and purposeful. He was orderly and neat; his shoes were shined as though he were expecting inspection. We talked a little bit about everything, about Grandma Mary, North Carolina and my daddy. Uncle Sammy asked me how I was doing in school, which is what all grown-ups wanted to know. I told him I was doing fine. Then he stood up to leave and said, "Oh, I got something for you, kiddo." He pulled a black leather-bound book out of a bag on the floor. "Here," he said, handing me the book.

It was his Marine book. My uncle had recently left the service. Sammy turned to the page with his picture on it. He was one of more than a hundred tiny specks, some dark and some white, but I could make out his face. I couldn't even say thank you. I just nodded at him.

I was smitten with the image of my uncle on the pages of this elegant Marine book. Sammy in uniform was tangible evidence that there was an important man in my life. At first when I showed Michael the book, he said, "I can't even find your uncle on here. Where is he?" When I pointed Uncle Sammy out, he said, "That doesn't even look like your uncle." I snatched the book away from him and he said, "Okay. Okay. I was only playing. It looks like him. Lemme see it again."

I took the book to school, where it was properly appreciated by Carol and Linda. They told me Uncle Sammy looked better than all the other Marines, which I already knew. I interrupted the Mole Street Club meeting so that everybody could take a look. Adam grabbed the book from me, saying, "That ain't no Marine book," but he had hardly gotten the words out before he was saying, "Daaaaag," which I took to be awe of the highest order. I even showed the book to Michael's Uncle Bobby. Michael's father hadn't been around since the time he came to the movies, but Uncle Bobby had been coming over some weekends and taking Michael places. When Uncle Bobby brought him back, Michael would do whatever Nana told him to without her asking twice, and sometimes he'd let me feel his ears when we were watching television at night. "See, that's my uncle," I told Uncle Bobby one day when he came to take Michael to a football game. My uncle was important and special, I thought, just a little smugly, when Uncle Bobby and Michael left.

By Sunday evening my mother was bouncing off the walls in anticipation. "Now remember to say 'Muh-lin-dee.' And speak slowly and distinctly. And project yourself. Remember, your voice has to carry. And don't say 'um.' " All I could do was nod as she whipped off a litany of don't-forgets.

Nana helped me get ready for the program. She dressed me up in one of her old-fashioned frocks that she kept in the back of her closet and wrapped my head in a rag and told me not to wear shoes when I went on the stage. I wore lipstick and she circled my eyes with black eyebrow pencil. "You look like a real slavery-time gal," she said, standing back and staring at me. I studied my face in the mirror wondering: Did slaves wear lipstick?

Nana and Mr. Robby rode to church together. Mommy, Michael and I rode with Anne and Pete. Aunt Ruth was in her housecoat playing Billie Holiday records and painting her toenails when we left. She didn't go to church. Period.

When I got to Faith Tabernacle I could feel my stomach churning around and getting fluttery. The program was downstairs in the basement, where Sunday school was held, and the auditorium was already pretty full. I sat in the front row with the rest of the people in the program. There were two singers, a pianist, a trumpet player, another girl who was going to recite a poem and me. Reverend Lewis started off with a word of prayer and then asked everybody to rise and sing "Lift Every Voice and Sing." He welcomed all the visiting ministers and turned the program over to Mrs. Dees, the superintendent of the Baptist Training Union. Mrs. Dees welcomed everybody all over again and prayed all over again and turned the program over to Mrs. Little, a Sunday-school teacher. The first person she called on was me.

I looked at Mommy when I heard my name and she made kissy-mouth at me, which didn't quell the creatures scurrying around in the pit of my stomach. Muh-lin-dee, I said to myself. My last conscious thought was of Miss Lesches telling the class to strive for enthusiasm. I don't remember walking up on stage, but I must have, because suddenly I was standing in front of everybody, the only sound my own heartbeat. When I opened my mouth, nothing but the pure-dee slavery-time dialect came out. " 'Lias! 'Lias! Bless de Lawd! . . ." Miraculously my trembling disappeared. I stole a glance at Nana; she was grinning. My mother's face was lit up like five hundred candles. "Don' you know de day's erbroad?" My mother was enthralled. I strutted across the stage with my hand on my hips. "Ef you don' git up, you scamp . . ." The audience started laughing. I could hardly keep from grinning. "Dey'll be trouble in dis camp. . . ." I was on a roll! When I was finished Mr. Robby and Pete stood up to clap before anybody else and then Nana and Mommy got up, and even Michael was smiling.

When my recitations were concluded, Reverend Lewis went onstage and said, "Faith Tabernacle has been blessed with talent. Abundant talent." After the rest of the program was over, all the visiting ministers came up to me and told me what a nice job I'd done and did I want to come to their church, and all that kind of embarrassing stuff. Pete told everybody he was going to be my manager. "This child's gonna make me rich," he said, shaking his head and smiling. Nana and Mr. Robby laughed, and everybody helped himself to the same red punch and assorted cookies always served after church programs.

On our way home I couldn't stop smiling. Capable, Miss Lesches had called me. Yes. I was. Mommy said, "Too bad your father couldn't have heard you."

That burst my bubble a little. I thought, Yeah, he missed it.

"Maybe you can recite the poems for him next time you see him," Mommy suggested.

Yeah, I could do that, I mused. I leaned my head against the backseat of Pete's car. But suppose I messed up when I said the poems for Daddy? Tonight had been perfect, not one mistake. I wanted my daddy to hear me say the poems perfectly and hear the audience clap and laugh and say "Amen." The next time I saw him wouldn't be the same. Why did he always have to miss everything?

Uncle Sammy brought his fiancée to visit one evening during the week. Irma was the color of a sweet potato. She was pretty, a cheerful, functional kind of pretty. She talked and laughed a lot. It was after dinnertime and we all sat on the sofa as Sammy and Irma talked about their wedding plans. They said they were having a big wedding in July. "Mama's coming up. And your daddy," Sammy told me. Suddenly Sammy and Irma started talking just to each other. They didn't change the subject and they weren't rude; they just talked only to each other. Everything around them seemed soft and my mother leaned back into the sofa and smiled to herself. I didn't feel left out. I felt as though I were being allowed to watch a grown-up, romantic movie.

I began to daydream about their wedding. I couldn't wait! My father, mother and I would sit together. My mother and father would say things only to each other. Maybe my father would be walking. My father walking and Mommy, Daddy and me together. This was the real dream.

Three nights later I lay in bed and watched my mother dabbing at herself in front of the mirror. Deep coral lipstick. Chanel No. 5. A touch of rouge. Rouge? I sat straight up. "Where are you going, Mommy?" I asked, my antennae rising.

"Nowhere."

When the doorbell rang, I crept to the edge of the stairs and waited. A big overcoat. Cigarette smoke. Deep mumbling. Haw-hawhaw, real low. Girlish laughter in response. Fear gripped me like handcuffs.

"Mommy!" I wanted water.

"Mommy!" Something scared me.

"Mommy!" I needed, uh, uh, a back rub.

She came each time, bending over my bed to soothe, rub, hold me. Then she wafted down the stairs as if on a cloud.

Nana appeared after the fourth call. Her green 'do rag was wound neatly around her head and in her hand she gripped a paperback. On the cover a man and a woman with bright red lips clutched each other in a passionate embrace. Nana peered at me. Her eyes were dangerous, narrow slits. One look and I ducked my head under the covers. She wasn't going for that. "Lissenyoulittlemonkeydon'tthinkIdon'tknowwhatyou'reuptoand Iwantyoutostopthisfoolishness*rightnow*. *Your mother has company*. Don't. You. Call. Her. Another. Time."

"Who's down there with her?" I asked from under the covers.

"None of your beeswax. Go to sleep."

"Tell me."

"No."

"Please. Tell me."

"A friend. Go to sleep." She shut the door.

But I couldn't sleep. I put my thumb in my mouth and reached up to pull on my ear. I cracked the door a little after I heard Nana go in her room. What were they talking about down there? I could hear the low rumbling. Hawhawhaw. What did that laugh want with my mommy?

UNCLE SAMMY AND AUNT IRMA'S WEDDING WAS BEAUTIFUL, BUT THE magic I expected didn't happen. Uncle Norman and Uncle Joe pulled my daddy's wheelchair up the cement steps into the church. Mommy and I stood back a little until he was inside, then she and I found a pew and sat down. Daddy said he wanted to stay in the back so he wasn't in anybody's way. "Go on up front," he urged us.

"I'll see everything before you do." We sat together at the reception in the church basement and I fixed my daddy's plate while Mommy sat quietly with no expression on her face. "Well, how'd you like that wedding?" Daddy asked. "Wasn't that something?"

"Uh huh," I said, but what I was thinking was this: When is my daddy gonna start walking?

DADDY TOOK GRANDMA AND ME TO NORTH CAROLINA RIGHT AFTER the wedding. Somehow I knew the summer would go quickly. Knew it that first night lying in the bed next to my father, who had fallen into a hard sleep as soon as he dragged himself under the covers. Why hadn't it happened? When would it happen? I snuggled into the sheet thinking I was going to wake up one day and be older and Daddy would be older and none of what Grandma Mary promised would have come true. None of it. So I pushed for everything in my ninth summer: long baths with Bunnie, with tons of bubbles; world-class wars with Jimmy and Johnny under the ammo tree; dressing to kill with Belinda.

Daddy let me spend three nights with Eugenia. The week before I went he kept saying I was going to be staying with Dr. So-and-so and his wife. When Eugenia's parents came to the car to speak with my father they acted very friendly, but I could tell they didn't think my daddy was as important as he thought they were.

While I was at her house, Eugenia asked me, "What does your daddy do?"

Do?

"For a living, I mean."

I didn't know what to say. Words wouldn't come. What did he do? He was my father, that's what he did. He was in a wheelchair. I changed the subject.

On our way back home Daddy asked me if I'd had fun. "Yeah," I said.

"Don't you like that house?" he asked eagerly.

"It's pretty."

"Yeah, that's the kind of house I wanted. Want."

"Daddy, I want to eat crabs this year."

All summer long I asked my daddy to please, please put on his braces and try to walk. Please. He just laughed and said, "Girl, those things don't help." At night Mr. Abe sang his slave songs and Grandma quilted. The days went fast, just as I thought. And my dream didn't come true.

I begged and begged until finally, a week before I was to leave, Daddy let me walk to Cousin Emily's house all by myself. I felt grown-up and free trudging down the highway, tall corn at either side of me, dogs yapping when I passed. I yelled back at the dogs, my words propelled by childish bravado. "Shut up!" Anyway, what could some dumb ole dogs do to a big girl walking to her cousin's house by herself?

I passed Morgan's Corner and two old red-faced men I didn't even know stared at me. They were both dressed in overalls and hard high-top shoes, with old faded hats that dipped down into their eyes. Their florid faces glistened in the summer heat. The taller one called out "Hey" as I passed and then the other one said "Hey" too. I heyed them right back, a little surprised. In Philly strange white people never opened their mouths to a colored child. In Pasquotank County everyone spoke to everyone else. I kept on walking, then I heard one of the men talking to me. I stopped and turned around.

"You Aunt Mary's grandbaby? Is your daddy George, the one in the wheelchair?"

Aunt Mary? Why'd he call her that? I nodded.

"I knowed it. I knowed it," the man said, slapping his splayed fingers against his side and grinning as if he'd just heard an up-roarious joke. I walked on, waving as the man called out, "You be good, now."

Belinda and I dressed up in Cousin Emily's clothes all after-noon, playing grown-up. I headed back up the road around four o'clock. When I got a little past Morgan's Corner, Daddy came driving by. He slowed down and I ran across the road and jumped in the car.

"I was just coming after you," he said, grinning. "You have fun?"

I nodded, a little out of breath from running. "Where are we going?"

"You wanna go somewhere?"

"Just riding."

"I got crabs in the back," Daddy said eagerly.

"You do?"

"They'll keep. Let's go riding."

We went out Route 17, because Daddy knew it was my favorite road. Dismal Swamp lay beside us, deep and silent. I studied the water. Daddy pulled over to the side of the road. I looked into the water and thought about the slaves.

"Was Grandma Mary's mother a slave?"

"Naw."

"Grandma Mary's grandmother?"

"Uncle Johnny said there wasn't any slavery on Mama's side. He's the family historian." Daddy looked over at me. "Why you asking?"

"Just wondering. Some white man said hello to me when I was walking to Cousin Emily's house. He asked me if I was Aunt Mary's grandbaby."

"What'd he look like?"

"Kinda old. He had on overalls and a hat kinda like Mr. Abe wears in the field."

"I don't know who that was," Daddy said slowly, as if he were still thinking.

"How come he called Grandma Aunt?"

Daddy looked at me. He didn't seem to know what to say. Finally he said, "Oh, that's sort of an expression down here That's what some folks call old ladies. He didn't mean nothing by it."

Daddy and I went to Cousin Ruby's house and when we got back home it was after nine o'clock. Grandma and Mr. Abe were in bed and Bunnie had gone out. Daddy and I carried the basket of crabs into the house. I could hear them thrashing around, their bodies hitting one another. Daddy put a big pot of water on the stove and added green and red spices and a little vinegar. When the water started boiling he dumped the crabs into the pot, but two fell on the floor and started crawling out of the kitchen. "Get 'em. Get 'em," Daddy hollered.

I caught both of them in the living room and picked them up with a pot holder. Daddy put them in the water. After a while I told Daddy, "They're turning red."

"They need to cool," Daddy said, after he poured the water out of the pot.

We ate the crabs at midnight. I spread a bunch of newspapers on the small table on the back porch and Daddy dumped the crabs on top. He said, "Get ready for the feast, baby doll." After that neither of us said a word. We just tore those bad boys up. Daddy kept putting crabs on the table and lifting his eyebrows as if to say, "Can you handle some more?" and we kept gritting. From time to time we looked at each other and our mouths were so full we had to smile with our eyes. After I put away eight crabs I stopped counting. And I know Daddy ate at least fifteen. Probably twenty. After we were finished, we cleaned up the porch, and then sat in the living room talking because our stomachs were too full for us to go straight to bed. And Daddy said, "Well, you done had your crabs."

BUNNIE HELPED ME PACK MY CLOTHES. I INSISTED THAT WE PUT MY summer clothes in one suitcase and my new school clothes in another. "You're a nutty buddy," Bunnie said, laughing. "You think your old clothes are gonna contaminate your new ones?"

"I just don't want them together," I repeated. The truth was, as soon as I got to Philly I was going to unpack my new things, spread them out on the bed and stare at them. I just wanted to be able to get to my new clothes easily.

"You getting big," Grandma Mary told me when I was leaving. "You come back next summer and be a young lady. Ole Grandmama won't know you."

"Yes, you will," I said, hugging her. I wanted to ask my grandmother about my father's legs, if they were still going to heal as she said they would. But I didn't say anything. I just held onto her.

"Yeah, you growing up," she said softly. Then Uncle Otto and Aunt Lela honked the car horn and it was time to go back up the road.

Daddy rolled out to the car with me. "You gonna write me some more stories?" Daddy asked.

"You like those stories, Daddy?" I asked eagerly.

"I love 'em. I think you're a right smart writer, chickadee."

"All right. All right. Let's get this show on the road," Uncle Otto declared. I gave my father a quick hug then I got in the car. It was time to head north.

SAMMY AND IRMA MOVED INTO A HOUSE IN WEST PHILLY, NOT TOO far from her mother. When I got back from North Carolina in September they invited me to spend a weekend. My mother was happy to let me go and I was enthralled. It was different at Sammy and Irma's house. Their voices, one light and high, the other full and deep, bounced off each other. There was a rhythm to the house that I liked. Irma cooked breakfast; Sammy took out the trash. They teased each other and had pillow fights. This was good, I thought: the deep voice and the light voice bouncing off each other and surrounding me.

They took me shopping Saturday afternoon. "We want to buy you a present," they told me. We went to Strawbridge's and wandered through the girls' department until I saw what I wanted. I picked out a black shirt that buttoned down the front and had a button-down collar. When Uncle Sammy paid for it the saleslady handed the bag to me and said, "We'll let your little girl carry it." I took the bag and Sammy and Irma didn't say anything.

On Sunday evening Sammy was driving me home. I asked him, "What do married people talk about? Don't you ever run out of things to say?"

He laughed. "No, not really. You talk about your jobs and what happened at work. Or you talk about what you're going to do on the weekend. Sometimes something important happened in the newspaper and you talk about that. Or maybe you have children. Then you talk about your children, whether they're feeling okay or what they said. You know what I mean?" He glanced at me in the dark car, taking a quick, intense look at my face to see if he'd expressed himself well, if my question had been answered. I was confused. What Uncle Sammy was describing didn't sound so different from Mommy and Nana. But it had to be!

"Wait until you get married. You'll see. You and your knotty-headed husband"—I giggled at his description and he smiled—"will be sitting up in bed eating Cracker Jacks"—I laughed again—"and just talking your head off. You'll call each other up at lunchtime and talk. Eat dinner and talk. You'll see."

When we got to my house, there was a car parked out in front. Nana answered the door and I could smell the cigarette smoke behind her. At first I thought that one of her friends was there. Then I heard the low rumbling, the girlish laughter. Nana said, "Your mother has someone she wants you to meet."

They were sitting on the sofa. The skirt of my mother's green dress touched the man's thigh. His arm was draped across the back of the sofa and two of his fingers were lightly touching her shoulder. I felt my stomach quake.

"Bebe, this is Mr. Johnston."

The man stood up. I stuck my hand out. "Hello," I said, not looking him completely in the face.

"Well, hello there," Mr. Johnston said, grasping my hand in his. He wasn't so tall, not as tall as Uncle Sammy. He was thin, with very light skin and rust-colored hair. He gave my hand a couple of loose shakes. He wasn't looking at me while we were shaking hands: he was sort of grinning at my mother. I pulled my hand away. "So you're the Bebe I've heard so much about. I heard you were one smart little girl. Spell 'encyclopedia.' Try that one." Now he was looking at me.

Our eyes met and green darts flew in rapid crossfire. He was ugly, I decided.

"E-n-s-y-c-l-o-p-e-d-i-a."

"Wrong! It's e-n-c-y, not e-n-s-y," Mr. Johnston said triumphantly.

"Well, that's a pretty hard word," Mommy said. Her voice sounded soft, too soft.

I didn't say anything, just put my arms around my mommy.

Upstairs in my room, I put away my clothes and got in the bed. The door was open and I could hear my mother and Mr. Johnston talking softly. I thought about her skirt on his leg and his two fingers on her shoulder. "He's not my daddy!" I wanted to scream angrily. I wanted my daddy!

# CHAPTER 11

Little Miss Revlon went sailing through the air, then crashed into the base of the radiator. From my standing position in the middle of the double bed I shared with my mother, I hurled Betsy Wetsy in the direction of her sidekick. I leaped off the bed and landed screaming. I stood in the middle of the floor and yelled until I felt the room engulfing me like a sea. I was drowning in dangerous waters that threatened to wash away my fragile dream.

Nana dashed in, out of breath, wiping her hands on the neat checkered apron around her waist, then hiking up the waistband of the corduroy pants she liked to wear around the house. When she opened the door I could hear snatches of the Flamingos crooning, "I only have eyes, foooor, you-ooh-ooh jabatchaba . . ."

"What's the matter? What's wrong?" Nana's eyebrows rose in alarm.

My mother was right behind her. "What is it?"

Didn't she know? Of course she knew! I said nothing and continued to wail.

"Bebe, Bebe what is it?" my mother asked, more urgently.

"Girl, you better tell us what's wrong with you," Nana snapped, her patience thin and brittle as a communion cracker.

"Enhenhenhehnenh." I hiccuped out my response, the most coherent statement I could make. My shoulders were vibrating up and down.

*"Girl, what's wrong with you?!!"*

I ignored Nana. I looked at my mother. Finally, "Enhenhenhenhenh . . . you don't love me."

"Oh, please," Nana said, her voice dripping with scorn. Nana's Depression-era consciousness told her that sensible people cried only about life-threatening situations: no food; no heat; gunshot wounds. That I was standing in the middle of a warm, attractive bedroom with a full stomach, bawling about my mama's not loving me was hard for her to understand, or tolerate.

But my social-worker mother was truly alarmed. She felt . . . guilty, which was exactly how I wanted her to feel.

"What do you mean, I don't love you? Of course I love you. I love you more than anyone else on this earth." My mother grasped my fingers and pulled me to her. I snatched my hand away. "Why do you think I don't love you?"

"Enhenhenhenhenh." A thin trickle of snot was drizzling down to my bottom lip. I snorted to retrieve it, but couldn't stop the drip.

Nana shook her head and her gold hoop earrings danced and glittered in the light. She rolled her eyes at me as she handed me a tissue from my mother's drawer. "Umph, umph, umph. You need to stop this mess right now." I didn't look at her.

"Why do you think I don't love you?" My mother's voice was persistent, soothing and guilty. Ah. Guilty!

"Enhenhenh," I twittered.

Nana groaned. "She's just jealous. Standing up here, with her little fat, phony self, snorting and sniffing like somebody's killing her." She looked at me and rolled her eyes. I looked away. "Doesn't even want her mother to have a friend. Tsktsktsk." She turned to my mother. "Don't you let this child run your life. She's just trying to make you feel guilty, with her little fat, phony self." I could see my mother wavering. "You gonna let a child run your life?" Nana muttered. Then she said strongly, "I can't take any more of this mess," and walked out of the room.

As soon as Nana left, I turned away from my mother. Now I would really make her suffer.

"Bebe . . ."

"Why does *he* have to keep coming over here?"

"Who?"

"You know."

"Who?"

*"Mr. Johnston!"* I screamed furiously.

My mother's small smile was like kerosene on a smoldering fire.

*"Why does he have to keep coming over here!"*

"Oh, darling . . ."

*"I hate him!!!"*

"But he hasn't done anything to you. He likes you and . . ."

*"No, he doesn't like me. He hates me. And I hate him!"*

"I don't hate your friends," she continued in her soothing, social-working voice. "He's just a friend of mine, like Clara, or . . ."

*"No, he's not. It's . . . different!"*

"How? How is it different?"

"Do you kiss him?"

I could hear double-dutch ropes turning, slapping the pavement on the street below. The little girls outside were singing as they jumped: "Miss Mary Mack, Mack, Mack . . . All dressed in black, black, black . . ." Fear was creeping up my spine like a spider. I could hear my mother breathing, but I was scared to look at her. I wanted to yank back my question. I didn't want to know the answer. Maybe Mommy felt my silent retraction or maybe she just remembered who she was, because in the terrible instant when I looked into her eyes she zapped me. Flaming eyes. No lips. "How dare you?" blazed across her face. Then the storm passed and she was cool, generous and on her way out the door. "When you calm down you can come downstairs and look at television."

UNCLE EDDIE'S STORE WAS ONLY FIVE BLOCKS FROM OUR HOUSE. Whenever I craved a link to North Carolina I made a detour from the trail that led straight home from Logan Elementary School and visited my uncle. I braved those blocks alone, hoping the Turtle Lady wasn't lurking around the area. Not long after my outburst and not long after Mr. Johnston asked me to spell "aardvark," I dropped in on my uncle.

That day after school I stood quietly in the door of the market waiting for Uncle Eddie to notice me. The odor of fish was overpowering; I could barely smell the bananas and oranges displayed in a wooden bin. The store radiated Uncle Eddie's energy; his movements filled the place with eloquent commotion, a tribute to his passion for work. He pounded down on a piece of steak and the cereal boxes behind him shook. He cleaned four pounds of porgies for a dull-eyed, fat woman with three screaming kids, then shouted to his assistant to go downstairs and bring up a crate of orange juice. It was always rush hour at Eddie's Market. The customers moved around him searching the wall nearest them for Kellogg's Corn Flakes, the Argo starch I loved to nibble on, Carnation milk; they picked over the fragrant bananas and oranges, then peered in the long, low glass showcase and chose from the shimmery display of bluefish, trout, butterfish and others, and blood-red steaks and freshly ground beef. Uncle Eddie was, as always, immersed in a myriad of conversations, none of which he ever completed. At the candy section he talked to an old man about the weather as he handed him a box of Good and Plenty. He walked over to the meat counter and started arguing good-naturedly with a woman about how long to cook the roast she'd chosen and whether or not to bake or fry the whiting. He hollered at a bunch of kids who came in after school looking for candy, potato chips and sodas; his voice trailed off as they left.

Uncle Eddie looked up from the bloody slab of beef he held and saw me standing by the door, but he continued to carve away at the meat. Finally, when the crowd had thinned he looked in my direction again and blinked, his head bobbing back a little. That blink was full of appreciation; it said: Well, you came to see your uncle. Isn't that nice. He put the meat cleaver down and said, "Well, look who's here. Ole Be Be." And as he always did, he announced to the room in general, "My niece." Then he turned to me and said, "So, when's the last time you saw your big-head ole daddy, huh?" He grinned a lopsided grin that dazzled me.

We talked for only a few minutes. That's all the time Uncle Eddie ever gave anybody who came into his store who wasn't a paying customer. First things first. He nodded when I told him that everyone was doing well. Then he wiped his hands on his bloodstained butcher's apron and came from behind the meat counter, hollering to his assistant that he was going to the basement. Then he grabbed my arm and guided me down the narrow stairs, "Got something to show you, girl." When we got downstairs he said, "Look what I just bought." He pointed to a giant freezer, new and gleaming.

"That's great, Uncle Eddie," I said, walking around the huge appliance, acting as if I were examining it from every angle, because I knew this would please my uncle.

On our way back upstairs, Uncle Eddie spoke to me briefly about my father. "He had a sore on his butt. You know how you can get those sores from just sitting in one position all the time?" I nodded. "So he had to go into the hospital so it could heal," he said, "but he's okay now."

A new crowd had gathered in the store. "Take something you want," Uncle Eddie urged as he went behind the counter. "Okay. Who's next? That's my niece," he said, pointing me out to a small, neat-looking old woman. He flashed me that familiar, comforting smile, and I didn't take a thing.


MR. JOHNSTON CAME THAT EVENING WHILE I WAS GETTING READY for bed. I heard the doorbell ring and my whole body went stiff. There was a knock on my bedroom door. When I opened the door Michael was smiling at me.

"Your mother's boyfriend is here," Michael said maliciously, his large, dark eyes gleaming and his teeny-weeny nostrils quivering with delight at the opportunity to tease me.

"He's not her boyfriend!" I shot back.

"You're dumb if you think that," Michael said flatly.

"He's not!" I screamed. I searched my mind for some mean

retort to throw in Michael's face, but I couldn't think of anything to say.

Michael stuck the knife in a little further and twisted it. "I heard your mother talking to Clara on the phone. She said she was going to marry Mr. Johnston." My cousin told lies all the time, big jumbo whoppers, but I always believed him. I couldn't maintain even the semblance of being cool.

"Enhenhenhenhenhenh . . ."

Michael was smirking as he left.

I stood with my back pressed against the door, feeling the cold hard wood against my spine. I told myself that Michael was lying, teasing me the way he always did. Didn't Nana tell me I was simple for always believing him? But what if it were true? Could that happen, I wondered frantically. My stomach started dancing and jumping around. My childish imagination had never conceived of my mother marrying someone else or, for that matter, my father marrying another woman. I never realized my hopes for family togetherness could be assailed by forces beyond my control. In that instant I saw what a weak, pitiful wish I'd nurtured, kept alive only by a grandmother's magic words and my own foolish faith. I was stupid! That was the truth that was staring me in the face. I shut my eyes tightly so I didn't have to see it. That night I dreamed I was on a raft, all by myself, surrounded by the ocean. I faced no real danger, just endless floating.

A MONTH LATER THANKSGIVING ARRIVED. I WOKE UP SNIFFING THE excitement in the turkey juices that hissed and bubbled in Nana's kitchen. My mind wasn't on the kitchen, though; it was on the street. This year my father was joining us for dinner.

Out-of-season visits from my father were like watermelons in winter: sweet and exotic. Every blaring car horn sent me flying to the window. "Stop all that running. Your daddy will be here when he gets here. Go get Michael, and you two come help me chop this celery and fill these water glasses," Nana exclaimed as I whizzed past her.

There were too many horns blaring on the street. "You are

the fidgetiest thing," Nana said, exasperated. I just couldn't concentrate long enough to chop celery or put ice cubes in the water
glasses, chores I usually loved. My anxiety must have been catching. In our restlessness Michael and I fussed and giggled until we
broke a water glass, leaving shards and a puddle in the middle of
the kitchen floor. "Get out of here. Just go!" Nana yelled at us,
shaking a big wooden ladle in our faces. "Go somewhere and sit
your behinds down. My goodness."

We fled to the living room, flopped ourselves across the sofa
and watched the parade on television for a while. The year before,
Michael and I had left Nana behind in her turkeyfied kitchen. Pete
had taken us to the parade, and I had ridden his shoulders in the
thick crowd on Market Street, but this year it was freezing cold
so everybody decided to stay home. As we watched the crowd of
spectators on television I spied familiar faces. "Hey! They look
like your brothers," I said. All expression left Michael's face. I
wanted to call the words back, but it was too late.

Right before school had started that year, Nana, Michael and
I were sitting in the kitchen and Nana said, "Mikey, I have something to tell you. Personal," she said, looking at me.

"Tell me too," I begged.

"It's up to Michael."

"She can hear it."

"Ruth found out your father has some more children. You
have three brothers." Nobody said anything. "I think they go to
your school," Nana said finally.

Michael just sat there staring at his knees. He stood up. "Does
he live with them?" he asked Nana.

"Yeah. He does." Nana went over to the cabinet and began
rummaging around. She pulled out a box of Betty Crocker yellow
cake mix. "I feel like making a cake. Who wants to help me?
Who's gonna lick the bowl, huh?"

Michael's brothers did go to Logan. The twins were in second
grade and the little one was in first grade. They all looked alike
and they all looked like Michael. They had the same last name as
Michael, only they spelled it differently. Nana told us later that
Kenneth had married the mother of his other children, even though

he'd never divorced Aunt Ruth. Nana said he was a bigasome-thing.

"Make friends with them, Michael," I told him once at recess when we saw his brothers playing on the little kids' part of the playground.

He shrugged and walked down to the poplar tree. Later, though, I used to see him playing with them. He told them who he was, too.

When we saw Nana leave the kitchen, we crept back to the stove and stole handfuls of stuffing from the giant bird sitting on top. We were cramming our mouths full when the doorbell rang. We were nosier than we were hungry so we choked down the stuffing and ran to the door to see Nana's new boyfriend, Mr. Coty, coming in. He was wearing a plaid sports coat and a tie with more colors than I'd ever seen in my life. The way he had a cigar stuck in the corner of his mouth reminded me of Uncle Elijah. "Here comes Happy the Clown," Michael whispered, snickering. I had to laugh; his suit looked like 52nd Street on Saturday night. Under his arm Mr. Coty brought in a coconut cream pie and an apple pie, and after he said hello to everybody he went straight back to the kitchen with Nana. Mr. Coty was nice, but his voice didn't have the music in it that Mr. Robby's did. But then Nana was always switching boyfriends, so I learned not to get too used to any of them.

The doorbell rang again and I ran to the window, looking for my father. It was Clara and her boyfriend, Uncle Sonny, who put a bottle of Taylor's cream sherry on the kitchen table, along with three pies—pumpkin, sweet potato and lemon meringue. Nana grinned at him. "That's all right, baby," she said, flirting as she snatched up the bottle and put it in the refrigerator.

Anne and Pete came down bringing warm homemade rolls; the aroma of bread filled the house. "C'mon, you kids. Who can beat me at war?" I ran to the desk drawer and found the playing cards. I was vehemently declaring war on Pete when I heard a distinctive blare from outside. Beeeeep beep. My father's horn. No doubt about it. I dropped the cards on the table and leaped to my feet.

"Bebe, Bebe," my mother said, trying to calm me down, realizing all her attempts would fail.

I was already at the front door, running down the steps into the freezing air, no coat, no hat. No nothing. "Daddy. Daddy. Daddy!"

We kissed. Foreheads. Cheeks. Lips. Everything on our faces was brushed by each other's lips. I threw my head on his chest and put my arms around his neck.

"BebebebebebeMoore." I couldn't get close enough to him.

"Hello, George." My mother slipped my coat around my shoulders.

"Hello, Doris."

Their greetings were like the day, crisp, cool.

"Sonny and Pete are coming out in a minute to bring you in."

"All right." My father lit a cigarette.

"Mommy, sit down," I said, trying to get warm.

She paused. Smiled. Then she slid in next to me.

"So," Daddy began, looking at my mother, "how have you been?"

"Oh, just fine," she said in her cool voice. I shifted in my seat and stole a look at my dad. A sudden emptiness had crept into his eyes, but when he turned to look at me it was gone.

"Bebe . . ."

"Bebe . . ."

"You go first," my father said to my mother.

"I was just going to say that Bebe's doing really well in school this term." She smiled at me.

"Oh, that's good. That's good, kiddo," Daddy said, turning to me.

"What were you going to say?"

My father looked blank for a moment. "Oh, nothing. I forgot. It'll come to me."

Pete and Sonny knocked on the car window.

"Whatcha say, ole man," Sonny said jovially.

"Hey there, how ya doing? You know you kinda favor a doctor friend of mine," Daddy said thoughtfully. "You remember Doctor Winston, Doris?"

"Sonny doesn't look anything like him," my mother said, her mouth getting a little tight.

"*Good* friend of mine," Daddy said.

"Hi, George," Pete sang out cheerfully.

Sonny opened the back door on my father's side and pulled out his chair. My father opened his door and Sonny rolled the chair right next to him. "One of you guys, grab this pillow from under my behind," he said, chuckling a little. "Just be sure you don't grab my behind with it." Sonny and Pete laughed as Pete pulled the pillow and put it in the wheelchair. My father half slid, half jumped from his seat into the chair, then shifted his weight around on the pillow.

Six steps led to the front door. Pete took the top part of the chair and Sonny took the bottom and they lifted the whole chair up the steps, even though Daddy hollered at them just to get behind him and pull the chair up. "Y'all Negroes ain't young and I gotta lot of meat in this chair." But Pete said they'd rather lift him that way, because they didn't want to tip him over by accident. Some people who were going into Mr. Crawford's house stood and watched Pete and Sonny and my daddy. I didn't like their stares. Looking at Pete and Sonny made my knees knock. Don't drop my daddy. Don't drop my daddy. My father smiled without really looking at anyone. In fact, he mostly talked to me the whole time Sonny and Pete were carrying him up the steps.

Nana called us into the dining room just when the aroma of turkey, greens, candied yams and the rest of the food on the overburdened table made everyone feel overwhelmed by hunger. The group was quiet when we first sat down at the table, as though we were all secretly afraid the food would disappear. Daddy said grace; everybody held hands while he prayed. When he was finished, Nana began loading up the plates and passing them around, ignoring Clara when she asked her to put just a little bit on her plate.

"Aww, girl, what you talkin' 'bout?" Nana said, laughing. "You never see a fat woman without a man."

The sherry went around, with only my teetotaler mother and Michael and me not partaking. The voices at the table got louder and more boisterous. Nana reminded Anne and Pete about the paper sandwich, and Anne almost choked on her sherry she was laughing so hard at Pete, who was trying to pretend he was still mad. The Thanksgiving table was as laden with memories and tales as it was food. Old times. Bad times. Good times.

". . . I was on welfare for a hot minute," Nana confided as we all helped ourselves to seconds. "I got me a scrub brush and a bucket and got off that mess. Yes, darlin' . . ."

". . . What you talkin' 'bout? There ain't no cracker like a Florida cracker. They used to string up Negroes down there for breakfast, lunch and dinner. Soon as I could, I caught the first thing smokin' out of there," Anne said, spearing some greens, the juice oozing through the prongs.

". . . You didn't see the pictures. They ran them in the *Jet*. I'll never forget it long as I live. That boy's body was beaten beyond recognition. Own mother couldn't say who he was," Pete said, sipping on his sherry. "And those white men got off free as a jaybird. Umph, umph, umph. I tell you. . . ."

". . . It's gonna always be that way. . . ."

"Oh, no it ain't. Unh unh. Noooo . . ."

Michael and I sat at the table absorbing the words and histories swirling around us. Grown-up talk. It got louder as the evening spun on, words mixing with turkey bones, the pungent scent of Mr. Coty's cigar and Daddy's Winstons, the papery slap of pinochle cards flung down in jubilation.

Daddy eyed his hand, winked at my mother, who was his partner, and exclaimed, "Moving on in for a head rub. Hey, ole Sonny, man, your head itching? I'm a scratch it tonight, boy." He laughed that deep, Pasquotank County laugh and looked over at my mother and winked. Mommy laughed too, a free, high chortle. She said, "Oh, George," and sounded like a young, young girl. Then Daddy reached over and rubbed my head. It was supposed to be like this, I thought.

Later on in the evening, Aunt Ruth and her boyfriend, Rudy, a handsome Puerto Rican who looked like Kenneth, came by. Pete brought in more folding chairs and they sat down at the table and ate dinner while everybody else had pie and ice cream. Nana and

Mommy tried not to look at him. He was the one who gave Aunt Ruth a black eye. Only a few weeks before, Aunt Ruth had packed up her bags and gone back to him, taking with her the sound of Lady Day. Nana said that she didn't know what Ruth saw in him.

Aunt Ruth got silly, drinking too much of the Tanqueray gin they had brought, and Nana took her into the kitchen and made her drink some coffee. She didn't drink most of it, though. I peeked in the kitchen and she was sitting at the table laughing like crazy. I could tell she was making Nana mad from the way my grandmother was slamming pots and pans around. Nana was trying to sing, but Aunt Ruth kept interrupting her, saying stupid stuff, so Nana was really getting hot. I heard her say, ". . . come in here, embarrassing everybody. It's a disgrace." And then Aunt Ruth said, "Oh, Mama," or something like that. Michael wouldn't go near the kitchen. He went into the living room and started watching television; when his mother came in and tried to kiss him on the neck, he pulled away. So Nana told her to come back into the dining room. She leaned over me, trying to kiss me, and I could smell the Toujours Moi spilling from her bosom to my chest. I didn't move away or anything. She wasn't all that bad.

Later, Delphine and Bunny, two of Aunt Ruth's elegant girlfriends, dropped by, bringing more exotic scents and more laughter. I stared at their long, brilliant fingernails, their fur coats, the way they exhaled the smoke from their cigarettes. Still later, the doorbell rang again and my Uncle Norvel and my real Uncle Sonny, my mother's father's brothers, came in, accompanied by their two plump wives. As the night got louder and louder, arms reached out and pulled me closer, closer. What in the world were they trying to squeeze into me?

I stood on the bracers of my father's chair, my arms around his neck, my face snuggled into his cheek, happy to have him, dreading the moment when he would have to go. They seemed happy together, my mother and father. Happy playing cards. Happy eating dinner. I thought about my mother's high, girlish laugh. Let it happen, I thought. Please let it happen.

# CHAPTER 12

"One two, cha, cha, cha. One two, cha, cha, cha." Nana's ebullient singing filled our living room, bouncing off the maroon sofa, the marble coffee table, the two comfortable chairs near the television. Her voice was competing with the blended tones of the Shirelles warbling out of the radio. She took two bouncy steps up and then turned and took two steps back. "See, it's like the mambo," she said, moving close to me. Nana's Topaz cream sachet saturated the air around her.

Michael groaned. "It ain't like no mambo. That's some ole-head Brotherhood stuff you're doing. This is the cha-cha. The new cha-cha." Michael bounced forward three steps, wiggling his hips as he moved up, then twirled around and danced back.

"Now ain't that the same thing I did?" Nana asked.

"No," Michael and I said together.

"It was so," Nana insisted, fuming.

"This is what you did," Michael exclaimed, laughingly imitating Nana's more sedate dance. "This is the new cha-cha," Michael said, duplicating his own vibrant movements.

The last strains of "Our Day Will Come" faded and a quartet of harmonizers singing, "Carolina, the extra fine grain rice . . ." came over the radio. Michael reached over and switched the dial.

The drone of a news announcer's voice interrupted the music. "Senator John Kennedy's name has been mentioned as a Democratic nominee. . . ."

"We want to cha-cha," I whined. Nana sucked her teeth in mock disgust at our lack of interest in the political process, then flipped the station back to dance music. "What you call the cha-cha. That ain't nothing. All that butt shaking." She hiked up her corduroy pants and wiggled her behind. We all started laughing at the same time. "That ain't no cha-cha. Just a bunch of butt shaking. Bebe, I'm trying to teach you the real, honest-to-God cha-cha, not that mess."

"I want to learn Michael's way," I said, still giggling. Nana was a good dancer, for an "ole-head" old lady; but if I copied her style, people would think I was jive.

"All right. Go 'head. Do the butt shake. It's your world; I'm only living in it." She pulled out the dish towel that was tucked inside her waistband and playfully swatted me with it as she fled from our gyrations to the calm of her kitchen.

Michael turned up the radio until the music was screaming.

"Watch," Michael said. He towered over me by a head. He was thin and muscular and moved as if he didn't have a bone in his body. His feet were total staccato. Bam de bam de bam bam bam! I stood behind him and mimicked his quick movements. Bam de bam de bam *bam bam!* It wasn't a hard dance. "You got it," he said.

The strong voices from the radio filled the living room. Michael and I swirled and cavorted on the dark Oriental rug. This dance was different from the slop. The slop had light, dragging movements; this dance had softness in the swivel of hips, but our feet came down forceful and hard. The steps Michael showed me were intricate variations of the basic step. Jump up! Jump back! Heel click, heel click. Turn. "Ain't that cool?" Michael asked me. Oh, yeah. Bam de bam de *bam bam bam!* The music was rushing inside of us. Our heels were pounding the floor; the living room seemed to be shaking. The country would soon elect a new president. Next year would be my last one at Logan and I would embark upon a new path. Bam de bam de *bam bam bam!* My whole world seemed to be rocking to a harder beat.


THE BLARE OF MONDAY'S LATE BELL JOLTED THE LAST VESTIGES OF torpor from my bones. In September I had entered 5A. In January 1961 I skipped 5B and went to the sixth grade. Most of my fifth-grade classmates accompanied me to Miss Tracy's room. The Philadelphia school system, in order to end midyear graduations, had abandoned the A/B grade levels. In January most students were skipped into the next grade, although some were retained.

Miss Tracy nodded her head and held out her hand, letting her palms face her students; she drew her hands upward. I rose with the rest of the class and placed my hand over my heart, shifting my weight from foot to foot and staring straight ahead at the bulletin boards, which were still covered with red and green construction-paper Santa Clauses and Christmas trees. I acted as if I were speaking, but when the rest of the class said, "I pledge allegiance to the flag . . ." I only mouthed the words. Months before, Reverend Lewis had told the congregation that Negroes in the South were being beaten by white people because they wanted to integrate lunch counters at drugstores. A few weeks earlier, while Mommy, Nana, Michael and I were sitting in the living room watching television, the show was interrupted; the announcer showed colored people trying to march and white policemen coming after them with giant German shepherds.

"Now you know that ain't right," Nana had said angrily.

The day after I saw that news bulletin I was saying the Pledge of Allegiance in class and right in the middle of it my head started hurting so bad I thought it was gonna fall off and I felt so mad I wanted to punch somebody. I didn't want to say the pledge, that was the problem. I was afraid not to say anything, so I just kept opening my mouth, but nothing came out. After that I only pretended to say the words. If they were gonna sic dogs on Negroes then I wasn't gonna say some pledge and I wasn't gonna sing "The Star-Spangled Banner" neither. Not for them, I wasn't.

Sixth grade was rough. In the first place, I didn't like Miss Tracy. None of my friends liked her either. She was the meanest teacher I ever had, so full of rules and ultimatums. No talking. No erasures on spelling tests. No going to the bathroom except at recess. No this, no that. Always use her name when addressing her. No, Miss Frankenstein. Yes, Miss Frankenstein. She sent Linda out of the room just because she said "Excuse me" to me when she dropped my spelling paper. I mean . . . really. I could see Linda through the small glass window in the door, standing outside in the hall crying while we graded the spelling papers. Causing my best friend's tears was enough for me to start hating Miss Tracy, but I had other reasons.

It was a year of hot breathing and showdowns at Logan. We were sixth-graders, on our way out the door and feeling our oats every step of the way. Some of the boys began to sound a little bit like men, their upper lips darkened and their chests expanded. Among the girls, an epidemic of hard little bumps popped out on our chests. First Carol, then Linda, then me. We were embarrassed; we were proud. But the little band of Negroes at Logan felt something more than puberty. Fierce new rhythms—bam de bam de *bam bam bam!*—were welling up inside us. We were figuring things out. At home in the living room with our parents we watched the nightly news—the dogs, the hoses and nightsticks against black flesh—and we seethed; we brought our anger to school. The rumor flew around North Philly, West Philly and Germantown that Elvis Presley had said, "All colored people can do for me is buy my records and shine my shoes." In the schoolyard and the classroom we saw the sea of white surrounding us and we drew in closer. We'd been fooling ourselves. It didn't matter how capable we were: it was *their* school, *their* neighborhood, *their* country, *their* planet. We were the outsiders and they looked down on us. Our bitterness exploded like an overdue time bomb.

"Miss Tracy doesn't like Negroes," I announced to Carol and Linda when we sat under the poplar tree at recess.

Linda got excited. "How do you know that?"

"You ever notice how she never picks us to do anything? And she's always putting our names on the board for talking and she doesn't ever put David's name on the board and all he does is run his mouth and eat boogers."

"And try to act like his Elvis Presley," Carol added. Miss Tracy's always calling us 'you people.' And remember that time she sent Wallace to the office when that white boy stepped on his foot?"

"That doesn't mean she doesn't like Negroes," Linda said doubtfully. Carol and I looked at each other and shook our heads. What a baby.

"Well, what does it mean, then?" I asked Linda sarcastically.

"It means she doesn't like the Negroes in her room," Carol said dryly.

The skirmishes were slight affairs, nothing anyone could really put a finger on. A black boy pushed a white boy in line. A black girl muttered "cracker" when a white girl touched her accidentally. One afternoon when David was walking past our tree Carol yelled, "Elvis Presley ain't doing nothing but imitating colored people. And he can't even sing." David looked at her in astonishment. She put her hands on her hips and declared, "I ain't buying his records and I ain't shining his shoes neither!"

"Boys and girls, you're growing up," Miss Tracy said to the class one afternoon. Yes, we were. Something hot and electric was in the air.

The winter before I graduated from Logan Elementary, there was a disturbance in my class. Miss Tracy was absent and we had a substitute, a small, pretty woman named Mrs. Brown. She had taught us before, and all of us liked her because if we finished our work she would let us play hangman. We were spelling that day, going through our list of words in the usual, boring way. Mrs. Brown picked someone and the person had to go to the blackboard and write a sentence using the spelling word. We had three more words to go and I'd already been picked, so my interest in the whole process was waning. Hurry up, I thought. I was only half listening when I heard Mrs. Brown ask Clarence, who was wearing his everyday uniform, a suit and a tie, to stop talking. Clarence turned a little in his chair and frowned. He continued to talk.

"Did you hear me, Clarence?" Mrs. Brown asked.

"No."

Everybody turned to stare at Clarence and to check him for any outward signs of mental instability. Nobody talked back to teachers at Logan. Mrs. Brown coughed for a full minute, then stood up and asked Clarence to go to the board. Her voice was sharp. Clarence slouched in his seat. "No," he said almost lazily. Nobody breathed. Mrs. Brown said he would have to go to the principal's office if he wouldn't behave. All of us in class shuddered as if we were one body. Was Clarence crazy? I thought of my own dark trek to the principal's office. Nobody wanted to visit Jennie G. Clarence glared at Mrs. Brown so forcefully that she turned away from him. Clarence said slowly, "Later for the principal. Later for you. Later for all y'all white people. Send me to the principal. That don't cut no cheese with me."

Everything happened fast after that, after it was clear that Clarence had lost his mind. Mrs. Brown quickly dispatched one of the boys to bring Mr. Singer, who appeared moments later at the door. Mrs. Brown conferred with Mr. Singer hastily and then he took Clarence by the arm and ushered him out of the room. Clarence did a diddy-bop hoodlum stroll and showed not one bit of remorse as he left.

As soon as he was gone, Mrs. Brown leaned back in her chair and put the sides of her hands to her temples. The small diamond on her finger glittered in the sunlight. "Why would he say such awful things to me? Why?" she demanded, looking at the class. "Why?" she repeated, her eyes now focusing on every dark face in the class as if we alone knew the answer. Everyone was looking at Linda, Carol, Wallace and me, I realized. And they were . . . scared. Their eyes asked: Are you like Clarence? Are you angry too? Mrs. Brown tried to start the lesson again, but nobody was concentrating. Linda, Carol and I looked at each other cautiously. It was silently agreed: we wouldn't explain anything.

"That nigger's crazy!" Wallace whispered as we filed outside for recess. There was no more that could be said.

In the schoolyard, in our compact circle, we whooped like renegades. "He sure told Mrs. Brown off!" we exclaimed, falling all over each other in our excitement. "Later for all y'all white people," we repeated that single line, giggling as we slapped each other's thighs. I thought not of the dogs and the nightsticks, but of the ponytails and poodle skirts on *Bandstand,* bobbing and swishing off beat, twisting and turning so happily. Carol, Linda and I nodded at each other. The single vein of anger that was growing in us all had been acknowledged this day. We had a crazy nigger in our midst, close enough for comfort.

Clarence, of course, was suspended. A much more subdued boy returned to school flanked by his mother and father. The grapevine said that Jennie G. had said sternly to his parents, "We will not tolerate that kind of rude, uncivilized behavior at Logan. Is that clear?" When it was all over, Clarence had to apologize to Mrs. Brown and tell her he didn't know what on earth had gotten into him. But I knew.


I TURNED ELEVEN IN FEBRUARY. MY FATHER DROVE TO PHILADELPHIA to celebrate, and he took my mother and me to dinner at Horn & Hardart because the aisles were wide enough for his wheelchair. After we ate I got behind Daddy and pushed him, and we all went around the corner to the movies. The usher stared when Daddy came in, and said, "Now you aren't gonna block up the aisle, are you?"

Mommy looked straight ahead past the man. Daddy stuck out his chin a little, laughed and said, "Where would you like me to sit, mister?" I could tell he was mad. We ended up sitting in the back. Daddy hopped into the aisle chair and folded up his chair and leaned it against the outside of his seat. I sat next to him and every time something funny or exciting happened, I squeezed Daddy's hand until I was sure he wasn't angry anymore.

We came straight home after the movie. After my father parked the car in front of our house, my parents handed me a small box. Inside was a thin Timex watch with a black strap. I gasped with happiness and excitement. I was sitting between my mother and father, admiring my watch, basking in their adoration. I'd forgotten all about the usher. This is the way it should always be, I thought. When my mother said it was time for us to go in I said, "Kiss Daddy."

Mommy paused for a moment. My father looked awkward. He leaned toward my mother. She pecked him on the cheek.

"No. Not like that," I chided them. "Kiss on the lips."

They obeyed me and gave each other another brief, chaste peck. Why couldn't they kiss better than that? Mr. Johnston wasn't my mother's boyfriend anymore. He hadn't been around for several months. Why couldn't she love my daddy again? My mother and father didn't look at each other as they moved away.

I wanted magic from them, a kiss that would ignite their love, reunite all three of us. As my father drove off I looked down at my watch and stared at the minute hand ticking away.

Miss Tracy worked our butts off until just before graduation. She assigned us a health report and an arithmetic project, and we had to write a creative story using all the spelling words we'd had since January. On top of everything else, she gave us a book report.

Miss Tracy took our class to the school library and told us to find the book we wanted to do a report on and to make sure we told her what it was. I turned the library inside out trying to find a book I liked. The problem was, I'd read all the good stuff. So I asked Miss Tracy if I could get my book from the public library; she said that was fine with her.

Michael, Mommy and I went to the downtown library one Sunday after church. I searched in the young adult section for an interesting title. Then I went to where the new books were displayed and picked up one with a picture of an earnest-looking black boy in the foreground and a small town in the background. I started leafing through some of the pages and I couldn't put it down. The book was about Negroes trying to win their rights in a small southern town and how they struggled against bad white people and were helped by good ones. There weren't any bad Negroes and that fit my mood perfectly. As I was reading it, the thought hit me instantly: Miss Tracy wouldn't want me to do my report on *South Town*. She'd tell me it wasn't "suitable." I decided I wouldn't tell Miss Tracy; I'd just do the report.

The day I stood in front of the class to give my report, my

mouth was dry and my hands were moist. "My book is called *South Town*," I said, holding the book up so everybody could see the cover. The whole class got quiet as they studied the black boy's serious face; Miss Tracy's head jerked up straight. "This was a very exciting, dramatic book, and I liked it a lot, because every summer I live in a place exactly like the town that was described in this book," I said, my voice rising. I had my entire book report memorized and after a while everything came easily. I walked across the room, raising my hand for dramatic flair, feeling like a bold renegade telling my people's struggle to the world. I whispered when I described a sad part of the book. I finished with a flourish. "I recommend this book for anyone interested in the struggle for Negroes to gain equal rights in America. Thank you."

As soon as I sat down I could feel Miss Tracy's breath on my neck. "You didn't ask my permission to do that report," she said. Her hazel eyes were as cold as windowpanes in February. I had forgotten how terrifying Miss Tracy's rage could be. What if she gave me an F? Or sent me to the principal's office? Oh, Lordy.

"I'm sorry," I said, my voice drained of dramatic flair. I didn't feel like such a bold renegade anymore. I was scared.

Miss Tracy turned away without saying a word. Three days later she returned the reports. At the bottom in the right-hand corner of mine there was a small B. Emblazoned across the top in fierce red ink were the words: "Learn to follow directions."

I took the report home and gave it to my mother who, of course, asked, "What directions didn't you follow?" I told her the whole story; then I held my breath. The last thing I wanted to hear was, "Bebe, I'm disappointed in you." Mommy didn't say that; she just looked at Miss Tracy's comments again. Then she said, "Sometimes you eat the bear; sometimes the bear eats you," which sounded kinda strange coming from her, because Mommy wasn't one for a lot of down-home sayings. She put the report in the bottom drawer of her bureau, where she kept my school papers and grades. "Don't worry about it," Mommy said.

Three weeks later I sat on the stage of the school auditorium in the green chiffon dress my mother made me, underneath it a brand-new Littlest Angel bra identical to the one Linda's mother had bought her. The straps cut into my shoulders, but my mind was too crowded with thoughts for me to feel any pain. As Nana, Mommy, Michael and Pete watched, I walked across the stage to receive my certificate. Pete took pictures. I wanted my father to be there, but at least I could show him the photos.

Two weeks later I kissed Mommy, Nana and Michael goodbye and climbed into my father's newest acquisition, a blue Impala convertible. "BebebebebebebebebeMoore," Daddy sang out when he saw me, then, "I guess you're getting too big for that stuff, huh?" His eyes were questioning, searching. I didn't know what to say, afraid that if I said yes, Daddy would never again make a song of my name, and if I said no, he'd think of me as a baby forever. So I leaned my head back against the seat and smiled. The wind was in my face and I was heading toward a North Carolina summer that would deliver a heartbreak and a promise.

GRANDMA MARY WAS WAITING FOR US ON THE PORCH, SITTING IN HER rocking chair, her crossed bare feet resting on that day's *Daily Advance*. She gave me a tight, heavy hug. I ran inside, shouting my hellos to Bunnie, who came running down the stairs to greet me, and Mr. Abe, who was, as usual, singing in the living room. I ran into my daddy's room and put my suitcases on the bed. Then I opened them and started putting my clothes in the closet. I looked up when I heard Grandma at the door.

"You're not sleeping in here anymore," Grandma said. "You go upstairs with Bunnie."

I couldn't believe what I was hearing.

"But I want to sleep with my daddy."

"Big girls don't sleep with their daddies." Grandma's voice was patient, but resolute.

They don't? My mind clouded. I heard my father's chair behind me and whirled around to face him. "Why can't I sleep with you?" I demanded.

"Well," Daddy hesitated, looking from me to Grandma Mary. Finally he said gently, "I guess that's only for little girls. You're a big girl now and big girls don't sleep with their daddies."

"But I sleep with my mommy."

"That's different."

"Why?" I asked, tears beginning to form in my eyes. I blinked and one rolled down my face into the corner of my mouth.

My father looked at me, unable to answer the question. "Be-cause . . ." he began.

"Because you're too big, missy," Grandma said firmly. She picked up the heavier of my suitcases and stood waiting for me to follow her. "Now get your things and go on up to Bunnie's room."

"Can't I just stay here for this one last summer?" I begged.

"No," Grandma said, folding her arms. She waited.

I looked at Grandma, but her eyes revealed no mercy. There was no use talking with her. I'd lost the battle. I mournfully trudged up the narrow wooden stairs. Daddy said, "I'll miss ya, kiddo," as I left, but I didn't laugh. His words only made me sadder. Now Daddy and I wouldn't be able to have our night talks.

I cried that first night. No snoring. No mountain to lean against. Just more breasts, pressing, pressing, pressing.

The next morning I went to my father's room. He was awake, but not out of bed yet. I went to the closet and retrieved the dusty old braces. "Why don't you ever wear these?" I asked.

My father sat up. "Every summer you come here, you ask me about those things."

"You never put them on," I said accusingly.

"They're too heavy."

"But can't you walk with them on?"

He looked at me. "I can't walk, Bebe."

"Try."

My father said very softly, "I have tried. I can't."

"I never saw you try."

My words hung in the air like a heavy cloud. "You were too little then. That was back when I first got hurt. I was in the veterans' hospital in Memphis and the doctors were giving me physical therapy." He looked at me to see if I understood. "That's when I tried the braces, but they didn't do any good."

"If they didn't work, why did you keep them?"

"I don't know," he slumped back down in the bed and closed his eyes. When he didn't say anything else I left quietly, pushing away his words. I didn't want to hear them.

Grandma was in the kitchen beating up some eggs for breakfast with a fork. I could hear the steady plaplaplap as I got nearer. "Grandma, do you still think my daddy is gonna walk?"

"What?" Plaplaplaplap.

"You told me my father would walk one day." There was reproach in my voice that surprised both of us.

"I did?"

"Yes." Oh, yes.

"I did?"

My eleventh summer got away from me, zipped by in a blur. Miss Rosie from down the lane had company, a niece named Quay, who was Bunnie's age. Late one Sunday afternoon Bunnie and Quay and I put on our bathing suits and they baptized me in one of the muddy puddles in the lane. They grabbed me by my hands and feet and swung me over the puddles saying, "I baptize you in the name of the dog, the cat and the holy rat." Then they dumped me and I was one muddy mess.

I remember that the mosquitoes were frightful that year. Worst ever. My legs and arms looked like a war zone and I was forever itching and scratching. Daddy would look up from his Zane Grey novels and say, "Stop scratching. You make it worse." I had sores all up and down my legs and arms. I asked Daddy what would take the marks away and he said time. I must not have understood him, because I asked him how to spell it and he started laughing and said, "Time." And I said, "What?" And he said, "Time, you little knucklehead. T-i-m-e." We were both laughing then. He made up a big jug of water and mixed in some cream of tartar and made me drink it three times a day. I hated the taste of that stuff. Whenever I was anywhere near the refrigerator and he was around Daddy would say, "You had some cream-of-tartar water today?" and pour me a great big glass full. He'd sit there and watch me drink it.

Everybody came to reunion. Sammy brought Irma with him.

It was her first reunion, so she got introduced to all the millions of Moores who were giving her the once-over. Aunt Lela and Uncle Otto brought their neighbor and her daughter with them to family reunion. The girl and I were about the same age, only she wore her hair in a more sophisticated pageboy, while I was still in braids. One night she showed me how to cut strips from a brown paper bag and use the paper to roll up my hair. Before I went to bed, I put a clean pair of panties on my head to guard my rollers. In the morning I showed my father my new hairdo. It didn't look exactly like the girl's. Uncle Joe said I looked as if I'd stuck my finger in an electric socket. Daddy took one look at my face and then my hair and said, real softly, "Well, baby girl, you got you some hair, don't you? It's a little bit wild. Nice, though."

WHEN I LOOK BACK AT IT, MY ELEVENTH SUMMER WASN'T SO BAD. I played with Belinda a lot. Actually we did more talking than playing. And of course, Daddy and I rode down 17, under those kissing trees, and once or twice Daddy parked the car and we looked at Dismal Swamp in silence. I thought about the slaves, swimming for their lives. I don't know what Daddy was thinking about. He seemed restless.

And Mr. Abe sang all summer long. That must have been his singingest summer ever. His music was my friend. I remember that after I walked out of the kitchen that day and left Grandma inside beating the eggs, I heard Mr. Abe in the living room. Singing. And I started moving toward that music. Stumbling toward that music.

# CHAPTER 13

"Smile again, Nana," Michael said.

"Yeah, Nana, smile," I pleaded.

Nana sat on the maroon velvet sofa in the living room, looking out the window at the fall leaves swirling in the wind, pretending she didn't hear a word we said. We sat on pillows at her feet. She was still in her housecoat, even though it was after ten o'clock on a Saturday morning. She turned from the window and looked into the mirror, watching herself as she untied her head rag, revealing a neat French twist underneath. She patted her hair, then carefully rewound her head rag and tied a tight knot in the front. Aunt Jenana, Michael called her. She stretched her arms way up toward the ceiling, covered her mouth with her hand and yawned.

"Come on, Nana. Smile," Michael begged, pulling her hand as though he could yank a grin out of her fingertips.

"Why should I smile for you?" Nana said, her lips twitching faintly.

"Aww, c'mon, Nana. Do it again." Michael was almost whining. Nana gave Michael and me a steady gaze, moving her face lower and lower, closer and closer to ours. When her cheeks were almost touching ours, she smiled, revealing an expanse of pink, naked gums. Michael and I convulsed. We collapsed help-lessly against one another.

"Funny, huh?" Nana asked wryly, chuckling a little with us. She turned to peer again into the mirror behind her.

"Do it again," we begged.

"No, that's it."

"Please."

"No more."

When the dentist first told Nana that she had pyorrhea, she didn't believe him. I heard her say to my mother, "I brush my teeth every morning and night. There's nothing wrong with my teeth."

Mommy said, "It's not your teeth; it's your gums." Then she told her to go to another dentist if she didn't believe the first one. Nana did and the second one told her the same thing. So she went back to the first dentist. It took him a couple of months to take all of her teeth out. He pulled them one or two at a time, depending on how loudly Nana was yelling that day. First the back ones, then the front ones, until she didn't have any left. Each week she came home from the pullings looking more and more sunken in, more and more defeated. It hurt her feelings, losing thirty-two perfectly straight white teeth on nature's whim. Nana had gotten used to being Madam Mambo, Queen of the Broth-erhood, a pretty woman people took to be at least ten years younger than she was. With each extraction she began to sink a little, as though she'd lost her place in the world and didn't know how to find it.

The day Nana's new teeth were ready she went straight from the dentist's office to the hairdresser, and when she came back home her hair was full of new auburn highlights and her mouth was full of dentures. Nana went into the bathroom and put on lipstick and powder and filled in her eyebrows with Maybelline eyebrow pencil. When she came downstairs for dinner she kept saying she felt like a new woman. Every time I looked at her she was smiling and asking me how her teeth looked.

"Good."

"You sure?"

"Yep."

"I should believe you, huh?"

"Yep."

At dinner that first night Nana bit into something chewy and a few minutes later when she opened her mouth her teeth fell out. They didn't fall all the way out, they kinda hung off her gums. Michael and I just about died laughing. Michael's mouth was full of milk and he sprayed it out all across the table. Mommy tried to act dignified, but she ended up laughing so hard that tears started running out of her eyes. Nana shoved her teeth back in and started laughing. She told us, "Quit it now." But nobody could stop. When we wouldn't stop she got a little mad.

Church was the first place Nana went after she got her new teeth and learned how to chew so they didn't fall right out of her mouth. Not Faith Tabernacle, because Nana wasn't all that crazy about Reverend Lewis ("Never met anybody so blowed up with hisself in my life") and she didn't like churches that held long services ("You think God wants everybody holed up in some church for four hours, whooping and hollering and carrying on? Puleez!"). Nana went to a Baptist church right down the street from my Uncle Eddie's store. One cold Sunday morning, when the wind was whipping torn pages of the *Bulletin* and the *Inquirer* down the street, Michael and I went to church with Nana.

Nana's church was tiny inside. The building was brightened only by the vibrancy of the people who sat on the wooden benches in upright attention. All the men in their dark suits and ties and the women in bright-colored dresses were squashed together in the pews. The choir didn't even have a stage to stand on, just a teensy area in the front of the church, where the short, dapper minister stood behind a scratched-up lectern. Behind him was a lopsided picture of Jesus. In this picture Jesus was a white man with a tan who had brown hair that hung to his shoulders.

We pushed our way down an aisle, carefully stepping over

cheap high heels and black "old-man" comforts, saying " 'Scuse me" three or four times before we finally reached empty seats. When Nana sat down the first thing she did was open her pocketbook. Nana always carried gum and I could smell the strong odor of mint. I stuck out my hand and silently begged her with my eyes. She took out a piece of Doublemint and gave me half and Michael the other half. "Don't chew it," she whispered to us, "just hold it under your tongue." Nana had her own rules of etiquette. No person with an ounce of home training ever actually chewed gum in the House of the Lord. We settled into the pews as the small choir assembled in the front rose to sing several rousing stanzas of "Packing Up." Two or three women in the back responded to each verse with a loud "Amen" and "Thank you, Jesus." I held my chewing gum, sucking at the sweetness from under my tongue, while the choir sat down and the minister began preaching.

About halfway through the sermon the women in the back began to get louder, and when I looked over at Nana she was crying. I gave Michael a nudge, guiding him with my eyes to Nana. His head jerked a little when he saw her tears. We hadn't ever been to a church service with Nana, so we had no idea how she reacted to a sermon. Michael and I were used to my mother's spiritual reserve. What was next, I wondered, feeling alarmed. Suppose Nana decided to jump up and get happy like Miss Hat. I wasn't ready to see my grandmother lose control in this tiny room full of strangers. Tears were trickling down Nana's face, but she wasn't showing any signs of getting the spirit. Her lips weren't twitching. Her foot wasn't even patting the floor. Just the tears. Even so, I didn't want to take any chances. The thing to do was to annoy her a little, so she couldn't concentrate on what the minister was saying. "Nana," I whispered, "where's the bathroom?"

"Just wait," she whispered back, dabbing at her eyes.

"I have to go now," I whined. Whining got on Nana's last nerve.

Nana glowered at me. "Just hold it," she said. Her words sizzled out between the edges of her dentures like steam from a radiator. I could see Nana wasn't crying anymore, so I slid back into my seat and sucked my gum contentedly.

BEFORE I HAD GRADUATED FROM SIXTH GRADE MY MOTHER RECEIVED her master's degree in social work from the University of Pennsylvania. She already had a master's in sociology. Soon after, she was promoted to supervisor of homemaker services for Philadelphia's Department of Welfare. The new tag carried with it the responsibility for managing the predominantly female corps of temporary homemakers who substituted for parents who were unable to take care of their children. Nana immediately set up a telephone marathon to let all her henna-headed cronies know the new glory that was now crowning the head of her eldest child.

"Don't brag, Mother," Mommy said, shaking her head and pressing her lips together.

"All those white folks down on that job and you get the promotion, and you tellin' me not to brag? Humph!" And Nana went right on down her list, greeting each of her old-head partners with, "Honey, let me tell you . . ."

The promotion resulted in longer hours for my mother and occasional late-night calls when emergency services were needed. She received a raise and our family climbed another rung of upward mobility. That meant leaving 16th Street.

North Philly was becoming a little shabby around the edges. Oh, there was still joy. The Popsicle man, the ice cream man, the huckster came as always. The big kids still managed to turn the fire hydrant on three or four times a summer. The water gushed out, drenched squealing children, made everything feel cool and nice. But the rushing waters couldn't wash away the signs of change. Many of the longtime residents whose paychecks had jumped into double digits during the prosperity of the Eisenhower era were now anxious to buy a place with a lawn and some roses, a place reminiscent of their southern origins. Some sold their homes, but others were forced to cut up their magnificent brownstones into apartments and rent them out to tenants who were less prosperous than they. When Helena and her German mother and black father left, their little house on Mole Street was simply boarded up. Even the Turtle Lady was abandoning the area. Nobody had seen hide or hair of the she-monster for more than a year. For my mother and Nana the final straw came when North Philly failed to offer any educational options other than an overcrowded Gillespie Junior High. "We're moving," Nana declared resolutely. My mother set her sights on a neighborhood that would offer a continuation of my Logan experience. What the white children learned, that's what her child had to learn. But I wasn't ready for a new terrain.

"You want to move?" I asked Michael.

"Sure. Don't you?"

"Unh unh."

"Don't be dumb. You'll get your own room."

I said nothing. It wasn't that I didn't want my own room; I just didn't want to lose my old one. I'd already endured too many losses that year. I'd come away from North Carolina in a wounded daze, with a crumpled dream for a souvenir. I had trouble looking at my father that summer. His steel chair hurt my eyes. I couldn't dream away his paralysis anymore. I was too big for that. When I thought of Daddy that summer, when I looked at him, in my head I had to say, "Oh, yeah!" remembering that there was something different about him now, something irrevocable that I would have to grow into: he was never going to walk again. And now I was faced with another hard change. After I returned from North Carolina, we moved to a neat, tree-lined neighborhood called West Oak Lane.

My separation from Logan and North Philly was painful. Jackie, Jane and Adam disappeared from my life. Slowly, my friend Carol did too. And the men, so many men were gone. I left behind Reverend Lewis and the deacons and trustees of Faith Tabernacle, Mr. Watson and my Uncle Eddie's store. The year before we moved, Anne and Pete bought a house in Germantown. Our families visited back and forth, but over the years my beloved Pete became someone I saw at holidays with the rest of the annual dinner guests.

West Oak Lane was beautiful. Besides the ancient oaks that

bordered the streets in many of the backyards, there were mulberry, peach and even cherry trees. Mommy and Nana chose a wide street of brick rowhouses, bordered by small patios amid lawns. I took one look at the spacious new house and our roses and azaleas, and knew that West Oak Lane was a step up.

Our house, like the others on the block, was built shotgun style, with the living room, dining room, breakfast room and kitchen all flowing behind the sun porch. Upstairs there were four bedrooms and a single bathroom. My own room was bright and girlish, but I still crept into my mother's bed at night when I craved snuggling. The basement had great possibilities. "We'll turn it into a rec room," Mommy promised. Michael and I screamed with enthusiasm. A rec room meant parties and dancing!

Rosenfeld's Drugstore took up one corner, but the rest of the block was strictly residential. The L bus, which came at regular twenty-minute intervals, stopped in front of the drugstore and again at either corner. The bus took Mommy to and from the Broad Street subway stop six blocks away. West Oak Lane's commercial strip was at Broad and Olney. Nana walked there to the post office, the A&P, the Esquire Movies, Esquire Drugstore, Luria's women's discount clothing store, all part of the jumble of buildings that filled the three-block radius near the subway. There was also a blue building that mystified and intrigued me: "Wagner's Ballroom," the sign said. Every morning clumps of children in various age groups walked or rode to Pennell, the elementary school, or Wagner, the junior high, or rode the bus to Olney High School. To the casual observer West Oak Lane was a pleasant, bustling neighborhood.

But beneath the calm surface there was tension. Like North Philly, West Oak Lane was an area in transition. In North Philly, Negroes were moving away from their own territory; in West Oak Lane, whites were fleeing from brown-skinned newcomers. To the left and right of us, down the street and around the block, whites were reducing the prices of their homes and leaving amid a colorful profusion of "Sold" signs. The neighborhood synagogues were sold and transformed into Baptist churches. The kosher foods in the market were replaced with chitterlings and fatback. But the Great Dragon Restaurant on Broad Street remained. The Esquire Theater remained. And so did Wagner's Ballroom.

One Sunday afternoon when Michael and I were walking from our house to Old York Road we saw a line of white teenagers lined up outside Wagner's Ballroom. "It's like *Bandstand* in there," Michael said, "only it's not on television."

Anything that had to do with dancing and having a good time got Michael's undivided attention. His teachers at Wagner were already calling my mother about his lack of motivation and preparation in class. But Michael was always prepared to go to the teenage parties that had begun to dominate his existence. We both stood and stared at the profusion of slim skirts and tight jeans, of dark hair and dark eyes. "Those are Italian kids from South Philly," Michael said casually.

"How come they ride all the way up here?"

" 'Cause it's boss in there. I'm going there," Michael announced, full of a thirteen-year-old's bravado.

"Dancing with all those white kids?" I scoffed at the idea. What was he thinking about?

"See if I don't."

I dismissed Michael's ambitions, but when I saw Wagner's after that I began to think: Well, why not? Why the hell not?

Once a week I was dispatched to bring home three loaves of bread: raisin, whole wheat and rye. One day when she was watering our grass Nana met Mrs. Feldman; when the old woman told Nana she sold discount bread from her home, Nana immediately began to patronize her.

I hated going to the Bread Lady's house; it was dark and creaky and smelled as leftover as the bread she sold from a large wooden crate. The furniture and dingy carpet were old and stained. The windows were dingy. In the winter it was freezing and in the summer the house was shut up and stifling. Mr. and Mrs. Feldman creaked and smelled too, although Mr. Feldman simply sat in a beat-up kitchen chair, not saying a word. Occasionally his wife, a small, fat woman who wore too much rouge, would speak to him loudly in Yiddish and he would answer her with an angry snarl. But when I came to buy bread, Mrs. Feldman gave me her complete attention. Why, I couldn't figure out.

"You speak very nicely," she told me once after I repeated Nana's order. What? Hello, Mrs. Feldman, I'd like three loaves of bread?

"That's a very nice jumper you are wearing," she said another time, getting close enough so I could smell the fried potatoes she'd eaten for lunch. "What's this fabric?" she asked, feeling my skirt between her thick fingers.

She was curious about our family. What did my father do? Oh. What did my mother do? Oh, really? For the city? Oy! So, then, had my mother been to college? Penn? Oy! Oh, graduate school too? Two master's degrees. Her narrow, dark eyes widened in astonishment and then disbelief. What year did she graduate? What graduate school? Where in City Hall did she work? How long had she been there?

"I remember when there weren't any colored people in this neighborhood," Mrs. Feldman told me one afternoon after school. On my way to her house I had been singing "In the Still of the Night" and I was still full of doo-wahs and harmony. I shifted from foot to foot, anxious for Mrs. Feldman to give me the bread so I could leave her stale house.

"A lot of my friends are gone now," she continued. "They moved to the other side of Broad Street. The northeast."

I nodded. Why couldn't she stop talking, wrap up the bread and let me get out of there?

"I been in your house," she said suddenly. She reached into her bag of bread and pulled out three loaves. Mrs. Feldman's wig slid down on her forehead when she leaned over the bag. She handed me the bread with one hand and adjusted her matted wig with the other. "It's very clean," she said solemnly.

What, I thought, the bread? I hesitated. "The bread?"

She laughed, said something to Mr. Feldman in Yiddish, then they both laughed.

If West Oak Lane didn't offer exemplary race relations it did present me with new girlfriends. Vivian lived next door; Barbara and Diane were sisters who lived two doors down. We played jacks and double dutch and walked to Broad and Olney together for ice cream cones and sodas, trips to the movies. We also, on one regrettable occasion, chipped in our pennies and nickels and bought a pack of Chesterfield cigarettes, smoked them in a nearby park and nearly choked to death. Some weeks after our nicotine rendezvous, we gathered in Vivian's sun porch and tried our best to emulate the Shirelles, the Chantels, the Ronettes and the Marvelettes. We were like every other Negro teenage girl in America: we believed fame and fortune could come through our vocal cords. If the Marvelettes and the Shirelles could be stars, why not us? If our harmony was a little off, our spirits were right where they should have been.

The songs took me right to the threshold of womanhood. I had outgrown my Littlest Angel bra and it had been a year since I'd officially become a woman. The combination of doo-run-runs and puberty was too strong to ignore. As soon as I entered Wagner Junior High I promptly fell in love with Mr. Dickerson, my seventh-grade science teacher and the first Negro teacher I ever had. Mr. Dickerson was boss! Mr. Dickerson was fiiiine. Beau fine. I memorized the leaves of every maple, oak, birch, gingko in Fairmount Park, but my love was unrequited. I did, however, get an A+ on my term paper, and inside the cover of the folder that contained my report card Mr. Dickerson wrote: "You are a terrific young lady. Keep up the excellent work." I got an A for the year. Still, my crush had been deep. I nursed my hurt for a whole year. By the time I was in eighth grade I had healed and was turning my attentions to a younger man.

My piano teacher, Mrs. Clark, lived right around the corner from our house. She was an enormous woman with smooth dark skin and full cheeks that plumped up even more when she smiled. Mediocrity was a sin in Mrs. Clark's basement. No matter if we weren't gifted, all of us students still had to practice and polish our piano pieces so that even the easy-to-play ones were performed brilliantly. And shame on our behinds if we didn't. Mrs. Clark had a thin stick that she would on rare occasions wave around (nobody ever actually got hit) while her relentless metronome kept the beat. The threat of Mrs. Clark's brown friend rode through her basement like a ghost. "Work!" Mrs. Clark shrieked. "Work hard!!" She informed us regularly and matter-of-factly that we had to be twice as good as white children in everything we attempted in life. "That way you got half a chance of making it." Mrs. Clark certainly lived her credo; she was a one-woman money-making machine. With four children to rear, she enthusiastically supplemented her husband's income, not only by giving piano lessons but also by selling spaghetti dinners and all-occasion cards, sponsoring skating parties, and taking children on trips in the summer, all for a nice little fee.

Anthony was one of Mrs. Clark's prized pupils. He was thirteen years old and he could play Bach and Rachmaninoff as if his fingers were on fire. When Anthony played, all the students seated in Mrs. Clark's basement were absolutely silent. I heard Mrs. Clark tell Anthony's mother that he was a child prodigy and that with her skill and the help of the Lord he would do great things.

There was a park across the street from Mrs. Clark's house and sometimes when she was backed up she would give her students permission to go play there. Anthony and I took our lessons on the same day, and one Wednesday afternoon when Mrs. Clark was making one hapless student play "The Moonlight Sonata" fifty-eleven times, she told Anthony and me that we could go out. "Come back in fifteen minutes," she shouted.

We ran into the park feeling wild as reindeer. Anthony and I hid from each other among the overgrown oaks and birches. We raced through the grass playing tag, our excitement growing each time we touched each other. First I chased him and then, after I tagged him, he chased me. Finally we sat down under a tree. I was suddenly shy. I had never been anywhere alone with a boy. Anthony looked at me and I immediately looked at the ground.

"So, where do you go to school?"

"Wagner. Where do you go?"

"Cooke."

"What grade are you in?"

"Eighth."

"Oh."

"What grade are you in?"

"Eighth."

"So how long you been coming to Mrs. Clark?"

"A few years."

"You wanna walk over there?" He pointed to a clump of trees. I nodded. I was going wherever he wanted to go. I felt very warm, as though I had a motor inside of me, sometimes purring slowly and sometimes speeding up without warning. When we sat down again, our shoulders touched accidently.

On the following Wednesday afternoon, as Anthony the magnificent slid out from the piano bench and I slid in, he slipped me a note. I opened it on my way home. "Baby, do I stand a chance?" Daaaag. The next week I passed back my answer:

> *Dear Anthony,*
> *I will be your girl. You don't have to* Shop Around *and there's no* Maybe *about it. Everytime I see your face you make me want to* Twist and Shout. *I will love you way past* A Quarter to Three. *I will love you until it's* Madison Time *in heaven. I'm not a* Bad Girl. *Baby,* You Can Depend on Me.
>
> *Love,*
> *Bebe*

Anthony called me every night after dinner. My mother wouldn't let me go to the movies alone with him, but twice she let him come over on Sunday afternoons.

When Anthony visited we sat on the sun porch and played Scrabble. Once when we were playing, Anthony announced to my mother that he had won. After he left, my mother asked me if I let him win. Let him win? "Why would I do that?" I asked incredulously. Mommy only smiled.

School closed on Fridays with a flurry of weekend house parties that started at seven-thirty and ended at ten-thirty. I bopped, cha-chaed, twisted and pop-eyed until the sweat turned my body into a teenybopper waterfall. I was more hesitant when it came to dancing when the host or hostess put on "Soldier Boy" by the

Shirelles. The thought of slow dragging with a boy made my knees knock. Despite my mother's "Now You Are Growing Up" booklets, from what Michael had described, slow dragging was at least as dangerous as sex.

"So when are you coming back?" Anthony asked me as I walked him to my front door the Sunday before I was due to leave for North Carolina.

"September," I said, feeling a little glum.

"And you're not going back to Wagner, huh? You're definitely going to Girl's High in the fall?"

"Yeah," I said with a long sigh.

"Well, have a good time," Anthony said softly, moving closer. "Write me, okay?" I nodded as his face came nearer to mine. "I'll see you when you get back, okay?"

"Okay," I said softly. Anthony quickly looked behind himself. So did I. We were alone. His lips brushed against mine, so soft I hardly knew they were there. My first real kiss. As I walked into the house I was thinking that it would be nice if I could put off going to North Carolina for maybe a month.

# CHAPTER 14

Grandma Mary stood up so quickly and with such force when I came through the front door that the rocking chair behind her kept swinging back and forth. She was still holding the bowl of string beans she'd been snapping when the screen door slammed behind me. "Okay if I walk down to Cousin Emily's, Grandma?" I asked.

"Young ladies don't wear shorts when they go down the road." Grandma uttered this gravely, without the least hint of a smile.

My thirteenth summer and Grandma Mary was on the warpath. Grandma Mary, who prior to my teenage years had never said no to me, who always let me do exactly as I pleased, suddenly was turning into a tyrant with rules and regulations for my every move.

Actually, Grandma Mary's first no had come during the summer she banished me from my father's room because I was too big. The following year the pendulum swung in the opposite direction. At eleven I was too young to stay out half the night with my father. Too young for the short skirt at Belk and Tyler's. By the time I reached twelve, I was too old again. Too old to be throwing green balls at Jimmy and Johnny. Too old to sic the dog on the chickens. But not old enough to go to town by myself.

At thirteen, I was again too big. "Young ladies don't go to church with bare legs. You're too big for that." "Young ladies button their blouses all the way up."

Her outbursts were tied to the three new bras and the box of sanitary napkins I'd packed in my suitcase. I knew this instinctively and immediately. It was the same in Philadelphia, with Nana and Ruth debating on new ways to keep me locked up until I was twenty-one or married or both. "I wouldn't let that boy come over here," Nana warned my mother. "You letting her go to another party?" Ruth asked, wide-eyed.

I sighed and went back into the house to put on a skirt. Philadelphia, with its summer rock-and-roll shows, its weekend house parties, offered more freedom than Grandma's watchful eyes would permit. Grandma didn't even want me to play the radio! And to make matters worse, my father was working in Richmond, three hundred miles away, fixing toasters and televisions at an appliance-repair shop. He could see me only on weekends. Bunnie had moved to Philadelphia. Miss Rosie didn't have any visitors. There was nobody around but my Uncle Joe's wife, Cookie, and his two young children, who were spending the summer with Grandma too. July wasn't halfway over before I sat down and wrote my mother a desperate, impassioned letter. "Please make up some excuse for me to come home. It's boring down here."

My mother's return letter was filled with a social worker's diplomacy. "Your grandmother is getting older. Try and be patient, dear." Then she slapped on a little guilt for good measure. "You know your father and grandmother love you very much. I'm sure you can entertain yourself for a few weeks."

I tried, I really did. I read *Marjorie Morningstar, Hawaii* and stacks of *Seventeen* and *Ingenue*. I played with my little cousins and even planted a garden in a sunny plot just off the backyard. There weren't any animals to fool around with except for the chickens and I didn't like chickens. Frosty had died and Grandma and Mr.

Abe didn't keep pigs anymore. North Carolina was boring.

I walked down to Cousin Emily's in the morning and messed around with Belinda until dusk. My cousin and I didn't dress up anymore, of course. There was a house near Cousin Emily's where teenagers went to dance in the evenings and sometimes hung around during the day. Grandma Mary disdainfully called it the "piccolo joint," because it had a jukebox; it was obvious to me that Grandma believed the road to hell was paved with such places. Sometimes if Belinda and I had money, we walked over to the shop, as we called the place, played records and watched older teenagers shoot pool. But even going there got boring. I lived for the weekends when my father came.

Early in August Daddy picked me up and drove me to Richmond to spend a week. "I'm taking you to stay with a doctor friend of mine," Daddy announced, emphasizing the word "doctor." It turned out that the doctor was the husband of one of our cousins, but to hear Daddy tell it, he and the doctor were best friends. Maybe they were, but it sounded like name-dropping to me. I hated it when Daddy bragged. Sometimes I wanted to say, "Knowing them doesn't make you rich or important," but I never did. Our cousin lived in a middle-class black settlement, a tight little enclave of beautiful old houses bordering Byrd Park. "Everybody who lives around here is professional," Daddy crowed. It was clear that he held such surroundings in high esteem.

Around lunchtime every day Daddy honked for me and we'd go get hamburgers and French fries. After we ate we drove to the small store where Daddy worked for an old man named Mr. Poole. There were just the two of them in the shop. They called each other by their last names without the "Mister"; I could tell they liked each other. And I could tell that Mr. Poole trusted Daddy by the way he let my father do his work without checking up on him.

There wasn't much space in the shop. Behind the counter where Mr. Poole waited on customers was a small room with two tables, two chairs and a bunch of shelves on the walls. The shelves were full of radios, clocks, toasters and portable televisions.

On the table on the right side of the room, the finished items were tagged and bagged, waiting to be picked up. On the table on the left, everything was in different stages of being repaired. I sat in one of the chairs and read while Daddy worked. It was hot in the back of the shop, and in no time there were wet rings under Daddy's arms and he had to keep wiping his face with a rag he hung over the arm of his wheelchair. This wasn't my father's first job, of course. I knew he had been a county farm agent before he got hurt. After his accident he had been a counselor at McGuire VA Hospital, helping wounded soldiers adjust to their injuries. I had been very young when he had that job, so I couldn't really remember it. And he used to drive people places for money. I remember when I was six or seven he sometimes spoke about getting a check and as I got older I figured out that he meant Social Security. For several summers my father had been idle, and now, as I watched him put broken radios back together, was the first time I remember seeing him on a job. I liked being in that small, hot room with my father. Looking at him busily assembling nuts and bolts I realized that he was happy, far happier than he had been during the summers when we sat around in the yard with nothing to do.

"Where'd you learn to fix all this stuff?" I asked him once.

"Goodwill," Daddy replied, not looking up. "Don't you remember when I was at Goodwill in Philly? Remember the Christmas party and the Santa Claus?" He waited, then when I didn't answer said, "You were little."

I must have been four or five. Daddy was living in the house on 16th Street with us and learning a trade at Goodwill during the day. At Christmastime Goodwill gave a dinner for all the handicapped men and their families. I sat at a long low table with a bright red tablecloth and everywhere I looked there were men in wheelchairs, men with hooks for arms, men with one leg or no hands, men with unflinching expressions, but with sadness seeping through their eyes.

"I remember," I said softly.

"Yeah," Daddy said. He looked at me quickly. "You having an okay time?" His eyes were a little anxious.

"Uh huh."

"Isn't Richmond a beautiful town?"

"Yeah."

He looked out to the other room, where Mr. Poole was waiting on a customer. "I could get a place like this," he said eagerly, his chin jutting out a little. I nodded. "Make aplenty money, too. What do you think about that, huh? We could get us a nice little house."

On my last day, we drove to McGuire VA Hospital, where my father stayed whenever his kidneys started acting up. The hospital was a vast assortment of flat, low buildings. We parked outside Ward 38, where people with spinal cord injuries were kept. "I want you to meet somebody," Daddy said.

Tank Jackson was sitting in his wheelchair by his bed looking at a baseball game. When he saw us coming, he started grinning.

"What you know, ole man?" Daddy called out. "Know who this is?"

"Be Be," Tank said. He looked at me. "I seen your picture a million times." He held out his hand. I shook it.

Daddy and Tank sat next to each other in their wheelchairs and watched the ball game. I sat in the chair near Tank's bed. Daddy did most of the talking and Tank did all the laughing and smiling. But neither one of them had much to say. It wasn't like the times Daddy got together with Uncle Eddie or Uncle Norman and they would talk about making money in deep, hungry voices. Uncle Norman was always telling my daddy how he was tired of working in the knitting mill and he wanted to have his own factory. The last time Daddy and I had visited Uncle Norman I heard him tell Daddy that he had bought two old knitting machines and that he was making sweaters and was going to take them down south to sell them at some of the colored colleges. And Daddy had leaned toward him, all excited, and they talked numbers and dollars all night long. But it wasn't like that with Tank. They just sat in their chairs, looking at the ball game, sometimes calling each other names in teasing voices. When we got ready to leave, Daddy said, "Your sores heal up?"

"Almost."

"You make sure those nurses turn your black butt over."
Daddy put his hand on Tank's shoulder.

Tank said to me, "Be Be, tell your daddy to bring you around
to my house next time you come."

ONCE DADDY BROUGHT ME BACK TO NORTH CAROLINA AND LEFT, I
felt as cooped up as ever. "How come my daddy didn't get a job
in Elizabeth City?" I asked Grandma one August afternoon. My
words came out sounding irritable and curious; I was both. We
were sitting in the living room, which was rare for us to do during
the day. Grandma had a bag of rags at her feet and we both held
needles in our hands. Quilting was the peaceful oasis of my thirteenth summer.

"Jobs don't grow on trees. You gotta go where the jobs is,"
Grandma explained.

"He coulda looked. I bet he didn't even look in Elizabeth
City."

"Maybe 'Lizabeth City jobs don't pay as much as them in
Richmond. Richmond's a big place."

"They've got big cities in North Carolina," I argued, just for
the sake of having the last word.

"Well, mebbe he didn't wanna work in North Carolina 'cause
he can't get no driver's license here."

I held my needle in front of me motionless. "What do you
mean? My father has a driver's license."

"Well . . ." Grandma had stepped into deep water, I could
feel her struggling to get out. I knew instantly that she was hiding
something from me about my father, something important. "Look,
let me show you something about . . ."

"My father doesn't have a North Carolina driver's license?
How come?"

Grandma looked at me. "It got took away because of the
accident," she bent her head and started sewing.

"You mean when he got hurt."

Grandma looked up. "No. The other accident."

My father had been in another car accident? I was surprised. And curious. "What happened?"

"Oh, I don't rightly know," Grandma said, her eyes avoiding mine in a way that told me she did know.

"Well, was my daddy driving?"

"Uh, yes, he was driving. Look here, hand me that red scrap right there. No, the other one."

"Was he by himself?"

"No."

"Did anybody get hurt?"

Grandma put down the piece of red cloth she'd been holding. She looked at me and took a deep breath. "A boy was in the car with him and he got hurt. Real bad."

I could scarcely breathe. "What happened to him?"

"I think . . ." Grandma's voice trailed off. Then she looked me straight in my eyes. "He died."

My hand froze on the piece of tattered cloth that I was holding. "Was it my daddy's fault?" I whispered.

Grandma picked up her needle. She stuck a piece of thread in her mouth and took it out, poking around the needle with it. She couldn't find the eye. "I don't know." She peered at the thread and fumbled again with the needle. "Mebbe he was driving too fast. I don't know."

"What about, what about when he got hurt? Was he going fast, too fast?"

"Mebbe."

"Was he?"

Grandma looked at me long and hard and didn't answer. Maybe? I thought about Daddy's dark green Pontiac, the blue Impala swiftly careening down Route 17, the wind in our faces, my hair flying, my daddy smiling and laughing in the wind. I understood. It was all his fault. He wasn't a nobly injured prince. He was reckless. My father was a person who had ruined lives, his, mine, others'.

I looked at my grandmother and I couldn't hide what was in my mind. Maybe she saw something in my eyes that scared her.

All I know is that her voice was low and suddenly vicious. "Your mama didn't want to stay with George after he got hurt. She must have wanted her a man what could walk."

Her words didn't register for a minute; they just floated in space until finally they penetrated my brain. I could feel the surge of blood. I looked down, and between Grandma and me the red scrap of fabric stretched wide as a road. "She didn't," I said quickly. I stood up and my breath came out in little jolts of air that made me dizzy. A silent scream rushed through me like vomit. I stood up. "Don't. Don't talk about my mother."

# CHAPTER 15

The photograph was in the bottom drawer of my mother's bureau. It was an old-fashioned **picture**; my father's face wasn't on paper but was embossed on **thick** plastic with a heavy cardboard backing glued to the photo. The face in the photograph was young, smiling, innocent. He was wearing a tan soldier's uniform. "To My Beloved Wife, Love George," read the inscription. I stared at the picture for a few moments, my fingers clenching the border tightly, then I pulled out the scissors from my mother's top drawer. The point of the thinner blade was sharp enough to draw blood.

It was his fault! Those words had kept echoing in my head throughout the remainder of my southern summer as I trudged down the lane to Cousin Emily's, as I kneeled to listen to Mr. Abe's monotone during Sunday-morning prayers, as I pumped water for my bath. His fault. I stole looks at my father while he read the paper or shined his shoes, and I saw a guilty man.

I returned to Philly with my head full of questions. How? Why? When? I asked my mother. She was stunned by my intensity. Mommy hemmed and hawed, murmured and paused and told me absolutely nothing. My mother was funny about her business.

Nana. Nana was another story.

"Such a big shot." She spit the words out. "Him and his fancy cars. So fast. He always had to move so fast. I went down to those sticks where they lived and he had your mother in a shack, a shack. Eating off a, a, a wooden box. No table. No chairs. And him with his big shiny car sitting outside that shack!"

All of her pent-up rage came rushing out. "He called you a split tail!"

"A what?"

"A split tail. That's what ole country niggers call a girl baby. I heard him say that when you were born. He told somebody, 'Awww, man, it's a little ole split tail.'

". . . Wouldn't be surprised if he had some woman in that car with him."

"Did he . . . ?"

"Did he?! Ha!"

MY MOTHER CAME INTO MY ROOM. "DID YOU DO THIS?" SHE ASKED, holding up the picture. It was full of holes and slashes.

I shrugged. Was she going to punish? Lecture? I didn't care.

"What are you so angry about? Did your father do something to you? Tell me!"

"No, he didn't do anything to me."

Months later I was sitting in the sun porch when I heard the horn. My heart froze. And for a moment I didn't get up. For a moment I kept flipping through the pages of a magazine without reading them. Then the horn blared again and it reminded me of Thanksgiving and Christmas and the good summers of long ago when my father was an innocent man, a noble prince. I got my coat, my gloves. When I went outside, Daddy was sitting in front of the house in a new car. A beautiful cream-colored Buick. I slid in beside him and we drove to Fairmount Park. He switched the engine off and turned to face me. "Are you mad at me or something?"

"No, Daddy."

# CHAPTER 16

My world was trembling. I lay across the studio cot close to my door, looked up at the ceiling and tried to ignore the shaking inside of me. The Supremes were singing from my transistor radio. "Baby, baby, baby, where did our love go?" I pushed my loud, strong soprano right in the middle of the Motown sound; sometimes I "baby-babied" with Diana and sometimes I "baby-babied" with Flo and Mary. In my room the sound of my own voice, straining to reach the high notes above my range, gave me something to concentrate on. I didn't want to think about Anthony's cool disengagement tactics on the telephone. "Well, like, you know, I quit you." And I certainly didn't want to think about my father and betrayal and the side I had finally chosen.

I could see why Mr. Abe sat in his living room chair all evening doing nothing but mumbling one song right after another. I understood how Nana's beating up a song could keep her from knocking Michael and me into the middle of next week (which she was always threatening to do and never ever did). Mr. Abe and Nana were healing themselves. Stretched across my studio cot with Motown sounds blaring around me, that's exactly what I was trying to do. It was funny the way I could dig down inside myself, squeeze out the notes and make them do what I wanted them to do. I wanted to control my thoughts in the same way, but I couldn't. At least I couldn't control the thoughts I had about my father, ideas that invaded the music.

How could my father not have been who I always thought he was? That was the recurring question that swam through music, high school classes, skating parties, Sunday school, even emerging on the banks of my quiet times. The question was most often a silent one, but once I spoke it aloud to Michael. My cousin was both sympathetic and gleeful that my "good" daddy had fallen from his pedestal to land in the mire next to Kenneth. His responses varied, depending on how happy or sad he was feeling at the time. Once, when I was really upset and crying, Michael patted my back and told me, "Aww, don't worry about it. Your dad's been pretty nice to you." Another time he snarled at me without warning, "Your ole wheelchair daddy messed himself up." It didn't help me to rationalize that Michael hadn't seen his father in years and that Uncle Bobby didn't come around anymore either. Knowing that Michael spoke out of pain didn't help vindicate my father. He *had* messed himself up. And me. My mind had painstakingly woven the image of his innocence; now that tapestry was slowly unraveling, leaving me angry and confused.

When I compared him to other fathers who were away from their children he wasn't so bad. I recalled when I sat under the poplar tree in the yard at Logan and Carol described her father riding around in a shiny automobile and her with no Easter clothes. Humph! I thought of Kenneth and his irresponsible absence, the sly set of his head, the crookedness of his smile. What a bum. Didn't I have the good father? The one who sent money and bought my clothes, the one who came for me at the beginning of every summer.

But everything had changed. Grandma Mary's and Nana's words had snatched away my father's innocence, not from him, but from me. No demon had cut him down on the road. He'd done it himself. He was the demon behind the wheel. He had betrayed my image of him.

After I returned to Philly I didn't write my father. He mailed me several scribbled pages about Grandma Mary, Cousin Eula, Belinda, the weather, and said at the end, "I can't wait to hear from you."

Mommy watched the mail, what came in, what went out. She asked me, "Have you answered your father's letter?"

"I will," I lied. But I didn't.

Besides, there was promise in the September breeze; just breathing in the times took my mind off my absent father. For one thing, the March on Washington had just been held that August and the air was still heavy with Hope! Pride! and Dreams! On the days I wasn't melancholy I was feeling inspired. Up, Ye Mighty Race! That's what I felt like. When I walked past Wagner's Ballroom these days I said to myself: only a matter of time.

Reverend Newsome, our new minister, told the congregation at Corinthian Baptist Church that they had to hold onto that marching spirit. Everybody said amen because the truth was, nobody wanted to let go of the potency and unity that had emanated from that gathering. I wanted to go to D.C., but my mother told me, "Don't worry about marching. You just get good grades and nobody can keep you out."

Not everybody believed in the dream, of course. A man in line at the A&P behind Nana and me told us, "So what the hell difference is a march gonna make? They gonna start hiring some Negroes to do more than mop their floors and shine their shoes? That's what I wanna know."

But I wasn't listening to any nasty man. I had Hope!

That Labor Day after the march, when my uncles gathered together at reunion, I could sense their new mood. They stood in a clump around their newly shined automobiles and spoke about the march. "Well, yeah, some more jobs are gonna come out of it."

"Damn right, they gonna pass that civil rights bill. 'Cause if they don't, these cities are gonna burn up."

"A lot of things done changed already. And I tell you, in a few years, the South is gonna be the place to be." As always I crept to their border, wanting to be closer to them. They still fascinated me, my uncles standing together.

I could see changes already. Even before I left North Carolina that summer, most of the "Colored" and "White" signs in Elizabeth City had disappeared, and the ones that were left, nobody paid any attention to anyway. It was as though somebody forgot to take them down, but everybody understood they didn't mean anything anymore. But even I knew there were invisible signs on the minds of people that would take years to destroy. Maybe forever.

I SAT WITH THE LARGE GROUP OF INCOMING FRESHMEN GATHERED IN the auditorium of the Philadelphia High School for Girls looking frantically for Linda. I had left Wagner Junior High at the end of eighth grade; my A− average qualified me for Girls' High, one of the city's two academic high schools—the other was Central, for boys—that started in the ninth. Uncle Sammy thought it was wonderful that I was going to a ritzy high school. Pete sent me twenty dollars in a graduation card when I left Wagner, even though I didn't actually graduate. But sitting in the midst of so many new faces I felt all my joy and excitement replaced by trepidation.

I was awed. My eyes were unaccustomed to such splendor. The tour of the school had revealed a place where everything seemed to gleam, from the luxurious pink marble hallways to the cafeteria with its stainless steel stoves and sinks. Even the classrooms were bright, spacious and airy. The entire facility was imposing. The building sat right on top of the subway at Broad and Olney and rose up on a hill, then fanned out to a sprawling campus that included a grand front lawn and enough acres behind to accommodate the gym classes which came outside for calisthenics and field hockey.

On the stage, Dr. Klein, the principal, a fair, fiftyish woman with cottony blond hair, was telling us that we were now part of a proud tradition and had to live up to Girls' High standards. She gave her message in a clear, northeastern accent, trilling her rs and enunciating her ts in a crisp, frightening way. Next to her, the vice-principal, Dr. Thompson, nodded and smiled at us. I stole a hesitant glance around the room and saw faces as awed and anxious as my own. What I didn't dare ask aloud was written clearly on the faces I saw: Could I make the grade? I knew the question was on my face as well. The teachers we had met at our orientation were methodical, no-nonsense educators who took their task of bringing knowledge to some of Philly's best and brightest very seriously. "They never grade on the curve," someone behind me whispered. "A lot of girls flunk out," someone else said. Shiiiiit. Slowly my eyes wandered around, searching for a friendly face. Seated in the auditorium were students from all over the city; every ethnic group in Philadelphia was represented: Jews, Negroes, Italians, Ukrainians, Irish, Chinese, Japanese, Puerto Ricans, Polish and regular white people with last names like Wilson and Smith. Girls' High was a melting pot for achievers. There were people seated in the crowd who, four years later, would garner 1600 on their SATs, become Merit scholars, sail off to Ivy League universities with full-paid scholarships. Two future White House fellows, both Negro, were seated in that room. Of course, I didn't know that then. All I knew was that everyone in the auditorium was smarter than I. Waaaaay smarter. In the aisle across from mine, I finally spotted Linda. I sighed with relief to be reunited after two years of being at different junior highs. Linda and I had been Logan's brightest scholars! I saw two girls from my homeroom at Wagner. I was instantly buoyed. Aww, shoot, I knew as much as they did.

MICHAEL TUGGED THE STOCKING CAP OVER HIS HEAD WITH A FIRM yank, as I stood in the doorway watching him. His stocking caps were the tightest in the Negro world. He always stitched a one- or two-inch tuck in them, decreasing the circumference of the band of the stocking so that it barely fit over his head. According to my dapper cousin, a smaller stocking cap made better waves. Whenever he took off his cap, there would be a little red ridge that circled his forehead; but his gleaming waves were uniform, and as long as Michael's waves were slick, all was right with his world.

"Hey, Michael," I called softly from the door.

"Miguel," he corrected me.

"Oh yeah, I forgot you deserted the race," I said, laughing. Michael only grunted and stared at himself in the mirror as he began brushing his hair.

Michael's waves were slicker and his stocking cap was even tighter ever since he had become Miguel. He had adopted the name after he began studying Spanish in high school. For more than a year he'd been calling himself Miguel. At first it was funny, Michael sitting down at dinner and acting as if he didn't understand Nana, Mommy or me, because he spoke only Spanish. He *was* being funny. But then it wasn't so funny, because gradually Miguel started popping up away from the dinner table and his new persona wasn't just for laughs.

"Why do you tell everybody your name is Miguel?" I asked him once when I overheard him introducing himself to a girl.

But he only shrugged, which was what he'd begun doing whenever he was confronted with a question that required the least bit of introspection and truth. Gradually I began to understand the answer, even if Michael wouldn't admit it. He was becoming Miguel because he didn't want to be Michael. He was running, just as fast and as far as his little slick waves and *por favor*s would take him. That's what I thought.

Michael wanted only to *be* Spanish; he certainly didn't want to study it. In fact, he didn't study much of anything. Whereas the grades on my first-semester report card were decent (not wonderful, but not horrible either), Michael's grades at Olney High School were awful. Michael was an underachiever of the highest rank and the report cards he brought home demonstrated just how unmotivated he was. My mother's and Nana's pleading fell on deaf ears.

And so did Aunt Ruth's. Nana called her at work, demanding that she come see her son's report card. I was sitting on the front patio when Aunt Ruth got off the bus. The bus driver could hardly take off for looking at her. As she crossed the street all the men on the block stopped whatever they were doing and watched her.

Their eyes confessed that they'd be only too happy to drink Aunt Ruth's bathwater.

Maybe it was the clarity of the Ds and Fs on Michael's report card, seen through an unkind sobriety, that enraged her. Aunt Ruth preferred to look at problems in a haze. She grabbed Michael by his shoulders and shook him hard. "I send you to school to learn," she shrieked.

Michael pulled away. He shrugged. "Like you care," he told her.

He wouldn't even listen to me and I certainly wasn't any naggy grown-up Bosom, but even I knew that Michael would eventually reap the useless seeds he was sowing. What kind of future would even a Puerto Rican, a Mexican, a damn Argentinian have with his Ds and Fs? "Boy, what's wrong with you?" I finally asked, after everybody else was finished cajoling and threatening.

"Nothing."

"Well, you better . . ." I started, sounding more like Nana than I could stand. Then I stopped. Michael's eyes were murderous.

"I better what?"

I didn't say a word.

"You just keep bringing home your little As and Bs, okay? Okay?"

Our academic performances were the beginning of a gap that would yawn wider and wider as months passed. But if Michael and I didn't have a great deal in common scholastically, there was, for the time being, part of our lives where our ambitions didn't matter. Our grades made no difference on the dance floor.

Parties, of course, didn't just happen; they had to be petitioned for, planned, sponsored. Since a social life was too fundamental to teenage happiness to leave to the whims of benevolent parents (far too often prone to take away the privilege of using their rec rooms when they discovered minor indiscretions), organizations sprang forth for the sole purpose of letting the good times roll. Michael joined Gamma Phi Omega, a West Oak Lane fraternity whose members all attended Olney. I joined the sister sorority,

Lambda Phi Epsilon. In addition to partying and cutting eyes at cute Gamma Phi Omega brothers, my sorority was supposed to serve the community. I vaguely remember an early Saturday visit to an old folks' home, the feel of the old women's hands grasping ours, the surprisingly strong antiseptic smell in the place, the soft, faint odor of urine that clung to some of the real old ones. We sang a couple of Supremes songs, and the old ladies in their chairs and beds really ate it up. They were smiling and grabbing at our hands when we finished.

Under the auspices of Alpha Kappa Alpha, my dignified mother continued to adopt deprived children informally, raise money for scholarships for needy students and volunteer for everything under the sun. Lambda Phi Epsilon was a little more decadent. The visit to the old folks' home is about the only social service I recall the sisters of Lambda Phi Epsilon rendering. Not that we didn't care about the world. We did. But the part we cared most about began and ended with our feet. We were some seriously party-crazy women. When we weren't collecting dues money to rent halls or dues money to buy matching pink shells and skirts and socks to wear to dances, then we were helping our brothers sell tickets to their functions.

The city was our dance floor and we arrived at the various hot spots via the generous chauffeuring of some soror's father, who always admonished us to be outside and ready to go home at precisely eleven, and never failed to add, "Now don't get so wrapped up in these funky boys that I have to come in there. Hear?!" We hung out in a North Philly hall located at Broad and Stiles. We partied down the street from Temple University at the Blue Horizon, so named for the sky-blue color of its exterior walls. We partied at the Imperial Ballroom in West Philly. My sorors and I were frenzied dancers, crossfiring, pop-eyeing, Boston-monkeying, dogging the night away. Somehow Michael always wound up in the middle of the floor with a crowd around him, as he leaped into death-defying splits, spins and flips with some double-jointed and equally limber partner.

At Gamma Phi Omega's anniversary dance, we jammed all night long at Broad and Stiles. The party was boss! I was steadybopping the night away. But while my feet could party, my hair couldn't hang. After one particularly energetic session I felt my hair: the heat had turned my little Dippity-do curls into fuzzballs. I rushed into the bathroom and took a fast look in the mirror. Despair. Grief. Why was my hair so, so . . . ugly?!! My flip had flopped, gone back, as in home, as in Mother Africa. I frantically raked a little ten-cent comb through my savage knots. I heard Marvin Gaye's "Can I Get a Witness," which was my stone jam. I gave my hair a final pat then rushed out to dance. Those frantic three minutes of doing the crossfire completely undid my repair work. Back to the bathroom! One look in the mirror told me it was time for serious action. I wet down my brush and swirled what was left of my pageboy into a tight, defensive French twist. This was Superknot: no heat could penetrate it. But I had to sweep my bangs off my face and now my big, retarded-looking forehead was showing. The hall was dim anyway, I told myself as I walked outside.

The slow strains of "Darling, Forever" hit me as soon as I came outside. I stopped walking and looked around. My strategy was to stay near the bathroom, that way if some ugly boy started walking toward me I could say, "Ooops, sorry. Nature's calling." I knew from experience that if the wrong guy grabbed my hand I might spend three of the longest minutes in history with my nose pressed right under some basketball player's funky armpits, or worse yet, have my face jammed against some conkhead jitterbug whose Nu Nile was dripping down my cheek. Or some little sawed-off dude might grind into my kneecaps so hard I'd be walking bowlegged for a week. A quick glance revealed *plenty* of wrong dudes in the hall. I was looking for the right dude, so I could close my eyes, lay my head on his shoulder and fall in love without ever having a conversation. Let the music do my talking. Yes, darling, forever. I scanned the hall quickly. The right guy was standing right across the room. Beau fine. Wouldn't mind getting *him* in my corner.

The song was coming to the bridge and nobody had asked me to dance. I was starting to ease away from the bathroom and scope on some of the ugly guys when I felt a tap on my shoulder.

I took a step back toward the bathroom and then looked up. Mr. . . . Not Bad was right up in my face. "Youwandance, mama?"

But for all the fun I had at the Blue Horizon and the Imperial, I still looked with longing at my neighborhood dance hall. *My neighborhood.* For almost the entire year I was in ninth grade I walked past Wagner's on my way to and from school. On Sunday afternoons the long line of outsiders stretched down the block. When I looked there were never any dark faces waiting to get in. But I knew the time was coming.

Michael came in my room one Sunday evening, pulled me aside and whispered, "Guess where I been?"

"Where?"

"Wagner's."

I gasped. "How'd you get in?" What I meant was, how had Michael gotten past the litany of excuses that the managers of Wagner's routinely used to keep us out? How had he evaded "We're too crowded" or "Membership only" or any one of a thousand jive lies?

"You know that white boy, Paul?"

I nodded, feeling instantly suspicious. The sandy-haired boy, Michael's schoolmate from Olney, had come to our house once or twice. Paul was soft and vaguely girlish.

"He goes there all the time. He got me in."

"Were you the only Negro?"

"Yep."

"So who'd you dance with?"

"Who you think I danced with? Girls, dummy."

White girls! Whoa. "Slow drag?" I asked incredulously.

"Nah. I didn't even bop with them. Just fast dancing. I'm going back next Sunday," he said casually.

I was instantly jealous. Michael had been to the exotic and forbidden land and I hadn't.

But my cousin was in a generous mood. "You can come too. I met the owners and they said I could come back as long as I didn't bring any colored people with me."

"He said that?"

" 'Now Mike, don't tell any other kellurd keds, okay?' "

Michael said, sounding just like a white man. "Like I'm supposed to go there and be the only colored person there with a whole room full of white people." Michael's eyes lit up. "I'm going back and I'm taking a bunch of folks with me."

The following Sunday there were eight of us waiting outside Wagner's. Only weeks before, President Kennedy had been shot and I had walked past the hall bawling my eyeballs out. Now the occasion was a happy one. We were the first in line and when the usual dancers arrived we could hear them buzzing behind our backs. We heard the shock in their voices. When we turned we saw fear and anger in some of their eyes. Those eyes said: Hey! This is ours. Get back! But we had our own eyes of fire.

When the manager opened the door, Michael's friend Paul whispered a few words to him. The guy gave us one long stare, as if we were something put out on the curb. Then he took our money and we went in.

It was nice inside, as I always thought it would be. It was dimly lit and there were mirrors all around and plenty of space. But of course, the music they played was kind of corny. Frankie Valli. Gene Pitney. Lesley Gore. Wah wah wah. "It's my party and I'll cry if I want to, cry if I want to, cryyyyy . . ." I couldn't dance to that stuff. Every once in a while they put on a real jam, some Martha and the Vandellas, the Temptations, Marvin Gaye and Tammi Terrell, and then the eight of us would cut loose as though we were at the Blue Horizon. When we were getting down, the Italian kids were steady checking us out. Watching our moves. When Michael realized he had an audience, well, naturally he showed out. And then they just looked some more, moving closer and closer to us.

Michael and I started going to Wagner's whenever we felt like it. Being there wasn't any more fun than being at the Imperial, but it made me feel more powerful. They couldn't keep us out anymore! That's what I thought, when I was hitchhiking and Philly-bopping to their corny music, looking at myself and my partner in the mirror.

It cost money to party, and Doris C. Moore was not sponsoring my good times. I baby-sat regularly for the Myers, a young

Jewish couple who paid me seventy-five cents an hour. A night's work paid my entrance to Wagner's or the Imperial Ballroom. When the Myers moved to Boston, the good times stopped rolling. Empty-pocket blues. When Mommy mentioned that a soror of hers, Mrs. Logan, had a young son who needed a baby-sitter, I was only too happy to oblige.

Away from Wagner's, Michael was brooding and angry. He argued constantly with my mother and Nana, and was silent when Aunt Ruth came around. His rage exploded first on his face and then on his body in thick red welts. The hives were emotional, the specialist said. Mannish, that's how Nana described his behavior. Or to be more precise, "so damn mannish."

I thought it was an odd insult, to call a boy mannish. What else was he supposed to be? The word voiced Nana's outrage. Mannish was too grown, too fresh, acting too much as if he were in charge of her. "I'll tell you one damn thing," she said one night after dinner at the end of a long verbal battle with Michael about grades and parties and insolence, "if you're not going to go to school, you'll have to go to work. You're not living here off the fat of the land. I'll tell you that!"

"Aww, I go to school," Michael said lazily.

Nana flared up like a torch. "You're a liar, just like your father. Just like him."

"Mother," Mommy began, but it was too late. Michael's shoulders slumped. His defiance crumpled. His body swelled with hives.

When the third semester rolled around and Michael brought home the same Fs as before, there was no shrieking and lamentations from the Bosoms. Just silence. Maybe those stone faces were the beginning of resignation. Ruth came by that weekend. Michael handed her his report card. She dropped it on the floor and when she bent down to pick it up she had trouble getting back up. "Aww, sweetie," she gushed, giggling a little, "you hafta do better."

But he didn't. Didn't even bother about being Miguel anymore. Michael dropped out of Gamma Phi Omega and stopped hanging with his jovial, foot-stomping frat brothers and began associating with more Pauls, more soft, girlish-looking fellows. When Nana saw Michael with his friends she used to shake her head, go back in the kitchen and sing at the top of her lungs. Blues spilled out of the kitchen and flowed all through the house.

I heard the blues, smelled the sadness. I saw, but I didn't see. I was studying, dancing, buying bras in bigger sizes, trying to grow leg muscles, liking boys and fighting to keep my hair from going back in the heat. My life occupied a lot of space. I was attempting to fly with my own wings. I felt the weight of old breasts bearing down on me, trying to keep me in the nest, where it was safe. Nana was a pain. Our horns seemed to lock over the most minor infractions and anything that had to do with boys. She was relentlessly on patrol, trying to make sure I wasn't "doing it." She was wearing out my last nerve. "You watch yourself," she warned me whenever a boy came over. Woman, puleez. But I was no longer her little chick with fuzzy feathers.

I couldn't help my cousin. He wasn't going to school. And those boys he hung out with. I couldn't bring myself to name them, what they were. My horror surfaced one night. "You need to just stop," I shrieked at him.

"Stop what?" he asked coolly.

"You know what. It's bad," I said lamely.

"Bad, huh?"

I couldn't have stopped him if I tried. I wasn't what Michael needed. I was beginning to think it was too late for what Michael needed.

I STAYED IN RICHMOND FOR MOST OF MY FOURTEENTH SUMMER. Daddy had a new job as an employment counselor in a downtown office. When we went there he introduced me to his coworkers and took me to where he sat. "This is my desk," he said, caressing the last word. Daddy also had a girlfriend, a widow with three sons and a great-aunt and a niece who lived with her in a rambling two-story house right outside the city. I liked Lillian. And I liked staying with her and her rambunctious, athletic boys. But the strain between my father and me hadn't disappeared. Daddy and

I didn't have much to say to each other. And when I did speak, my anger was sitting on my tongue like a bold, hungry rat I couldn't control.

Once when we were sitting on Grandma Mary's porch Daddy said 'They was' and I said 'They were' without thinking. He brought his hands down and folded them in his lap. His right leg leaped up in sharp spasms. He grabbed his leg, kind of laughing, the way he always did whenever he had a spasm. When his leg stopped moving he looked at me and when he spoke it was almost to himself. His voice was low and thoughtful. "Lookahere. You know your mother used to correct me. She corrected me in front of people." He left a space for me, an invitation.

I heard his question. Wasn't that wrong of her? Wasn't she wrong? "She corrects everybody," I snapped. "Besides, what's wrong with speaking properly?"

Daddy didn't say anything. He looked out over the cornfield that edged up toward the highway. I gazed at the cotton field behind us.

Another time we were driving fast down Route 17. Daddy had on a short-sleeved shirt and I could see the muscles in his arms dancing a little as he applied pressure to the hand accelerator. Dismal Swamp was an inky ribbon, flying past. Too fast. Way too fast. My shout was sudden; I had evil intentions. "Slow down. What are you trying to do, get us killed?"

ONCE I WAS BACK IN PHILADELPHIA, THE STEADY ROUNDING OF MY body suddenly brought me the attention of strange men. Linda and I had our hair done at a beauty salon in West Philly. With our new 'dos, we looked older than the tenth-graders we were. Men passed me by on Philadelphia streets and eyed me with such open, common lust that instinctively I lowered my eyes at the violation. All my life I had seen these men thrust their erect attentions upon any woman who passed them by.

"Hey, baby!"

"Hey, sweetness."

"Can I come with you, momma?"

They called out as if their lives depended on a prompt, accepting reply, an exchange that would affirm them for the day. I was astonished that nature had quite abruptly pushed me onto their terrain.

Once when an older teenager spoke to me with lazy-tongued licentiousness, I panicked and responded with nervous silence.

"Bitch," the boy spat at me.

I was stunned. There in the middle of a street full of cars and buses, stray dogs and loose, unattached people, I felt so unprotected.

As I approached the end of tenth grade a boy asked me to go with him. Tall. Thick-lipped. Wide shoulders and strong arms. He looked like a man. I fell in love. Not that puppy stuff; real, French-kissy, hickeys on the neck, sho'-'nuff love. My boyfriend wanted to do it. Have sex. My body said yes; my mind said no. Exactly what my mind said was: Hell, no. Girl, are you crazy? You will get pregnant. Nana will beat your butt. You will go to hell. You will not go to college. You will miss the prom. I told that sweaty boy: Listen, you can touch me here and here, but not there and there. No, don't touch me there. I told you *no*.

He told me I was giving him the blue balls and quit me for a hot mama.

After school I would sit in the basement crying and singing. And none of those bubble-gum tunes either. "Come and Get These Memories" wasn't gonna suffice. I had me some serious woman's blues. "You're no good, heartbreaker, you're a liar and you're a cheat. . . ." 'Retha was on the right track. I dug up Aunt Ruth's old Billie Holiday and Dinah Washington albums, her Gloria Lynne records, and I wore them out. "Trouble is a maaan. . . ." Now Gloria knew what I was talking about.

The Bosoms were full of advice. Nana told me to join a club and learn to play pinochle. "That's a lot of fun," she said with a straight face. Right.

Mommy sat me down on her bed and held my hand. She gave me her social-worker tone. "Well, darling, these things happen. If he was pressuring you, then he was the wrong boy for you." Yeah, Mom.

Aunt Ruth had moved in with us again and one morning when she was on her way to work she grabbed my arm and pulled me into her chest. She spoke fast, urgently. "Lissen. I've been watching you moping and mooning around here. I know you're crying about that boy. Forget him, honey. The guy wants to be a play-er. Let him play. Find somebody else. Now here's what you do: call up a coupla your girlfriends, tell them you'd like them to fix you up with somebody. I don't like to see you moaning and groaning over some guy. Don't start out that way."

I liked my beautiful aunt talking to me in a clear voice early in the morning. She was wise early in the morning. She was right.

The Bosoms had plenty of advice, but they couldn't offer me any protection against the pain of love. Maybe a man could. But who? Pete had moved out of my life. My Uncle Norman had just opened his knitting mill and was working around the clock with his knitting business. My Uncle Sammy was immersed in family life.

I didn't want to ask my father about love. Or protection.

When Mommy's soror Mrs. Logan called one night and asked me to baby-sit, I was still thinking that there was no one who could make sense of all my damp yearning and fear.

# CHAPTER 17

Mr. Logan taught me how to fry chicken one evening when I was baby-sitting his son, Butch. He stood in front of the stove, holding the handle of a black iron skillet; inside, the oil was bubbling. "You just make sure that the grease is hot, but not too hot. Know what I mean? Come on over here, girl. Lawd have mercy. You can't be scared if you're gonna cook." Mr. Logan's voice was like him: jovial and energetic.

Butch was sitting at the table. He was eight. Cute. Smart. Beaver and Eddie Haskell all rolled into one. He said, "Boy, I'm not eating that chicken. Nosirbuddy." Then he made the weirdest face imaginable.

Mr. Logan looked over at Butch and gave him a quick smile. "All right now, son. Lighten up."

"Dad, she's gonna poison us. We're gonna diiiiie."

Butch slumped forward in his chair and let his head fall softly forward onto the table. Then he put one hand on his heart and started making gurgling noises, glugluglugluglug, his interpretation of the death rattle. I started laughing. He did sound as if he were dying.

"All right, you're gonna be sorry, Butch," I said, composing myself. "This is gonna taste better than the Colonel's and you're not going to get any." I carefully stabbed a thigh and flipped the chicken over. I looked up hesitantly at Mr. Logan, who nodded at me. Butch just moaned louder.

Mr. Logan was in his forties, a tall, brown, broad-shouldered man who towered over his wife. He called his wife Hon. Mrs. Logan was studying for her Ph.D. in education and took evening classes. On the days when I baby-sat, Mr. Logan usually picked me up late in the afternoon after he finished working his shift at the post office. He stayed at the house with Butch and me until it was time for him to leave for his evening job. At night he parked cars in a garage downtown. He'd eat a little, mess around with Butch, then go to work.

I was sixteen, and not too pleased with myself. My skin was too pimply, my body too chubby and my hair too bushy for the sleek, sophisticated styles I saw in *Seventeen* and *Ingenue*. My hair. Every day the Lord sent, I wanted to burn my hair.

"Awww, now you got a new hairdo. That looks nice, doesn't it, Hon?"

"You don't need to be on any diet, girl. You're gonna have skinny legs, and the boys like big legs, ain't that right, Hon?"

If Mr. Logan said I looked nice, I knew he wasn't BSing me, because if he didn't like something I was wearing or the way I fixed my hair he'd just say, "Well, I don't know about that style." "Well, I don't know about that" was one of his favorite lines.

Mr. Logan encouraged me to do everything. He'd come in after midnight, see me collapsed across his kitchen table, a pile of books and papers on one side, an empty coffee cup on the other, and say, "That's right, girl. Hit those books," as if he thought it was great that Girls' High was whipping me. But that wasn't it. He thought it was great that I could hang.

"Just do your best," he'd tell me. "You young Negroes have a lot of opportunities now. Gotta take advantage of them." Mr. Logan was very big on the opportunities afforded to young Negroes.

Once when Butch had something to do after school and Mr. Logan and I had an hour to kill before picking him up, he took me to the home of one of his "boys," John. As we were sitting down in John's kitchen, Mr. Logan said, "See, you didn't know I had a daughter, did you?"

And John kind of laughed and said, "Naw, that's one on me." He smiled shyly at me. I extended my hand.

They drank Old Crow while I sipped Coke. When the man mentioned his daughter, a nurse, Mr. Logan casually disclosed my lofty future plans as though they were already faits accomplis. "Yeah, Bebe's, uh, planning on being a psychiatric social worker."

On our way to get Butch, Mr. Logan said, "Now John's basically just a dude off the corner. He come up hard, you know what I mean? You have to learn how to deal with all kinds of people, Bebe. There's a way to deal with everybody."

Mr. Logan taught me how to do that between his shifts. In rambling discourses that lasted into the night, he explained the differences between men and women, black folks and white, the educated and the illiterate. I inhaled Mr. Logan's teachings eagerly and found that his wisdom could be applied to daily life. One night he told me, "Those dudes on the street, they're just looking for acceptance, same as anybody else. Thing is, they're expecting not to get it. They're already mad. Know what I mean? So you surprise them, see."

How?

"You just speak first and keep walking."

On the streets, surrounded by leaners and loungers who expressed their macho with the challenge of "Hey, baby," I learned to do what Mr. Logan suggested: smile widely and speak first with the solemn, no-nonsense air of a social worker who is slightly hard of hearing. For the most part, to my surprise, the strange men on the corners let me be.

AUNT RUTH HAD A NEW BOYFRIEND. CLARENCE HAD A WIDE GAP BE-tween his front teeth and wore his hair in a towering process. He had been a boxer and still had the build, but now he did construction work. He spoke in monosyllables and ate a great deal at one sitting. At the dining room table my mother, Nana and I just looked at each other as he ate.

Clarence was up on slang. "For days," he said whenever anything pleased him. He declared that Nana could cook "for days" and that Michael could dance "for days." Was Muhammad Ali the baddest fighter around? For days!

"Where does she find them?" I whispered to my mother later.

"Don't ask me."

"He must be great in bed," I suggested. Mommy gave me one of her "And how would you know?" looks, but didn't say anything else.

Michael quit school in the twelfth grade, soon after Aunt Ruth left us again to move in with Clarence. I can't say that we were terribly surprised, because Michael's grades had been getting worse and worse and the school counselor had called many times about his truancy. Nana and Mommy lectured Michael until they were dizzy. "I give you up to the hands of the Lord, 'cause I done fought the good fight," Nana would say every time she and my cousin started to get into it. Nana had become a steady churchgoer since we moved to West Oak Lane, and she frequently called on the Lord when Michael was getting on her last nerve. While she was waiting on the Lord she'd slam through the house, singing at the top of her lungs.

"What are you going to do to support yourself?" my mother asked when Michael announced that he had formally severed his ties with Olney High School.

"I'll get a job," Michael said, dragging out the word "job" as if it had two syllables.

"You need a high school diploma to sweep the floor, these days," Nana wailed.

Michael shrugged.

"You can't stay here and not contribute, Michael," my mother warned him. Her voice was brisk, businesslike. He might have been one of her clients. "We will support you if you're in school, but you cannot just lie around and do nothing. So you'd better start looking for a job, dear."

Maybe Michael didn't take my mother seriously, but I did. If it had been up to Nana, Michael might have been able to live a lush life. Nana talked a good game, but inside she was soft. Mommy had a social worker's love of humanity, but she knew a lost cause when she saw one. And she knew how to play hardball. There was nothing my mother worshipped as much as productivity; being nonproductive was going to earn Michael a one-way ticket away from our house. "She's not kidding, Michael," I told my grinning, nonchalant cousin. "Keep it up. Mommy's gonna put your ass out of here."

For the first couple of weeks after he left school Michael just lazed around like a fat cat, sleeping until noon, getting up to eat, going back to bed and then finally dressing after six o'clock, just in time to be picked up by one of his soft, girlish-looking friends. My mother let Michael stay for six weeks in all, weeks full of dire and very specific warnings that my cousin failed to heed. Then she put him out.

"Are you going over to your mother's house?" I asked Michael before he left.

"Nah." His tiny, delicate nostrils were flaring softly.

I was silent for a while. Finally I said, "So, Michael, where are you going to go?"

"Don't worry. I got some place to go."

But I did worry. I worried a lot.

IN THE YEARS WE HAD LIVED IN WEST OAK LANE, THERE HAD BEEN A steady exodus of white families. Even the Bread Lady and her husband finally moved away, taking their supply of day-old rye, whole wheat and raisin bread with them. By the time she left all I wanted out of life was a fresh loaf of Wonder bread from the A&P.

West Oak Lane was still seething. Below the surface of polite smiles and superficial conversations that whites and Negroes engaged in was a we/they mentality that eschewed closeness. Even while the remaining whites anxiously sought buyers for their houses, they made no pretense of equality. They assumed that they were our superiors.

"The lady across the driveway told me they're having a big dinner party at her house next weekend," Nana told Mommy and me one night while we were eating dinner.

"What lady?" I asked.

"You know, that white woman that has the two big kids about your age."

"Oh." I was immediately not interested.

"She wanted to know if I'd wash dishes for her," Nana said casually, spooning seconds of rice onto her plate.

Mommy and I put down our forks and stopped chewing our food. "She asked you to do what?" we said in unison.

Nana started laughing at us. "She wants me to wash dishes."

Mommy's hand came down on the table hard and made the dishes clatter. "The nerve! Tell that woman to call an employment agency if she needs a maid. The nerve! She sees a Negro woman and assumes"—my mother said the word as a cultured English woman would—"immediately assumes she's a domestic." My mother was gathering dignity as her words picked up speed.

Nana laughed.

"I hope you told her that slavery is over and she can wash her own daggone dishes," I said in my iciest voice.

Nana just laughed louder.

"I mean, really, Mother!!" Mommy said. "What did you say?"

"Nana told that woman off, didn't you, Nana?"

"I told her that I didn't do that kind of work anymore, but that maybe my granddaughter would." Nana looked at me and smiled.

"*Me!!!* I'm not washing dishes for any . . . Why . . ."

"You baby-sit for them," Nana said calmly.

"Yeah, but that's . . ."

"Thirty dollars. She wanted to pay twenty, but I said you wouldn't consider it for less than thirty. For a couple of hours' work. Didn't you say you needed some new clothes?"

"Thirty dollars?"

"Go 'head over there. Make the money," Nana said, smiling into her plate. Mommy was silent. She was leaving it up to me.

I looked at Nana. Thirty dollars versus my pride, my dignity, my sense of "we shall overcome" . . .

I had never seen so many dishes in my life. Mountains of dishes. Oceans of dishes. Dishes for days! Everywhere I looked in Mrs. Brown's crowded kitchen there were dishes with gunked-on beef and mashed potatoes, dishes with apple and cherry pie. My head ached from looking at the mess in front of me. How the hell would I ever wash all those dishes? Why had I said I would?

It was different from baby-sitting. Baby-sitting was all soft, sweet voices. "We'll be at So-and-so's, Bebe. Here's the number. There's ice cream and chips. Have fun!"

Dishwashing was all "Do this, do that." People floated in and out of the kitchen all night long, but no one ever spoke to me. "Here's some more for you, girlie." That wasn't speaking to someone. All those anonymous faces thought I belonged at that sink, that I would be there forever.

In the dining room the voices of Mrs. Brown's dinner guests were boisterous, grating. The party had been going on for several hours and showed no signs of letting up. The dishes just kept coming. Big serving platters, full of grungy gravy. Slick, greasy plates. Bowls. Glasses with lipstick around the rims. I washed dishes for five solid hours. "I need a couple more forks," Mrs. Brown said, poking her head into the kitchen. She and Lucille Ball had the same dye job. I pointed to the table. When she left I looked down at my hands. I had the hands of a five-thousand-year-old gray woman. Every ounce of blood had drained away from my fingers. All around me on the counter were more dishes. Greasy, gunky dishes. A thick, hairy hand reached over my shoulder. When I looked into the water, the chewed-down tip of a cigar was floating amid the suds. Ugh!

The dishes kept coming until way after midnight. When I was finished, Mrs. Brown handed me three ten-dollar bills. "So maybe I'll call you again," she said.

Unh unh, lady. The kid is hanging up her dishpan hands. Ain't busting no more suds. "Well, I'm gonna be pretty busy, Mrs. Brown. School, you know."

Nana was waiting up for me, watching a late movie on the tiny black-and-white portable in the breakfast room and talking on the phone to her latest sweetie, Mr. Boyd. When she saw me, she said, "Lissen, dollin', I gotta go," and made a bunch of kissy sounds into the receiver before she hung up.

"How'd it go?" she asked, yawning widely. She dipped her hand in and out of a big bowl of dry Cheerios in front of her.

"Honey chile, I don't see how you survived," I said, grabbing a handful of Cheerios. I sat down and looked at Nana. "Seriously."

"She tip you?"

"You kidding?"

"Cheap," Nana said disdainfully. "Go to bed."

"Nana, how long were you a maid?"

She laughed. "All my life."

"Damn."

"Go to bed."

But I sat there with Nana and we ate Cheerios and watched the movie. All her life? No. Not all her life.


EVERY YEAR THE *PHILADELPHIA BULLETIN* SPONSORED A COVER-GIRL contest. Entrants were seniors from area high schools with enough nerve to send in their pictures. Needless to say, there had never been a Negro cover girl in the history of the contest. So when my mother suggested I send in my picture, I looked at her as if she were just slightly nuts. "Do it. See what happens," she insisted.

Well, why not? I had been relaxing my hair with a home permanent. My hair was now straight enough for me to have a Beatle haircut, which all my friends said was boss. I could get as funky as I wanted at parties; my hair stayed straight. Nana said the relaxer was going to make me bald-headed, but at the moment I still had hair.

"See," my mother said, "see," when the letter came from the *Bulletin* telling me that I was one of the semifinalists and inviting me to a dinner where the winner would be chosen.

Aunt Ruth was even more excited than Mommy about the contest. "My gorgeous niece," she kept saying over and over one Friday evening when she and Clarence had dropped in. Nana wouldn't give her anything to drink except ginger ale, but I could tell by the way she kept slurring her words that she had stopped off at a bar before she came by. Clarence kept nodding his head up and down and grinning. "I wanna buy your dress," Aunt Ruth said before she left.

Aunt Ruth called me and told me to meet her at the downtown Bonwit Teller on Wednesday evening. As soon as we walked into the junior misses' department she went over to a rack and picked out a deep-cranberry dress that was a little low-cut in a demure, debutante sort of way. Aunt Ruth had an eye for fashion. "Ohhhh," she murmured when I put the dress on, "that's the one. Baby, you could be Miss America in that dress."

As it turned out, I didn't even get to be Miss Bulletin, but I did make the court. And so did another Negro girl named Carol, who also went to Girls' High. The cover girl's picture appeared on the front of the Sunday magazine and the court appeared on the second page. The day the magazine came I examined my photo carefully, staring at my Beatle haircut: short hair, long bangs, my wide nose and smile. The face that Philadelphia loved!

It wasn't every day that Negro beauty was affirmed by the Philadelphia press. That Sunday the phone rang off the hook. All my uncles and aunts called. Mr. Logan told me I looked better than the girl on the cover and Pete called to say I should run for Miss Universe. My mother came into my room that night and handed me a copy of the magazine. "Send this to your father when you write him." I just looked at her. "Or do you want me to send it?"

"You can mail it to him."

"What's going on, Bebe?"

"Nothing." I would wait to tell my mother that I wasn't going to North Carolina in the summer.

Several months later, Girls' High was aflame with Contest fever. Contest was the annual sports competition that pitted Girls' High's finest junior and senior athletes against one another. Physical education specialists from all over the city came to judge the week-long series of gymnastic events.

The gym was silent as a lithe girl balanced her body on the rings. From the bleachers I watched girls shimmy their way to the top of thick ropes, leap across stationary horses and swing like trapeze artists from ring to ring. They were mesmerizing, but what claimed my attention wasn't on the floor. At the top of the bleachers, walking around with a scorecard, was a dark, long-necked woman, her body supple as a snake's. She was wearing her hair in a shocking halo of kinks. The woman's looks were raw and . . . African. Long earrings dangled from her ears. Bold colorful bracelets trapped her wrists. I couldn't take my eyes off her. My mother had several records by Odetta and I had seen the tight web of kinks that crowned her head on album covers. But this woman was real. And she had a lot of hair, hair that couldn't shrink up or go back, because it was already back; it was already there. A lot of nappy hair. From a few aisles away I caught Linda's eyes. She had seen the woman too. I could tell by the "What do you think?" look she gave me. I didn't know what to think. What was the meaning of that hair, I wondered.

MICHAEL LIVED WITH A ROOMMATE IN AN APARTMENT IN WEST PHILLY. It was clear he didn't want anybody to see the place, because he never invited us over and when we invited ourselves he made excuses. He visited us on weekends at first and ate like a stevedore whenever he came. "My God, boy," Nana said, watching him fill and empty his plate. He looked a little scruffy, but otherwise okay.

My mother and Nana and I hadn't given up hope that he would go back to school. "Whatever you're doing, you'll have

more of a future with at least a high school degree, Michael,"
Nana pleaded when he visited. "Don't go backwards. This family
has a college graduate. You should be following in those foot-
steps."

Michael mostly said, "Yeah, uh huh, sure," and kept stuffing
himself with food whenever Nana embarked on such discussions.

Between visits Michael usually called, but as the school year-
wore on and summer approached, we began to hear from him
less frequently. By the time school was out, three weeks had passed
without a word from Michael.

"Come on," Nana said one afternoon in June.

"Where are we going?" I asked.

"To Michael's apartment."

We took the Broad Street subway and then caught a bus on
Market Street. We got off at 57th and walked over to Walnut
Street. The apartment building was old and dingy and didn't have
an elevator. We walked up four flights, stopping at each landing
so Nana could lean against me and catch her breath. When we
finally reached Michael's apartment we knocked for about five
minutes before the door cracked open. A sliver of light flickered
out and an odd burning odor assailed us.

"I'm Michael's grandmother," Nana said. "Is Michael here?"

The door stayed cracked, but we caught a glimpse of the
young man's face and recognized him as one of the friends who
had come to our house with Michael. "Michael don't live here no
more," he said sourly.

"Do you know where he lives now?" Nana asked.

"No."

"How long ago did he leave here?"

"About three weeks ago," came the obviously bored reply.
I could still smell the burning. The odor was like Johnny smokers,
the old imitation cigarettes Michael and I used to buy at Pagejo's
when we lived on 16th Street.

From behind the door we could hear another voice, irritated
and whiny. "Hey, baby, close the door."

"Look," Nana said, sticking her foot in the crack, her eyebrows knotting together, "if you see Michael, please tell him to call home, that his grandmother needs to talk with him. It's important."

"Okay."

The door closed and Nana's shoulders slumped. "They're in there smoking that reefer," she said.

"What's reefer?"

Nana gave me a surprised look. "You don't know what reefer is?"

"What is it?"

"It's stuff that grows like tobacco and people smoke it to get high. That's what that smell is."

"What does it do to you?"

"Eats up your brain and makes you crazy, that's what."

"You ever smoke any?" I asked.

"Don't you smoke any," she snapped. Then her shoulders slumped and her face sagged and she grabbed me by the hand.

"Come on, Nana," I said, taking her hand and leading her down the stairs. "Don't worry about Michael. If he gets too down-and-out you know he'll come home." But secretly I wondered and worried too.


THE ALPHA KAPPA ALPHAS WERE GOING CROSS-COUNTRY. THEIR BOULÉ was being held in Los Angeles, and AKAs from every corner of the Negro world were going to meet there. Instead of flying, some of the sorors and their families planned to tour the country by bus. Mommy announced that she and I would join the bus group, which I knew was yet another one of her attempts to expose me to the grand landscape of America. She wanted to educate me. Seeing the Midwest and Far West was culture! That was fine with me. I didn't have anything planned for the summer.

Mr. Logan drove Mommy and me to the bus station. When we got ready to get on the bus he handed me a ten-dollar bill. "Here's a little something out of your future wages," he said, laughing.

My mother started to protest, but Mr. Logan wouldn't hear her at all. "Awwww now, you know I hafta lay something on my buddy here."

We *were* buddies. I looked after Butch and Mr. Logan watched after me. "I notice that lumphead Negro ain't been calling around here," he had said after I broke up with my boyfriend for the second time. "Well, don't worry about that. He'll be back."

He would? Nobody had told me that before.

"Sure he will. Just keep hitting those books. Make something of yourself. He'll be back. Then you can tell him you don't want to be bothered. Then you won't be able to get rid of him. That's the way that works."

Hmmmm.

I loved traveling. The sight of new streets and buildings, different faces and twangs excited me. In Cleveland we toured a Job Corps training center that the AKAs helped fund. When we got to Chicago we rode through the South Side and went to see a play. Once we were outside Chicago we left civilization behind, as far as I was concerned. A traveling band of Negroes created quite a stir in the hamlets of Iowa, South Dakota and Arizona. Our bus driver was a white man named Gene, a North Carolina hillbilly whose twang was a lot thicker than his hair. He called our bus his wagon train. Whenever the bus jolted to a sudden stop his toupee would slide forward and my mother would nudge me.

Gene always stopped at restaurants to see if they had room for us. If it was okay, he'd come back to the bus and yell, "Okay, settlers, chuckwagon's ready," which used to crack me up. What wasn't so funny was the people inside the restaurant. Time and time again when our group walked into a restaurant the whole room stopped eating just to stare at us. The little white kids had zero cool; one of them just about jumped into my larynx trying to get a look. As far as they were concerned we had all zoomed in from another planet.

"Dag, they sure are checking us out," I heard one of the

younger kids in our group say when we were near the Corn Palace in Iowa.

His mother said, "Shhhh," trying to hush him up. As if he were being rude.

When we got back on the bus the boy told the driver, "Gene, you gotta talk to your people, man. They're getting on my nerves with all this staring."

Gene turned all kinds of red. He said, "I know. I know,son. Some people, well, they don't mean no harm. Just excuse them."

Las Vegas was the most lit-up city I'd ever seen. "Okay, settlers, I want you to hold onto your wallets. If you can't trust yourself, give me your money," Gene teased as we left the bus.

Somebody yelled, "Don't bet your rug, Gene." And the bus driver just about died laughing.

My mother wasn't much on gambling, so our first evening in Vegas we walked around and looked at the casinos and night-clubs, had dinner and then came back to our hotel room. We watched television until I could almost feel myself dozing, then I heard Mommy say, "So when are you going to North Carolina?"

I said sleepily, but carefully, "I don't know if I'm going this year."

Mommy came over to my bed and sat down beside me. "What's going on?" she asked.

"Nothing."

"Well, then . . ."

"It's boring. There's nothing to do down there. Did you like living in North Carolina? When you were married, I mean?"

I could see in my mother's eyes the question: What brought this on? But she didn't ask it aloud. "I hated the South," she said flatly.

I sat up, intrigued by her frankness. "How come?"

"It was a mean place in the forties and fifties. For me, coming from Philadelphia, it was a difficult transition. I remember once going to the optometrist, and I walked into the waiting room for whites and the nurse nearly had a stroke before she hustled me out of there. Then when I got to the colored waiting room and I had to sign in, I wrote 'Mrs. George L. Moore.' And she asked me what my name was. And I kept saying, 'Mrs. George L. Moore.' I wasn't going to let that redneck twerp call me Doris."

"What did she call you?"

"When it was my turn she said, 'Moore.' " Mommy laughed. "So that was my victory, but it was a constant struggle. And I hated it. George kept saying the South was going to change and it would be the place to be, but it wasn't changing fast enough for me. And we were in a little country town, a farming community. No library. No museums. Nothing. I didn't have anything in common with the people. I hated it."

"Mommy, how did my father get hurt?"

My mother watched my face, my eyes. "In a car accident," she said, her voice even and firm.

"I know that, but how? Whose fault was it?"

"Well, nobody else was involved. . . ." Her voice trailed off.

"He drove fast, didn't he? Too fast."

"Sometimes, yes. Sometimes he would speed."

"So what happened that day, the day he got hurt?"

"Oh, God. It's been so long ago, Bebe." She paused. "He was supposed to be at home, doing his farm reports. You know we had a little restaurant with another couple. Your father was very, very ambitious."

"I know," I said, laughing. "He's always thinking of ways to make money."

"Your father loves money. He was determined to be rich. It's a shame; he would have been rich too. Anyway, it was my turn to be at the restaurant. He drove you to the baby-sitter's, then he dropped me off. He was supposed to go home and do his reports. But"—my mother's voice wavered—"he didn't.

"He went to a football game with some friends. It got later and later. And I got worried. We had a little radio at the place and I remember that the music went off. Nothing but static. It was time to close up and he still hadn't come. You had to be picked up too."

"Did anyone call you?"

"We didn't have a phone. People in the country didn't have phones then. No, nobody called me. And then I got really scared."

"Were you afraid he'd had an accident?"

"Yes. I was very afraid. Finally one of George's friends came. I can't even remember the man's name now. Anyway, he came and told me what happened. He took me to get you. Then he drove me to the hospital. Your father must have been rushing to get home from the game," my mother said with a clipped laugh. "He didn't want me to find out he'd been having a good time instead of working."

Neither one of us said anything for a minute, then I said, "Did Daddy ever have a, a girlfriend when you were married?"

My mother's back stiffened. "Who told you that?"

"Nana."

She looked at me, her back full of iron, her eyes alert. "I don't know why Mother has to . . ." Mommy looked at me.

"Did he?"

"I don't know." Her voice was firm. Don't push me, her voice said.

"Yes you do."

She stared at me, her eyes a steel vault slammed shut. Bette Davis eyes. Claudia McNeil eyes. The room was full of dignity. "Oh. You're going to tell me what I know. Is that it?"

Right away I felt like squirming. She put her hand on my wrist. "I don't know what happened between you and your father last summer, but if you're looking for reasons to hate your father, pick something he did to you, not to me. He's been a good father to you. Whatever he did wrong, whatever mistakes he made behind the wheel, he's paying for them, believe me. And Bebe, I made mistakes too. I want you to love him. Don't blame him for not being the god you made him out to be."

She must have seen the astonishment on my face. "You've always been a daddy's girl," she said, smiling.

"Does Nana hate my father?"

"She doesn't. Look. Nana's father wasn't . . . nice to her. And I guess my father was a disappointment. She's . . . Listen.

Just forget about what she said. You have no reason to be angry with your father and I don't want you to feel that way. When you go to North Carolina . . ."

"I may not go this summer."

Mommy looked at me. "That's entirely up to you," she said.

I saw the Pacific Ocean when I got to Los Angeles. We went to Alvarado Street and toured a bunch of old Spanish missions and, of course, Disneyland. Disneyland was wild and crazy. I sent a postcard to Aunt Ruth. I would have sent one to Michael, but I didn't have his address. I picked out a funny one to send to the Logans.

I thought about Mr. Logan's prediction as we drove home through hot, dry land. The Petrified Forest. The Mojave Desert. The Grand Canyon. We drove miles and miles with wheat and corn on either side of the highway. Maybe my old boyfriend would come back.

"Okay, settlers, this wagon train is coming on home!" Gene said as he pulled into the bus station in Philadelphia. He got off the bus and stood outside so he could help people get off. As the passengers filed out with their carry-on luggage they handed Gene money. After a while he had a wad of dollars as thick as his fist. He looked at all the bills he was holding and started crying. One soror's husband grabbed him in a bear hug, then a few more people came up and started patting him on his back. Gene really started boohooing then. "Y'all are just the nicest people, hunhunhunh. I ain't never met none nicer, hunhunhunh." He kept saying that over and over, sounding just like Andy Griffith from Mayberry, shaking his head as if he just couldn't get over how nice we were.

Mommy and I took a cab home; we didn't get in until three o'clock in the morning. It was ninety-three degrees and Nana had every window in the house open. She woke up when Mommy and I came in, and we stayed up nearly an hour telling her about everything we had seen. My mother fell asleep as soon as her head hit the pillow, but too many thoughts crowded my mind. Daddy's girl. Was that what I was?

I didn't wake up until noon the next day. Nana was sitting in the kitchen eating her lunch when I came down for breakfast. "We caught up with your cousin."

My heart lurched. "Where? Is he okay?"

"He was in Atlantic City, dancing at some go-go joint. Ruth and Clarence went down there and got him. He's real thin." Nana shook her head. "I don't know. I just don't know. You do the best you can, but it ain't enough. Boys need fathers. It's always left on the women," Nana said bitterly. "These men make a baby, zip up their pants and walk off into the sunset. Kenneth and your father . . ."

I felt my head shaking back and forth. NoNoNo. My head was still moving when I stood up, when I opened my mouth to speak. NoNoNo. "Nooooo. Don't say that. My father's not like Kenneth. Noooo. If you don't know the difference between the two, I do. Kenneth is a dog, Nana. My father . . ."

Nana looked startled, as though I'd hit her. "Your father . . ." she began.

"My father takes care of me," I said. And I thought yes. Yes.

I visited Michael at his mother's house the next day. Nana was right. He was very thin. And there was a hardness in his face that hadn't been there before.

"Guess who walked into the bar where I was dancing?" he asked me.

I shrugged my shoulders. "Who?"

"Kenneth."

"You're kidding."

"Yep. Kenneth." Michael's laugh sounded like a choke, as if he were gagging and laughing at the same time. I flinched. "I'm sitting at the bar having a drink and I notice this guy looking at me, so I start checking him out. And we're staring at each other, right? And so he gets up, comes over to me and starts smiling and he says, 'Do you know who I am?' And I look the mother-fucker dead in his eyes and say, 'No, who are you?' *Who. Are. You?* And you know what? He didn't say a word. Just got up and left."

I looked at my thin cousin. His eyes were brimming with anger.

" 'Do you know who I am?' " he repeated, his voice quivering with irony. "Naw, man, introduce yourself. Tell me who the fuck you are."

WHAT WAS LEFT OF GRANDMA'S CHICKENS SCATTERED AS THE BLACK Ford approached the front yard. Aunt Lela said, "There's Mamawaiting for us." It felt weird, going to Grandma's house at the tail end of summer instead of the beginning. Grandma's zinnias were in full force, but the corn was already harvested and there were only a few watermelons left in the field next to ours. Mr. Abe was fixing the fence that bordered the front yard when Uncle Otto pulled up. He called out, "Hey, y'all."

Grandma Mary was standing on the porch when we drove up; Daddy was sitting next to her. When I got out of the car, she took one look at my Beatle haircut and grabbed me by head and shook me till my brains were rattling. "My baby done cut off all her hair. Every bit of it!" I knew she was going to say something like that. Grandma believed that a Negro girl needed some hair to get her through life.

"It's the new style," I said, smiling a little. She was going to give me the business.

"Style!" She circled stiffly around me, then patted the back of my head with her hands.

"Your boyfriend like your hair?"

"I don't have a boyfriend right now."

"Uh huh," she said, and we both laughed.

I kissed my father on the cheek and he patted my hand. He said, "Well, Miss Globe-trotter." I couldn't believe it was nearly September and I was standing on Grandma Mary's porch touching my father as if it were June and the whole summer were spread before us, open like a picnic blanket. I heard a phone ring behind us.

"What's that?"

247

"I done got a phone," Grandma Mary said.

Daddy wanted to know all about my trip. "Did you see the Pacific Ocean?"

"Yep."

"Disneyland?"

"Uh huh."

Late in the afternoon Daddy started squirming. He turned to me. "Want to go off?"

"Okay."

We drove to Cousin Emily's house. It was breezy, almost cool. Some of Belinda's uncles and some other guys were standing around in the yard. A football lay on the ground. My father got out of his car and rolled up close to the house. The men began to play a lazy game of touch football, long, leisurely throws back and forth, running when they felt like it. They were falling down and laughing a lot. Loud, raucous laughter. I sat next to Belinda on the porch, mostly talking to her and half watching the game. We yelled at the players from time to time, trying to say funny things. I looked up when Cousin Emily came out of the house to hand my father a big glass of water. He didn't see her at first; he was too busy looking at the men throwing and catching and running. His two fists were balled up tight, which made the muscles in his forearms bulge.

I looked at my father's face. His eyes were wide open and full of pain and terrible longing. I'd never seen that agony before, not in my father's face. Gazing at my father's face reminded me of the time Reverend Lewis took me under. Him in his high fishing boots. Me in my see-through white robe. Maybe I expected the Holy Ghost to reach up from the church pool and grab me. What I felt was Reverend Lewis's hand on my back, holding me, his hand on my chest, pushing me under. The water splashed up against me, then it engulfed me and for a minute I thought I was drowning. That's what it was like looking into my father's eyes: like I was drowning in his pain.

"Girl, you shaking," Belinda said.

"Here's your water, George." Cousin Emily handed my father the glass and when he took it he was smiling. Daddy saw me watching him. He grinned widely, the lopsided, roguish grin that comes from leading a determined life. "Bebebebebebebebe-Moore." I walked over and stood on the back of his bracers and put my arms around his neck. The back of his head pressed against my breast, then he let his head fall against my arm. We stayed like that, quiet and close, for a long time before he said softly, as if thinking aloud, "Well. We still gotta get your school clothes. What you want ole Daddy to buy you?"

# CHAPTER 18

The blare of the horn made me jump even though I'd been expecting the sound all morning. I ran to the window and waved at Daddy and Uncle Norman. "They're here!" I yelled upstairs to Mommy and Nana. I looked in the large mirror over the sofa, smoothing the front of my white dress, pressing down my bangs. The mantel was crowded with graduation cards. The Logans had sent me a healthy check. When Mr. Logan saw my report card he said, "Now that's all right. Knew you could do it." I applied a little more lipstick. Behind me I heard the firm, businesslike click of my mother's heels on the stairs and then Nana's slower, plodding steps. "Come on," I said, "it's time to go." I was about to graduate and I was in a hurry.

When we got to Irvine Auditorium on the University of Pennsylvania campus, where the ceremony was being held, I showed my family where they could sit. Then I rushed into the throng of nearly five hundred girls, all wearing white dresses, who were milling around backstage. A hostess gave me a red rose to carry. One of the teachers signaled that we were supposed to line up. Gradually the unruly crowd merged into two straight, silent lines. An organ began playing "Pomp and Circumstance" and we marched in, filling up the middle section of the auditorium with the scent of roses.

The graduates listened attentively as Dr. Klein stood on the vast stage and told my class that our lives were just beginning, that the world held promises that only we could fulfill. I absorbed her words, breathing them in with the cologne in the air. Dr. Klein wasn't a very emotional speaker; her voice was a little monotonous, but I didn't care. When she spoke I tingled. When the class sang "Climb Ev'ry Mountain," chills danced up and down my back. I started crying.

I had wanted to graduate in an afro, and in fact two nights before, I had stood in the bathroom and created a natural that was the eighth wonder of the world. I turned my hair into a towering spectacle of crinkles and naps. Well, maybe not so towering, but there was enough hair standing all over my head to crowd the tiny mirror on top of the medicine cabinet. Even I was awed. I stared at myself, trying to recollect the way the gymnastics contest judge had looked, not quite sure if I approximated her standard of natural beauty. When my afro was only twenty minutes old, it was hard to adjust to the new me. At many a party, the image I saw before me had sent me running to the bathroom for emergency repairs. "Black is beautiful," I kept telling the new me. "Black is baaaaaaad."

Nana started screaming like a wild woman when she saw my hair. I knew she was going to act up.

"You don't like my new hairstyle?" I was going to be calm no matter how ignorant my grandmother acted.

Nana whooped. "You gotta be kidding me. Don't tell me you're planning on going out the house looking like . . ."

"Looking like what?"

She stuck her face in mine. "Queen of the electrified Zulus."

"You rather I go around burning my hair up trying to look like people I'm never going to look like?"

"What's wrong with you? You ain't no African."

"I am a black woman." Aha! I had said it.

"You hear that?" she said to my mother, who was trying her best not to laugh. Nana got right up in my face. "Where are you black? Where? You're a nice light brown. Cinnamon. Black! Do you think somebody's gonna give you a job if you walk in looking like that?"

"I already have a job with Uncle Norman." Which was true. Uncle Norman had hired me for the summer as a secretary/receptionist at his fledgling knitting factory.

"Your uncle's just starting out in business and you gonna go up there and scare off all his customers," Nana said, laughing.

"I'm proud of the way I look." I knew I sounded shaky. I was shaky.

"Oh, Lord." Nana looked at my mother. "Talk to this child. Talk to this yellow child. 'Cause I give her up to the hands of the Lord. I done fought the good fight."

I looked at my mother. "Now, Bebe," she said, soothingly, "maybe if you cut it and let some of your curls show."

They were missing the whole point. "Oh, never mind," I said, and stomped back up to the bathroom and slammed the door shut. I washed my afro down the drain, feeling real pissed off. And a little relieved. But I told myself, as I sectioned off my hair, applied the Dippity-do and wrapped strands around pink rollers, that one day I would have an afro as big and angry as the sun. And soon.

So I wore my hair in a Beatle for graduation, patting on my bangs for the hour it took before Dr. Klein called my name. When it was called I marched across the stage to get my diploma. At last!

There was a mad rush of kissing and hugging after the ceremony. I pushed my way through the sea of white dresses and roses, searching for my clan. I spotted them standing at the back of the auditorium, looking confused and happy. They all started waving and grinning when they saw me. As we made our way out of the building, Mommy and Nana were chattering like two bright parrots. My daddy wasn't smiling or saying much. I'd never seen him look so serious. "You go first," he told me. And he rolled cautiously behind me, letting me take the lead. Uncle Norman was at his side.

Outside the auditorium, girls in white dresses were swarming all over the lawn and sidewalk. In the crowd that had gathered, my father was the only one in a wheelchair. I was conscious, perhaps for the first time, of glances that came our way from strangers. I was shocked to realize that some people bestowed on us piteous smiles and that their eyes darted quickly away from ours. What was the meaning of their sadness?

Friends rushed up to me. They knew Mommy and Nana so we all squealed and embraced with a warm familiarity. Then I broke away. "I would like you to meet my father, George Moore, and my uncle, Norman Moore."

Daddy shook hands solemnly. "Nice to meet you." Why wasn't he smiling?

My friends told Daddy they'd heard a lot about him. He nodded.

During the ride home I sat in the back of my father's car with Nana and my mother. Mommy and Nana were passing around my diploma and the program. After he parked, Daddy turned around to me. "So, you're gonna be a working woman this summer, huh? Be so busy working for Uncle Norman you won't have time to come see your ole daddy. Then off to Pitt, huh." His voice sounded happy, but his eyes weren't.

"I'll come see you, Daddy," I said.

"Well, you better had."

Uncle Norman laughed softly. He said to Daddy, "What you gone do, man? She's grown now."

MR. LOGAN TOOK ME FOR A RIDE IN FAIRMOUNT PARK TWO WEEKS before I was to leave for the University of Pittsburgh. He cleared his throat fifty times, sucked his teeth and ran his fingers through his thinning hair. "You're a nice girl," he told me, "and smart too." He coughed. He seemed uneasy, not at all like the jovial buddy who every once in a while would pop in at my house when he was in the neighborhood, just to chew the fat. I could sense a speech coming on, but I hadn't the slightest idea what it would be about. "Now I don't know what you've been doing as far as sex is concerned; I don't know about that."

The birds and the bees, I thought incredulously. I started to put my hand on his, to say, "Mr. Logan, not to worry, the kid knows all about it." Not that I did. I was just kind of . . . embarrassed.

". . . I don't know anything about these birth control pills; they're kinda new, but there's foam, diaphragms and rubbers," he said.

My eyes opened wide. Birds and Bees, Part II. ". . . so you have to make sure there are no holes in them."

He told me things I'd never in my life thought to ask anyone, not my daddy, my mother, my grandmothers, my girlfriends, not anybody. "Now, some fellas will try and impress you with a whole lot of huffing and puffing, but if it's done right, it might not take but five minutes. The point is, honey, you should feel good when it's over."

I looked at the dashboard, the floor, my shoes before I looked up. His face, even more than his words, said he wanted me to make the transition from girl to woman intact, unharmed. "You know, we're all pulling for you," he said, and started the car.

# CHAPTER 19

Four years after King was assassinated, Aunt Ruth died of breast cancer. It was 1972; I was teaching elementary school in Atlanta. The doctors kept her pretty drugged up toward the end. She didn't really suffer; that's what Nana would tell me when I called home and asked about my aunt. But what I know about mothers is this: What they tell you about their children is sometimes what they desperately want to believe, with no foundation in facts whatsoever. In that hospital bed Ruth must have had enough lucid moments to think, to stare her past life straight in the eye. Nana was fooling herself.

Two years before she died, Ruth had had a radical mastectomy. The doctors cut all up under her arm, but I think it was too late even then. Clarence had found the lump months before and she waited too long before having someone check on her. By the time she went to the doctor, pus was oozing from her breast.

The doctors took her right breast. Her right arm swelled up fat as a mushroom after the operation and never went down. My Aunt Edith, who's a nurse, told me that wasn't a good sign. But she really didn't have to tell me anything. When I went to see

Ruth in the hospital and I saw her color, almost green, and how thin she was, I knew she wasn't going to get well.

The scar from the operation ran from the middle of her chest to way up under her arm. Ruth insisted that I see her scar. She had just finished the chemotherapy when I dropped by the apartment she shared with Clarence. I could smell coffee brewing when I went in. I wasn't halfway inside before she had me by the arm and was saying to me, "I want you to see how nicely my scar is healing." And before I could reply, she was pulling me into her bedroom. She took off her robe before I could say, Wait, lemme get myself together. Next thing I knew I was looking at this big gash, this place that used to be her breast. Never in my life had I felt so instantly, violently nauseated. I really thought I was going to vomit right then and there, but I prayed away the feeling. I started smiling at Aunt Ruth as if nothing were the matter, trying hard to look at the scar and think of something completely different, something pleasant and pretty like flowers, a day at the beach. But all I could think about was a three-legged dog that I saw once and how it howled. I smiled, though, and I didn't flinch; I sounded very calm when I told her, "Well, yeah, Aunt Ruth, yeah, that's not so bad. I don't know what I expected, but that's not so bad at all." She looked kind of relieved when I said that. She put her robe back on, and we went into the kitchen and she poured us some coffee. All the time I was drinking it, I was thinking to myself, how the hell could she have just ignored that lump? Why didn't she go to the doctor as soon as she found out? Nana said she let months go by. Months. But that was my Aunt Ruth, always leaving loose ends.

At the funeral my mother said to me, "I'll take care of Mother. You take care of Michael." Nobody was there just for him but us. Not his Uncle Bobby. Not his brothers. Nobody.

Michael was out of it, a limp, sobbing rag doll. I hadn't expected that. I thought he'd be stoic and maybe let a single tear trickle down his face at the end of the service. That kind of image came from watching too many Bette Davis flicks, maybe. Michael's crying filled the tiny funeral hall. Anne and Pete were there, and

Pete leaned over and patted Michael on the back. "Mike. Mike," he said over and over. I put my arms around Michael's shoulders and tried to hug him but he was wailing so loudly and his whole body was shaking and jerking so hard I couldn't really do anything for him. I was just there. A Bosom.

Months after the funeral we discovered that Ruth's financial affairs were a mess. When Michael applied for her benefits, he was told that he needed papers—either Ruth's divorce papers or Kenneth's death certificate. Ruth and Kenneth had never divorced, and as far as we knew, Michael's father was alive. Michael hired a lawyer, but he didn't get a quarter.

At Christmastime, when I came home again, Nana, Michael and I sat in the breakfast room talking about Ruth's money. Nana told him, "Listen. Call your Uncle Bobby and find out where your father is. Go to Kenneth and tell him you'll give him half of the money. Make a deal with him."

"Why couldn't he just be dead," Michael said. He laughed.

"Well, maybe he is dead," Nana said thoughtfully.

"Nah. He ain't dead," Michael said, his voice flat and dry. "He could get dead, though. I know people who'd take him out for three or four hundred bucks." Michael laughed again.

"Take him out? What do you mean, 'take him out'?" Nana looked at me, her eyes all squinched up. She had stopped putting henna in her hair and I couldn't get used to the gray.

"Kill him," I said.

"Who do you know would do something like that? You don't need to be hanging around anyone like that," Nana said sharply.

"One good shot right in the heart. Ping. Or maybe splatter his brains out, mess up one of his silk suits."

"Michael, shut up," I said, nodding toward Nana, whose eyes were heavy with shock and fear.

"Don't worry, sweetie," he said, pinching Nana's cheek, "I don't have enough money to put a contract out on Kenneth."

My father didn't come to Ruth's funeral. "What else could she expect from all that drinking"—that's what he said after saying he was sorry. At the time I thought that was pretty cold, but I put the thought to rest. I did just what old folks always tell young folks to do: I lived a little longer and kept my eyes open. Nana and Grandma Mary would die smooth as butter. Mr. Abe would go easy too. I guess Daddy had figured out that life is exactly the way some poet said it was: fair, but so uncool.

The truth is, Daddy didn't really like my aunt. Called her a barfly one time when I was still young enough to ask, "What's that?" and have in my mind the picture of an insect sitting on a piece of Hershey's chocolate.

"A person who hangs around bars all the time and drinks a lot of alcohol," he told me, his voice a little gruff.

"Alcohol?" What did he mean, like what the doctor rubbed on my arm?

"Whiskey."

"Oh."

"Don't be like your Aunt Ruth," he said gruffly. I knew he meant when I grew up. I was little, not more than seven or eight. It was the first time I knew he wanted me to become a certain kind of woman, that he had expectations of me. Years later I realized that his hopes for me were linked to his own dreams of immortality.

He wanted me to live a clean life, full of order and tradition. He as much as told me this once when we were together. I had flown from Atlanta to Norfolk and my daddy picked me up at the airport; we were going to Elizabeth City State's homecoming. In the car Daddy took a long look at me and said, "If I was a teacher making good money, I'd have me a better hairstyle than what you have. I'd go to the beauty parlor."

"You don't like my natural, Daddy?" He was the last holdout. Even Nana had gotten used to my hair.

"Black men like long hair."

I started humming the theme to *The Twilight Zone* good and loud to myself. What's this all about, I thought.

"You know, you need to start thinking about settling down."

Awwwww, shit. Stop the music.

"I'm only twenty-four. I'm having fun, Daddy," I told him.

"Fun? Girl, you done traipsed all over the world, to Africa, Europe, South America. That's enough fun. You better get yourself a husband."

I laughed right in his face. I almost said, "Nigger, puleez," but I caught myself, swallowed my neofeminist pride and said very softly, "I can take care of myself."

Daddy leaned in close to me. "Lookahere," he began, sticking his chin out a little, "it's hard out here for women alone. Teachers don't make that much money, you know."

"Tell me about it."

"While you're out there gallivanting and getting older by the minute, the smart women are taking all the good men."

The good men?

"The ones who're gonna make some money," he said, exasperated. "You don't think I want you to wind up with some sorry dude, do ya? Shoot, I want me some grandbabies."

Zing! Whoa! "You do?"

Daddy gave me a shocked look. "Sure I do. What you think?" His sudden grin was boyish and absurdly charming. "I want me a couple of grandkids."

"A couple."

"Yeah. Two or three. You not planning on having just one, are you?"

"That's all you had."

"Yeah, but I woulda had me some more if I hadn't got hurt. I woulda had four kids. Two girls, two boys."

"You think my career mother would have had some more kids?" I laughed.

Daddy's face was serious. "Sure. Doris wanted more babies. We talked about it. She wanted four kids too."

I drew a breath. "I guess you were sorry I wasn't a boy, huh?"

Daddy looked at me. "At first. Not sorry. Disappointed. You know how most men want sons for the first baby. But you know . . ."

"What?"

"I got used to you."

The funny thing is, I got married the following August. Hooked up with an old flame, the very same high school sweetie who used to moan and groan and swear I was giving him the blue balls.

"Didn't I tell you that lumphead Negro would be back?" Mr. Logan said.

"Your share of the wedding comes to a thousand dollars," I informed Daddy. He mailed the check to my mother. Paying for my wedding and giving me away, these were his last two official obligations as my father. Society cleared him after that. I suppose I did too, but I wanted something else from him. I was his grown daughter, but I wasn't finished being his child.

Funny, the things that crossed my mind while I was walking around humming "Here Comes the Bride." I thought about Reverend Lewis, of all people, even though I hadn't seen him in years. I hummed that wedding song and all of a sudden I was in my bare feet, wearing my slavery-girl get-up, standing on the stage in the basement of Faith Tabernacle Baptist Church reciting, " 'Lias! 'Lias! . . ." I sang some more and in my mind I licked the strawberry ice cream cones I used to eat after Sunday services and felt the cool drips trickling down my throat. But most of all, I recalled the strength of my minister's hands against my chest and back as he pushed me down, down, down into the baptismal waters. I thought of those hands pulling me out of the pool, holding me up. I remembered my minister's arm around my shoulder, his praise song in my ear. "Bebe, we're so proud of you." At twenty-five, with the perspective of a woman facing imminent marriage and eventual motherhood I was struck with a wave of nostalgia and something more substantial: an abiding sense of gratitude. What I realized at twenty-five I had taken for granted at eight: Reverend Lewis's words had been rain for my budding womanhood; he had helped me to grow healthy and whole. I wanted to feel his strength and support once again. I wanted him to participate in my most momentous occasion. "I'd like Reverend Lewis to marry me," I told Mommy.

Mommy vetoed my penchant for a reunion. She felt that because Reverend Newsome had retired that Reverend Adams, his replacement, should preside, especially since I'd been going to Corinthian Baptist for such a long time. "You don't ask a minister to come into another pastor's church and perform a wedding ceremony," she said firmly. Since Mother has always been the grande dame of Baptist etiquette, I didn't dispute her. As it turned out, Reverend Lewis couldn't even make the wedding. He stayed on my mind.

Daddy called me fifty million times during the week before the wedding. Mostly he wanted to know about my husband-to-be. "So tell me about his people," he said vaguely.

"They're nice. Regular. You know."

He was persistent. "Well, uh, what does his daddy do?"

What does his *daddy* do? Jesus. "I don't know. He's just regular."

"Well, uh, does he, uh, own a business? Is he a professional man?"

"Daddy?"

"Huh?"

"He's not rich."

"Oh."

Daddy called me two days before the wedding to tell me he was going to be looking sharp. "Girrrrl, your daddy has got an outta sight navy-blue suit and some snazzy shoes for your wedding." He laughed like a kid.

I didn't think about Daddy's outfit again until the actual day of the wedding arrived and my father showed up at my mother's house in a baad navy-blue suit and some of the loudest-looking navy and white country-preacher shoes I ever saw in my life. Beyond tacky. The saving grace was that I had a kind of a do-your-own-thing wedding. The groom wore an African robe, and I wore a traditional gown and a Nigerian headwrap. I told Daddy that he looked sharp and he started grinning all over himself.

Things got hectic after my father arrived. The photographer

came and took the wedding party to a nearby park for pictures. It was the same park where Anthony and I had chased each other while waiting for our music lessons so many years before. Now it would soon be immortalized in my wedding album.

The photographer was an "artiste." He arranged us like flowers on a dinner table and brayed high-pitched orders. "Bride and groom," he called, snapping his fingers smartly, "stand here! Here! Here!" My husband-to-be and I smiled into each other's faces until our lips ached. "Okay. Okay. Bride's family. Let's make nice. All smiles. Mother, you're not smiling. That's it. That's purrrfect."

The photographer put Daddy in the middle and had me place my hand on one of my father's shoulders, while Mommy touched his other one. Then Mr. Artiste told us to gaze lovingly at each other and smile. Mommy and Daddy were following the photographer's orders to a tee, staring intently into each other's eyes, smiling like an old married couple who knew each other very well. For all I knew, that was how they felt. Or maybe they were just very good at taking pictures. It didn't matter to me. I was in the middle of the portrait of family bliss I'd tried to paint for half of my life. I felt warm and happy standing there between my parents. But I felt no more love coming from them together than I had felt from them separately. The camera couldn't make us anything but what we'd always been: a family.

As soon as we got back home, Mr. Logan arrived to pick up Nana and Mommy. He had on a dark suit and a light blue shirt. "Hot diggety dogs," he said when he saw me. "You look beautiful, girl." He gave me a kiss on my cheek and I hugged him. Then he handed me an envelope. "Put this away somewhere. And be careful with your money. Sometimes you can get some uninvited guests, you know what I mean?"

My father was sitting in his car in the front of the house. I took Mr. Logan outside and introduced the two men. "You sure got a real nice girl here, Mr. Moore," Mr. Logan said. He put his arm around my shoulder. "I hope you don't mind that I borrow her for a daughter sometime."

Daddy said, smiling, "You can borrow her, but you can't have her."

I felt good standing on the curb next to my father's car and next to Mr. Logan, listening to them bantering about me. I thought about the nights Mr. Logan had encouraged me as we shared a cup of coffee and I struggled with geometry and chemistry. Good ole Mr. Logan, always in my corner. "Mr. Logan taught me how to fry chicken, Daddy," I said, suddenly remembering the evening I tentatively approached the frying pan at his urging. Borrowed. Yes. And it occurred to me then as I stood on the street in my long white gown next to Mr. Logan, not saying a word, that I might never be so sweetly borrowed again.

By the time we got to the church Daddy was getting nervous. We were standing in the hall outside the sanctuary and I was looking through the tiny window in the door into the church. I could see Michael sitting next to Nana and my mother. He was sitting stiff and straight as a piece of wood. Nana had her hand in his. An involuntary sigh flowed from me when I saw him. He was still thin, but he looked healthy, I thought. I wanted desperately to believe that he was healthy and happy and would one day finish school and go to college and be successful, productive, a model citizen. I needed to believe that childhood wounds could heal, that the love withheld from him wouldn't doom him. It was an ordinary wish that any sister might have wanted for her brother. I sighed again, looking through that tiny glass at Michael. His parents had bestowed uncommon beauty upon him, but what he needed was inner strength. *Do you know who I am?* The thought of Kenneth made me turn my head and stare at my bouquet. I didn't want to feel angry on my wedding day. I didn't want to feel loathing. I told myself that Michael at least had a job. He was working in a science lab at the University of Pennsylvania. He had his own apartment. I would feel joy on my wedding day. Joy. I heard Daddy behind me. "Where am I supposed to be?"

"Right here." It was the third time I had told him. The brother was spaced out. The music started playing and I said, "Come on, Daddy." He gave me a blank, helpless stare. I tapped lightly on his wheel spokes with my knuckles. "Roll it, Daddy." An usher opened the door and we started down the aisle together.

People say that when you die your whole life flashes before you. My whole life was sitting in Corinthian Baptist Church watching me say "I do." As we walked back down the aisle what I had was one giant flashback. My mother, Grandma Mary, Nana, Michael, all of my aunts and uncles, Linda—they were all there. There were some missing faces. Aunt Ruth was gone, of course. Reverend Lewis was absent. Anne was there, though my beloved Pete had passed away the year before. But I could see him sitting in a pew, his maroon scarf wound tightly around his neck. I smiled. My father and I proceeded slowly. People rose and cameras flashed. I had my hand on his shoulder. Daddy looked very, very serious, as though he were afraid of making a mistake in this last ritual of his fatherhood. As we approached the altar, Daddy looked at me; he took my hand and kissed it. There were tears in his eyes. "Who gives this woman to this man?" Reverend Newsome asked.

"I do," Daddy replied in a loud, clear voice. He rolled his chair away from me slightly and my groom stepped forward.

The reception was in the church basement. The wedding party sat at a long table on the stage. It knocked me out to discover that Nana and Grandma Mary were meeting for the first time. "You mean you all have never met before?" I asked them. They shook their heads. For some reason I'd always believed they'd known each other for years.

Grandma Mary settled back in her chair. She was being very quiet. "Can I get you anything?" I asked her.

"No. You gone bring your husband down to see me, ain't you?"

"You know I am."

Grandma patted my hand and smiled. "Doris looks good. She ain't aged a bit."

Nana talked my ears off. She had last-minute pearls of wisdom to sow in the hopes that I'd reap marital bliss. "Now I want you to keep a neat house," she whispered in my ear. "Men don't like sloppy women."

"All right." I looked up at her.

"Cook nice dinners. None of that frozen mess. Men don't

like that foolishness. You're down there with those Georgia gals. You can't be too careful. They'll take your man off you while you're closing your eyes to sneeze. Think I'm lying?"

I shook my head. "What else?"

"Sex."

"What about it?" I could hardly wait.

"Be generous." I whooped. Nana patted my back. "You'll do fine. You got me in you."

There was no real receiving line; people drifted by our table whenever they felt like it. One by one all of my uncles gathered around me. I looked up and John, Elijah, Eddie, Cleat, Joe, Sammy and Norman were standing over me. They were lined up in a dazzling row. They were unmistakably older, but still handsome men. When I looked up at them and saw their various shades of brown, the full and receding hairlines, the variations of their moustaches, their bellies rounder than they once had been, I still saw them as the splendid heroes of my childhood. My reverie was full: riding to reunions with Uncle John; the smell of Uncle Elijah's cigars; after-school trips to Uncle Eddie's store; Uncle Cleat's quiet ways; Uncle Joe's quick jokes; Uncle Sammy's Marine book gently bestowed; watching Uncle Norman's dream of business owner-ship come true. I thought of the homecomings of long ago and how I used to stay up all night long with Grandma waiting for them to come up the lane. Looking at them in their dark suits and paisley ties I remembered them bare-chested, gathered around their cars under Grandma's fig tree. I remembered the energy and the dreams that emanated from that place and the strong hands that reached out to me. My reverie was interrupted by their voices coming at me all at once, voices that confirmed their own memories.

"Girl, I changed your diapers."

"Bebe, you remember when I used to come get you and take you to the park?"

"Sure do look good, girl."

Someone whispered in my ear, "You not gonna have a whole bunch of kids, are you?"

"What you talkin' 'bout, man? Bebe ain't havin' no bunch of kids. She's got an education."

"You gonna keep on teaching?"

"Oh, I don't know. I like writing a lot. And I like business. I wouldn't mind, you know, owning a store or something like that."

Michael stayed only for a little while. He came up to me looking a little jittery. "I'm getting ready to go."

"Come by the house later," I pleaded.

"Okay."

I knew I wouldn't see him for God knows how long. "Come visit us in Atlanta," I said.

"Okay. Be good," he told me. He leaned toward me and whispered, "Tell that boy to treat my sister right." Then he kissed me on the cheek.

"You be good too," I said.

I introduced my uncles to my groom. They extended their hands and nodded at him warily. When I left the stage to speak with my mother, they had him surrounded.

"Well, are you happy?" Mommy asked.

"Yep. Thank you for everything." We hugged each other. She held my arms with both of her hands. "My dear little baby girl," she said. Her voice quaked a little.

"You're not going to cry, are you?"

My mother took a deep breath. "I don't think so."

From across the room I saw Mr. Logan and my father with their heads together laughing. The next time I looked up my uncles had scattered and Daddy was talking with my groom and they both had serious looks on their faces.

My new husband pulled me aside as I climbed back on the stage. "Your father, your uncles and that other guy . . ." he began.

"What about them?"

"They're all threatening to kill me."

A boy who tells a girl she is giving him the blue balls will grow up to be a man prone to exaggeration. What my father said to my groom was, "If you don't like her, send her home, but son, don't put your hands on her." A warning, that's all. Not a threat.

"Aww, that's just their way," I told him.

"Their way of what?"

AFTER I GOT MARRIED DADDY TOOK ME TO TANK JACKSON'S HOUSE once when I came to spend a couple of days with him. Everything in the house was made for a paraplegic; Tank had a drive-in shower and kept a wheelchair right inside the stall. When I saw this I said, "That's what you need, Daddy." Later I thought about the shower a lot, because I knew I'd need a place with a shower like that if I were to take care of Daddy properly when he got old.

While we were sitting in Tank's living room, I reached into my father's shirt pocket and took one of his Winstons, lit it and started smoking. Daddy tripped out when I smoked that cigarette. He didn't say a word, but he was tripping. His expression said: What's my little baby doing with a cigarette? I don't even smoke. I was just messing with him. As the evening wore on, with three drinks in him, he said to our host, but not to me, "Lookahere. Will you look at that. My baby is *smoking*."

The next morning we drove to Grandma's new house. The old one had burned down several years before, and now she and Mr. Abe lived in a small, one-story bungalow. At first I really missed the old house, but then I thought it might have been for the best. Grandma was getting old. She didn't need to climb stairs. And the new house had central heating. All the old house had to recommend it was memories. A lot has changed in North Carolina. It's funny. People and even places have drifted away on winds I can't take hold of. The family Bible burned up, and all the old pictures, but I have my memories.

What was quite marvelous and magical to me when I was small is that invariably at any of the houses my father and I visited, there would emerge a little girl about my age. She'd gleefully squeal, "Uncle George!" and start pushing my father's chair toward the largest shade tree in her yard, while I stood back and watched. She'd bring him a big glass of water, giggling as he ruffled her hair in thanks. Then, at her mother's or father's urging, she would turn to me and shyly lead me toward toys, comic books, kittens, whatever she had to fill the afternoon with pure delight.

Even as a child I realized that the girls were the children who filled his life when autumn claimed me. In the summer I was grateful to them, as I was grateful in the fall for Pete, Reverend Lewis, Mr. Logan and my uncles. When the missing element is human we are all dependent on the kindness of strangers.

Daddy and I sat in Grandma Mary's yard late that afternoon. "Lookahere. You know what I want to do?"

I shook my head.

"Start a cabulance company." He smiled.

"A cabuwho?"

"Cabulance. Cabulance." He leaned over in his chair and smacked my knee a couple of times. "It's a cab service for paraplegics and other people who can't get around too well. The van has automatic lifts to get folks in and out. You know how many people need a service like that?"

"Probably a lot."

"That's right. A lot." He was silent for a moment. "You can have all the marching you want. What it gets down to is economics," he told me.

I started to leave that alone. The day was too peaceful for a civil rights debate. But the words just flew out of my mouth. "It's more than economics, Daddy. What about human dignity?" I braced myself.

Daddy's chin jutted out; his eyes snapped wide open. "Dignity? Sitting next to white people in a restaurant doesn't give you dignity, same as not sitting next to them doesn't take it away. Hard as it was when I was coming along—and I'm talking about when they wouldn't sell life insurance to black folks, because they didn't want your children to do any better than you had—our people had dignity." His smile came from his gut. "Did you know that my daddy was the boss of every job he ever had?"

I shook my head.

"He was a contractor. The boss." Daddy leaned back in his chair. "You get dignity from your family."

We were quiet together. Then, "Say, you feel like getting these hairs on my chin?"

"Nope."

"Awww, you're not gonna do your ole daddy a favor?"

Mr. Pitiful.

In the early evening, while the Indian-summer sun warmed the yard, I plucked the ingrown hairs from Daddy's chin, then rubbed alcohol on the tiny wounds. I emptied his foul-smelling urine ducts, refused to wash his car ("Hey, car wash is right down the road, buddy"), and then stepped up on the bracers of his wheelchair, putting my arms around his neck while he read the paper. He looked up at me and said the same old silly daddy things to me, a grown woman, that he used to say to his little girl. "BebebebebebebebeMoore. Whatcha know, kiddo?"


AS MY FINGERS WANDER THROUGH HAIR I OFTEN LOVE AND I LOOK back, I realize that this is what I know: My father took care of me. Our separation didn't stunt me or condemn me to a lesser humanity. His absence never made me a fatherless child. I'm not fatherless now.

But I am lonely. I've come to a space in my life where the old men are too few and far between. I never thought they would be taken away so soon. I'm grown now. No strong hands reach out to boost me in ways that I was lifted before. My loss goes beyond the grave of my father; the void is vast and disorienting at times, causing me to grope and stumble until I feel the invisible props that will always support me. Long ago I realized that love is all that is required of fatherhood, that love will spark the action that it takes to mold a child. I have grown strong and whole from the blessings of my many fathers. Everything they gave me—roughness, gruffness, awkward gentleness, the contrast to my female world, their love—is as much a part of me as my bones, my blood. I was given a rich and privileged childhood, an American childhood, a solid foundation on which to stand and, yes, even go forward. I was guided by good men, powerful men. I was raised right.